# Frege on Definitions

# Frege on Definitions

## A Case Study of Semantic Content

John Horty

OXFORD
UNIVERSITY PRESS

2007

# OXFORD
UNIVERSITY PRESS

Oxford University Press, Inc., publishes works that further
Oxford University's objective of excellence
in research, scholarship, and education.

Oxford   New York
Auckland   Cape Town   Dar es Salaam   Hong Kong   Karachi
Kuala Lumpur   Madrid   Melbourne   Mexico City   Nairobi
New Delhi   Shanghai   Taipei   Toronto

With offices in
Argentina   Austria   Brazil   Chile   Czech Republic   France   Greece
Guatemala   Hungary   Italy   Japan   Poland   Portugal   Singapore
South Korea   Switzerland   Thailand   Turkey   Ukraine   Vietnam

Published by Oxford University Press, Inc.
198 Madison Avenue, New York, New York 10016
www.oup.com

Oxford is a registered trademark of Oxford University Press

Library of Congress Cataloging-in-Publication Data
Horty, John F.
Frege on definitions : a case study of semantic content / John Horty.
    p.   cm.
ISBN 978-0-19-531441-0
1. Frege, Gottlob, 1848–1925.   2. Semantics.   I. Title.
B3245.F24H67 2007
121'.68092—dc22   2007008578

9 8 7 6 5 4 3 2 1

Printed in the United States of America
on acid-free paper

*In memory of my grandparents—*

*Randall Rosenberry*
*and*
*Alice Woods Rosenberry*

# Preface

Every book has a history, and this short book has a long history—much of it, in fact, was written twenty years ago, as part of a dissertation on meaning in mathematical language. After completing this dissertation, I turned at once to an entirely separate line of research, centered around logic and artificial intelligence, and particularly nonmonotonic logic. One thing led to another, and as it turns out, I did not think about language or meaning again for nearly two decades, until a chance encounter with some of the more recent literature convinced me that the problems I had worried about had not been resolved, or even addressed in any detail, during the intervening period.

It is an interesting experience working with material that was originally drafted so long ago, and it is not an experience that I would recommend to a friend. Nevertheless, I do not propose to use distance from the material as any sort of an excuse. Although parts of the book are old, other parts are new. The older parts have been thoroughly rewritten, and I stand by both the arguments and the conclusions presented here.

As the title suggests, this book is very much a case study, entirely focused on the treatment of defined expressions in Frege's own semantic theory, although I hope the discussion will have some bearing on those contemporary theories with their roots in Frege's work. At various points, Frege considers a number of more contentious styles of definition, such as contextual or implicit definition, but I concentrate here only on the simplest and most pedestrian—ordinary stipulative definition. This form of definition can be illustrated by the introduction of the new predicate 'is prime', for example, into an arithmetical language through the stipulation that a number $x$ is prime just in case any number that divides $x$ is either equal to $x$ or equal to 1.

The book is organized around two problems posed for Frege's theory, and others like it, by languages that allow for the introduction of defined expressions like this.

Frege's semantic theory is based, first of all, on a notion of sense, or meaning, that is closely correlated with the psychological states of language users; but this correlation then forces a conflict between two of Frege's central theses concerning definitions. One of these is the thesis of eliminability, according to which a sentence containing defined expressions must share its sense with the sentence that results when each of these defined expressions is eliminated in favor of its defining phrase—so that the proper introduction of defined expressions cannot actually increase the expressive resources of a language. This is a standard view, which has been advocated by a number of writers as well as Frege. The second is the thesis of fruitfulness, according to which there must be the possibility, at least, that good definitions might allow us to prove things we would not have been able to prove without them. Although the exact interpretation of this thesis is a matter of dispute, it was clearly an important part of Frege's overall philosophy, and it has a good deal of intuitive appeal as well. Anyone who has engaged in formal work, or informal work of any complexity, is familiar with the way in which the judicious introduction of defined expressions facilitates conceptual advance.

At this point, we can see the general shape of the conflict between these two theses—fruitfulness and eliminability—simply by asking: if the introduction of defined expressions does not allow us to express any new senses, and if senses really are supposed to correlate with psychological states, then how can these defined expressions provide any cognitive leverage at all? How can they allow us to prove things we would not be able to prove without them? Providing a careful description of this conflict, however, and suggesting a resolution, is a complicated matter that requires a detailed discussion of Frege's views; the discussion occupies the first four chapters of this book.

The second problem I consider is centered around Frege's idea that the sense of a linguistic expression exhibits a determinate structure, and one that is isomorphic to the syntactic structure of the expression itself; a view along these general lines is shared by several contemporary advocates of the "structured meanings" approach in semantic theory. Again, however, this idea clashes with Frege's eliminability thesis, according to which the elimination of defined expressions cannot affect sense. Eliminability tells us, for example, that the sentence '17 is prime' must express the same sense as the sentence 'Any number that divides 17 is either equal to 17 or equal to 1', which is what results when the defined predicated 'is prime' is eliminated in favor of its defining phrase. But since these two sentences do not themselves share the same structure—one is a simple predication, the other a more complex quantificational construction—how could they possibly be isomorphic to the same sense?

The next four chapters of the book are devoted to a detailed examination of the issues surrounding this problem, both syntactic and semantic. A brief final chapter then compares the approaches taken in the two parts of the book and suggests some ways in which the work presented here might be developed.

\* \* \*

I am deeply grateful to Nuel Belnap, who directed the dissertation that led to this book, for his insight and critical attention, for the countless hours he spent with me at the time, and for his friendship ever since. I would also like to thank the other members of my original committee—Robert Brandom, John Haugeland, Dana Scott, and Richmond Thomason—for their help and generosity. In the intervening years, several people have discussed these ideas with me and encouraged me to return to the project. I thank them all, but I owe a special debt to Paul Pietroski, not only for encouragement, but for discussing the material with me in detail and for reading the entire manuscript, possibly more than once. Two anonymous readers for Oxford University Press provided valuable comments, corrections, and advice. My work was supported by a Fellowship for University Teachers from the National Endowment for Humanities.

# Contents

**Preface**          **vii**

**1 The introduction of senses**      **1**

  1.1 Frege's argument . . . . . . . . . . . . . . . . . . . . . 1

  1.2 Exploring the argument . . . . . . . . . . . . . . . . . . 3

      1.2.1 Propositional attitudes . . . . . . . . . . . . . . . . 4

      1.2.2 Information value . . . . . . . . . . . . . . . . . . . 7

**2 Sense identity**      **10**

  2.1 Models of the speaker . . . . . . . . . . . . . . . . . . . 10

      2.1.1 Ayer-Hahn monsters . . . . . . . . . . . . . . . . . 11

      2.1.2 Limited intellects . . . . . . . . . . . . . . . . . . . 14

  2.2 The strict interpretation . . . . . . . . . . . . . . . . . . 17

      2.2.1 Arguments for the strict interpretation . . . . . . . . 17

      2.2.2 Problems with the strict interpretation . . . . . . . . 24

**3 Definitions**      **27**

  3.1 Analyticity . . . . . . . . . . . . . . . . . . . . . . . . . 27

  3.2 Concept formation . . . . . . . . . . . . . . . . . . . . . 30

  3.3 Fruitfulness and eliminability . . . . . . . . . . . . . . . 32

      3.3.1 Explicative definitions . . . . . . . . . . . . . . . . . 36

      3.3.2 Stipulative definitions . . . . . . . . . . . . . . . . . 40

**4 Sense and meaning**      **50**

  4.1 The conflict . . . . . . . . . . . . . . . . . . . . . . . . . 51

  4.2 Resolving the conflict . . . . . . . . . . . . . . . . . . . . 53

      4.2.1 Indexicals . . . . . . . . . . . . . . . . . . . . . . . 56

      4.2.2 Language learning . . . . . . . . . . . . . . . . . . . 58

**5  A simple semantic model**                                          **65**

  5.1   Senses as procedures . . . . . . . . . . . . . . . . . . . . .   66

  5.2   Syntax . . . . . . . . . . . . . . . . . . . . . . . . . . . .   69

  5.3   Semantics . . . . . . . . . . . . . . . . . . . . . . . . . .   71

        5.3.1   Referents . . . . . . . . . . . . . . . . . . . . . .   72

        5.3.2   Senses . . . . . . . . . . . . . . . . . . . . . . . .  73

**6  Removal rules**                                                    **85**

  6.1   Incomplete expressions . . . . . . . . . . . . . . . . . . .    85

        6.1.1   The conflict . . . . . . . . . . . . . . . . . . . . .  85

        6.1.2   Resolving the conflict . . . . . . . . . . . . . . . .  91

  6.2   Defined expressions . . . . . . . . . . . . . . . . . . . . .   98

**7  Syntactic and semantic options**                                  **102**

  7.1   Syntactic options . . . . . . . . . . . . . . . . . . . . . .  104

  7.2   Semantic options . . . . . . . . . . . . . . . . . . . . . . . 111

**8  Senses of incomplete expressions**                                **118**

  8.1   A de re proposal . . . . . . . . . . . . . . . . . . . . . . . 118

  8.2   Complex incomplete senses . . . . . . . . . . . . . . . . . .  123

        8.2.1   Developing the proposal . . . . . . . . . . . . . . .  125

        8.2.2   Examples and equivalencies . . . . . . . . . . . . . . 134

        8.2.3   Evaluating the proposal . . . . . . . . . . . . . . .  137

**9  Afterword**                                                        **139**

  9.1   Developing the procedural model . . . . . . . . . . . . . . .  140

  9.2   Two approaches to defined expressions . . . . . . . . . . . .  144

# Frege on Definitions

# Chapter 1

# The introduction of senses

Gottlob Frege was the first practitioner of formal semantics—the first theorist concerned, for whatever reason, with the systematic assignment of semantic values, or contents, to linguistic expressions. In his early monograph, the *Begriffsschrift*, Frege relied on an undifferentiated notion of semantic value, which he described simply as "conceptual content" (1879, pp. 6, 12); much of his immediately subsequent work, particularly the *Grundlagen der Arithmetik*, was devoted to an analysis of conceptual content for expressions belonging to the language of mathematics. Sometime around 1890, however, Frege discovered an argument which convinced him that this simple notion of semantic value would not do. The point of the argument, first presented in his seminal (1892b), was that semantic value must be divided into two components, which he then went on to distinguish as "referents" and "senses." [1]

In this chapter, I review this familiar argument of Frege's, as he presents it in (1892b) and elsewhere, and begin to explore some of its underlying complications.

## 1.1 Frege's argument

In order to understand the argument, it is best to place ourselves in Frege's shoes: we should imagine thinking of semantic content, at first, as a single, undifferentiated notion, and then reasoning with the principles that convinced him it must be otherwise.

---

[1] I use 'sense' and 'referent' to render Frege's '*Sinn*' and '*Bedeutung*'. Although this translation—particularly the choice of 'referent' for '*Bedeutung*'—is problematic in various ways, it also allows for certain simplifications; and the problems should not affect our discussion here, which is entirely focused on *Sinnen*.

On the most natural reconstruction of the argument, there are two such principles. The first is simply the principle of compositionality—the idea, also due to Frege, that the content of a compound expression is entirely determined by its syntactic form together with the contents of its parts.[2] Although he had not yet formulated this idea as clearly as he would in later years, or examined its motivation as thoroughly, it seems that he meant to abide by it even as early as the *Begriffsschrift*.

The principle of compositionality serves to establish a correlation only between contents and contents: between the content of a compound expression, and the contents of its parts. By the early 1890s, however, Frege had apparently decided that an expression's overall semantic content—or at least one of its components—should be correlated also with the psychological states of language users. There are, in fact, a number of ways to achieve this kind of correlation, but Frege selected a method that relies crucially on a perceived distinction in what we might call the *information value* of different kinds of statements. Some, he thought, could properly be classified as informative, possessing real cognitive value; others must be classified as uninformative, or self-evident. Exploiting this distinction, Frege was then able to induce a correlation between semantic contents and psychological states simply by embracing, as a second principle, the idea that the semantic content of a sentence should determine its information value: if two sentences have the same semantic content, they are either both informative, possessing some cognitive value, or both uninformative, entirely self-evident.

We will return shortly to the notion of information value underlying Frege's argument; but let us see first how these two principles—compositionality, together with the principle that content determines information value—can be used to generate the conclusion that an expression's overall semantic content must be divided into distinct components.

What the principles provide, actually, are the materials for devising a very general criterion for determining whether two expressions can be classified as identical in their overall content. Let '$\Phi(\ldots)$' represent an arbitrary sentential context, or more generally, a mode of sentential composition. And suppose that '$E_1$' and '$E_2$' are expressions belonging to a grammatical category for which '$\Phi(E_1)$' and '$\Phi(E_2)$' are sentences—formed, as the notation indicates, from the placement of '$E_1$' and '$E_2$' in the context '$\Phi(\ldots)$', or more generally, from the application of this mode of composition to the two expressions. If '$E_1$'

---

[2]We will return later, particularly in Chapters 5 and 6, to consider Frege's views on compositionality in more detail.

and '$E_2$' are identical in content, then compositionality tells us that the two sentences '$\Phi(E_1)$' and '$\Phi(E_2)$' must likewise share the same content, since they are composed in the same way from content-identical parts; but in that case, since content determines information value, it follows that these two sentences must have the same information value as well.

This line of reasoning leads to what might be called Frege's general criterion for content identity: two expressions can be classified as identical in semantic content only if their respective placement in any sentential context results in sentences that have the same information value—either both informative, or both uninformative. The criterion is useful, of course, primarily for establishing *differences* in content. In order to show that two expressions cannot coincide in their overall semantic content, that they must differ in at least one component, it is necessary only to find some context in which their respective placement yields sentences distinct in information value.

The particular argument Frege presents in (1892b) can be seen as resulting from an application of this general criterion to a special kind of statement—a true identity of the form '$a = b$'. Since the identity *is* true, even though it involves distinct terms, he reasons that these terms must have some component of their content in common: '$a$' and '$b$' must possess, as he says, the same *referents*. But Frege also claims that this statement of identity is informative, that it holds some cognitive value, unlike the statement '$a = a$', which he views as self-evident. Since the two statements '$a = b$' and '$a = a$' do differ in information value, there is therefore some sentential context—the context '$a = \ldots$'—in which the respective placement of '$a$' and '$b$' yields a pair of sentences whose information value is distinct; and so these two terms cannot be entirely identical in semantic content. There must be some component of content, at least, in which these two terms differ; Frege calls these distinct components their *senses*.

## 1.2 Exploring the argument

Although this argument from (1892b) is familiar, it will be helpful before moving on to look a bit more closely at two of the issues it presents. The first concerns the relation of the argument as Frege presents it to our modern discussion of similar topics; the second concerns an important assumption underlying the argument itself.

### 1.2.1   Propositional attitudes

As we have seen, the need for senses, as an additional component of content alongside referents, arose ultimately out of Frege's idea that some component of semantic content should correlate with the psychological states of language users. This idea has elicited a good deal of sympathy among modern semantic theorists. However, in comparing Frege's argument with this modern work, we should note that the particular method Frege used to induce a correlation between semantics and psychology—by stipulating that semantic content determines information value—is different from that generally employed today. In modern discussions, there is little direct reliance on Frege's notion of information value. Instead, the link between semantic contents and psychological states is usually derived, almost as a side effect, from the more general principle that the semantic content of a sentence should determine its *truth* value: if two sentences share the same semantic content, they are either both true or both false.[3]

Using this more general principle, along with the original principle of compositionality, it is easy enough to arrive at a modern version of Frege's criterion for content identity: two expressions can be classified as identical in content only if their respective placement in any sentential context results in sentences with the same truth value. The link between semantic content and psychological states can then be derived incidentally, from the application of this new criterion to a particular range of sentences, those describing the propositional attitudes of language users. If the expressions '$E_1$' and '$E_2$' are identical in content, it follows from this modern criterion that any pair of sentences that differs only by containing one of these expressions in place of the other should coincide in truth value. We should therefore be able to conclude that a sentence of the form 'Susan believes that $\Phi(E_1)$', for instance, must share its truth value with 'Susan believes that $\Phi(E_2)$', that 'Karl hopes that $\Xi(E_1)$' must share its truth value with 'Karl hopes that $\Xi(E_2)$', and so on. If we are able to find any counterexample to this pattern—if it turns out, say, that 'Janet is afraid that $\Psi(E_1)$' is true, while 'Janet is afraid that $\Psi(E_2)$' is false—then this method of argument allows us to conclude that '$E_1$' and '$E_2$' must differ in some component of their overall semantic content.

Our modern interest is more sharply focused on the problem of specifying truth conditions for sentences like these—describing our beliefs, hopes, and

---

[3]This principle is described by Cresswell (1982, p. 69) as "the most certain thing" he knows about meaning; it is of course necessary to qualify the principle by insisting that the two sentences should be evaluated in the same context, as Cresswell goes on to do.

fears—than on Frege's original problem, which may even feel a bit antiquated, of trying to account for differences in information value. It might seem, therefore, that the notion of sense developed in Frege's writings would have little contemporary relevance. Why should we bother with a conception of semantic content explicitly keyed to information value, if what we really want is a notion that helps us compute the truth value of sentences describing psychological states? The answer, of course, is that these two conceptions are supposed to coincide. Although he came at it from a different perspective, what Frege was looking for in his notion of sense is exactly what we want today from a notion of content that can be used to specify the truth conditions of propositional attitude statements.

This coincidence between Frege's concerns and our own is sometimes just assumed, but in fact it needs argument. The easiest way to establish the coincidence is to show that two expressions can be classified as identical in sense according to Frege's own principles just in case they are also classified as identical in content by our modern criterion. One direction of this argument is straightforward. Suppose the two expressions '$E_1$' and '$E_2$' *fail* to satisfy Frege's criterion for sense identity: there is some sentential context '$\Phi(\ldots)$' such that '$\Phi(E_1)$' is informative while '$\Phi(E_2)$' is not. We can then conclude that the two expressions will fail to satisfy our modern criterion as well; there must be some context in which the placement of these two expressions will lead to sentences distinct in truth value. For consider the context 'It is informative that $\Phi(\ldots)$'. Since '$\Phi(E_1)$' is informative while '$\Phi(E_2)$' is not, it then follows by assumption—or very nearly so—that the placement of '$E_1$' in this context leads to a true sentence while the placement of '$E_2$' in this same context leads to a false sentence.[4]

The other direction of argument is more complicated, since there seems to be no direct route from the premise that two expressions fail to satisfy our contemporary criterion for content identity to the conclusion that they should also

---

[4]The reason for the qualification is that the slide between representing the concept of informativeness as a metalinguistic predicate and representing the same concept as a sentence-forming operator is not entirely trouble free. It is not entirely obvious that a sentence '$S$' should be classified as informative just in case the sentence 'It is informative that $S$' is true, for it sometimes does make a great deal of difference in logic whether a particular concept, such as necessity, is represented formally as a predicate or an operator. But I do not think that this difference between the two ways of representing informativeness would have mattered much to Frege; and, although he does usually represent the concept as a metalinguistic predicate, there are occasions (1914, p. 224; XIV11, p. 126) on which he seems to treat it instead as an operator.

fail to satisfy Frege's criterion. Even if we suppose that the replacement of '$E_1$'
by '$E_2$' does affect the truth value of some propositional attitude sentence—say,
'Susan believes that $\Phi(E_1)$'—it is hard to see how we could conclude directly
from this that there should also be some sentence in which the replacement of
'$E_1$' by '$E_2$' affects information value. At various points throughout his discussion in (1892b), however, Frege affirms some additional principles that allow us
to connect our contemporary notion of semantic content with his conception of
sense through a more circuitous route. The principles are: (i) that the referent
of a sentence is its truth value (p. 34); (ii) that the referent of a sentence is determined by the referents of its parts (p. 35); (iii) that expressions in contexts of
"indirect speech" take their "indirect" referents (p. 28); and (iv) that the indirect referent of an expression is its sense (p. 28). Using these principles, we can
conclude as follows that '$E_1$' and '$E_2$' must differ in sense just because they fail
to meet our contemporary criterion for content identity, even if we cannot show
directly that they fail to meet Frege's criterion. Because they yield sentences
with different truth values when substituted into the context 'Susan believes
that $\Phi(\ldots)$', we can conclude from (i) and (ii) that '$E_1$' and '$E_2$' take different
referents in this context. Because the context is one of "indirect speech," we can
conclude from (iii) that the indirect referents of '$E_1$' and '$E_2$' must be distinct;
and so from (iv), that they must differ in sense.[5]

These arguments justify us in moving back and forth between Frege's no-

---

[5] I have oversimplified by ignoring multiply indirect contexts. When an expression stands in
an ordinary indirect context, such as 'Susan believes that $\Phi(\ldots)$', Frege states, not only that
the expression takes as a referent its ordinary sense, but also that it expresses an indirect sense
(1892b, p. 28). Many writers, such as Carnap (1947, p. 129) and Linsky (1967, p. 33), have
assumed, therefore, that when an expression occurs within, say, a doubly indirect context—an
indirect context nested within another one, such as ($*$) 'Susan believes that Karl hopes that
$\Phi(\ldots)$'—it should take as a referent, not its ordinary sense, but its indirect sense. In fact,
Frege does not actually say this, but it is a reasonable conclusion to draw by analogy from
his treatment of singly indirect contexts. If the conclusion is correct, and if we could find co-
referential expressions '$E_1$' and '$E_2$' whose interchange affected the truth value of a sentence
only in doubly indirect contexts, such as ($*$) above, then the link between our modern notion
of content and Frege's senses would be broken. By our modern criterion, we would have to
conclude that '$E_1$' and '$E_2$' differ in content, since their interchange affects the truth value
of some sentence. However, Frege's principles would not necessarily force us to conclude that
they differ also in sense—but only in indirect sense. The link could be reestablished if we were
willing to adopt Linsky's assumption that, although ordinary and indirect sense might differ,
two expressions coincide in their indirect sense just in case they coincide in their ordinary sense;
or alternatively, Dummett's suggestion in (1973, pp. 267–269; see also 1981, pp. 87–101) that
we emend Frege's doctrine by identifying indirect and ordinary senses (this emendation was
also hinted at by Carnap). In what follows, I hope to avoid the complexities associated with
indirect senses by continuing to ignore multiply indirect contexts.

tion of sense and a notion of semantic content keyed to more modern concerns. Using his own principles, Frege *could* have supported his claim that certain co-referential expressions must be assigned distinct senses through a more modern method of reasoning—by examining the behavior of these expressions in propositional attitude contexts, rather than focusing directly on the idea of information value. In fact, however, he never did try to support the claim through this kind of argument, perhaps because of the additional complications that would have been introduced by appealing explicitly to the principles (i) through (iv). In studying Frege's own work on sense, we can, of course, consider only the arguments he actually presented, and all of these involve the idea of information value. Nevertheless, because of its connection with our modern concerns, we can evaluate Frege's ideas about sense very much as we would evaluate a contemporary proposal about semantic content—in part, by examining its consequences for the treatment of sentences describing our psychological states.

### 1.2.2 Information value

Returning now to (1892b), it is important to note that the argument Frege presents there relies, not only on the two principles we have discussed—compositionality, together with the principle that semantic content determines information value—but also on the further assumption, which Frege never tries to justify, that the statements '$a = b$' and '$a = a$' actually do differ in information value: that the first is informative while the second is not. And the assumption is not unique to this particular argument, from (1892b); each of Frege's arguments for distinguishing senses from referents follows a similar course. Each is grounded in the same general contrast between the informative and uninformative statements—between those possessing cognitive value (XIV11, p. 126; XV14, p. 152; XV18, p. 164), which he describes also as containing "valuable extensions of our knowledge" (1892b, p. 25; see also VIII12, p. 80) or "increas[ing] our knowledge" (1914, p. 224), and those without cognitive value, which he describes also as "self-evident" (XV14, p. 152; 1914, p. 224). Against the background of this common contrast, Frege then reasons in each of these arguments exactly as he does in (1892b), that a pair of co-referential expressions must differ in sense because there is some context in which the placement of one leads to an informative statement while the placement of the other leads to an uninformative statement.

For Frege, the difference in information value between statements like '$a = b$' and statements like '$a = a$' did not really seem to require justification or analysis.

The distinction was palpable, a perceived fact, and he never seems to have questioned it, or to have felt the need to explore it in any detail. Recently, however, it has been suggested by a number of writers that the very distinction Frege used to motivate his notion of sense has itself been misunderstood—that the distinction he perceived between statements like '$a = b$' and '$a = a$' results only from their pragmatic overtones, and should not be taken to indicate any real difference in the semantic content of these statements. In application to Frege's own work, this line of criticism has been developed most extensively by Nathan Salmon (1986), who argues, for example, that it is "by no means clear that the sentence '$a = b$', stripped naked of its pragmatic impartations and with only its properly semantic information content left, is any more informative in the relevant sense than '$a = a$'" (pp. 78–79).

This kind of objection raises large-scale issues, which I cannot go into here, about the appropriate trade-off between semantics and pragmatics in accounting for linguistic phenomena. Indeed, since the problems I want to explore in this book are largely internal to Frege's framework, I will simply have to suppose as a working hypothesis that the objection is incorrect—that Frege was not confused about the distinction he noticed between the informative and uninformative statements, and that it does reflect a real difference in semantic content. Still, the easy availability of criticisms like this shows that the nature of the distinction is not as straightforward as Frege might have thought; an analysis of some kind must be provided.

The particular analysis that will guide our work is, I believe, implicit in much of the literature in the area, but it is worth spelling out explicitly. I will suppose that Frege's notion of an uninformative, or self-evident, truth can be taken as an ancestor of the notion, subsequently explored by the logical positivists, of a *linguistic* truth, a statement whose truth is entirely determined by its meaning. Unlike the positivists, however, much of Frege's thinking about meaning was still conditioned by an orthodox, almost Cartesian view according to which meanings and their properties were supposed to be immediately apparent to the mind.

Although he had abandoned some of the traditional motives for this view, such as the conception of meanings as mental entities, Frege was able to maintain this much of the orthodoxy; and it led him to embrace a kind of *transparency principle*, according to which—in its simplest form—anyone who understands the meanings of two expressions, grasping the sense of each, must know whether or not they have the same meaning, the same sense.[6] I think it is reasonable to generalize this idea so as to apply, not only to the identity relation among meanings, but to any relation whatsoever; given Frege's rationalist assumptions, all of these relations should be transparent to the understanding mind. The result is a principle according to which: whenever the truth or falsity of a statement is entirely determined by its meaning—the meanings of its parts and the relations among them—then anyone who understands that statement, grasping its meaning, must know whether it is true.

With this notion of meaning transparency as background, our analysis of the uninformative truths as linguistic truths—truths determined by their meanings— as well as the corresponding analysis of the informative truths, can now be set out in the following way. A true statement '$S$' will be classified as *uninformative*, or self-evident, just in case any speaker who understands '$S$' must know that $S$; and conversely, if it is possible for a speaker to understand '$S$' without knowing that $S$, the statement will be classified as *informative*, possessing real cognitive value.[7] Given this analysis, the assumption underlying Frege's argument—that '$a = b$' but not '$a = a$' is informative—seems plausible, at least. It is just the assumption that anyone who understands the sentence '$a = a$' must know that $a = a$, while it is possible to understand '$a = b$' without knowing that $a = b$.

---

[6]My label for this principle is derived from Dummett, who endorses the principle as well as attributing it to Frege: "It is an undeniable feature of the notion of meaning—obscure as that notion is—that meaning is *transparent* in the sense that, if someone attaches a meaning to each of two words, he must know whether these meanings are the same" (1975, p. 131; for attributions of this principle to Frege, see Dummett 1973, pp. 95, 632; 1981, p. 323).

[7]This explication agrees with Dummett's (1973, p. 289) view of the uninformative truths as those that he defines as "trivially true." An explication along these lines is also advanced by Jeshion (2001, p. 953), who urges that the criterion should be based, not just on understanding, but on *clear* understanding, a clear grasp of senses. We will return in Chapter 3 to consider some of Frege's later ideas about the possibility of grasping senses more or less clearly.

# Chapter 2

# Sense identity

Frege's notion of sense is grounded, as we have seen, in his contrast between the informative and uninformative statements—those possessing some cognitive value and those that are, instead, entirely self-evident. In the previous chapter, I set out an explication of these ideas according to which a true statement '$S$' is to be classified as informative if it is possible for a speaker to understand '$S$' without knowing that $S$, and uninformative otherwise, if any speaker who understands '$S$' must know that $S$. Even if this explication is correct, however, it is still only schematic. As it stands, the explication cannot be used to determine the status of particular statements: it cannot tell us, for example, whether '$2 + 3 = 5$' is informative or uninformative. Because of this, the explication cannot be used to settle particular questions of sense identity: it cannot tell us whether expressions such as '$2 + 3$' and '$5$' share the same sense. Nor can it be used to settle particular questions concerning the identity of psychological states: it cannot tell us whether the state of believing that $5 = 5$ is identical with the state of believing that $2 + 3 = 5$.

In this chapter, I explore some of the options available to Frege for developing this schematic explication—options for classifying the range of particular statements as informative or uninformative, and so, for settling questions of identity both between the senses of particular expressions and between psychological states.

## 2.1 Models of the speaker

The classification of a range of statements as informative or uninformative embodies a set of standards for relating knowledge to understanding; it tells us, in part, what we suppose a speaker must know in order to understand these statements. As it turns out, these standards can be seen as reflecting a background conception of the speaker's psychology—particularly, the degree and kind of intelligence that we attribute to the speaker in our judgments of knowledge and understanding. If we suppose that speakers possess greater intelligence, we are more likely to presume that understanding entails knowledge: where '$S$' is some true statement, we are more likely to treat evidence that a speaker does not know that $S$ as evidence that the speaker simply does not understand the statement, and so we are more likely to classify '$S$' as uninformative, or self-evident. If our judgments are based on a conception of the speaker as somewhat less intelligent, on the other hand, we tend to accept a looser connection between understanding and knowledge: we are less likely to include a requirement of knowledge that $S$ among our standards for judging simply that the speaker understands '$S$', and so we are more likely to classify the statement as informative, possessing cognitive value.[1]

Because of this connection between our standards for relating knowledge to understanding and our background conception of a speaker's psychology, it is possible to explore some of the different ways of classifying statements as informative or uninformative in a roundabout way, by focusing on the associated models of the speaker's intelligence.

### 2.1.1 Ayer-Hahn monsters

To begin with, then, let us imagine a community of ideally intelligent creatures—creatures, like those described by some of the logical positivists, such as A. J. Ayer (1936, pp. 85–86) or Hans Hahn (1933, p. 159), whose reasoning is perfectly accurate, comprehensive, and instantaneous. Just by understanding a language, such a creature would have to know all of its a priori truths, all the truths expressible in the language that could be discovered through reasoning alone. Now suppose we were to take the contrast between informative and uninformative truths underlying Frege's notion of sense—his standards for relating understanding to knowledge—as grounded in a conception of speakers as creatures like these, Ayer-Hahn monsters. In that case, our schematic explication would force us to classify each statement expressing an a priori truth as uninformative, self-evident; and we can assume also, for the sake of simplic-

---

[1]A similar connection between the intelligence attributed to a system and the transparency of its propositional attitudes has been pointed out by Fodor (1979, p. 107), who argues that: "the more rational the system, the less opaque its belief contexts. The *more* we assume 'optimality of functioning,' the *less* intentionality, opacity, etc., we have to deal with."

ity, that any statement expressing an a posteriori truth could be classified as informative, possessing some cognitive value.[2]

An interpretation along these lines would naturally carry with it very loose standards for identity among the senses of particular expressions, and therefore, among the psychological states defined in relation to these senses. By Frege's criterion, there is reason to assign distinct senses to two expressions only if their exchange in some sentential context transforms an uninformative statement into one that is informative. According to the present interpretation, then, any two expressions that could be shown a priori to be co-referential would have to be assigned the same sense—since the uninformative truths are identified with those that are a priori, and there is no way to shift the status of a statement from a priori to a posteriori by exchanging a priori equivalent expressions.

Given the traditional picture of mathematics, for example, as a science whose truths are uniformly a priori, this interpretation would force us to assign the same sense to any two co-referential mathematical expressions. We would have to agree with Hahn that '5' has the same meaning as '$2 + 3$', or with Ayer when he says that '7189' and '$91 \times 79$' are synonymous. If '7189' carries the same sense as '$91 \times 79$', compositionality tells us that the two sentences '$7189 = 7189$' and '$91 \times 79 = 7189$' would have to express the same sense as well; and so the psychological state of believing that $7189 = 7189$ would have to be identified with the state of believing that $91 \times 79 = 7189$. Or to take a more extreme example, since the four color theorem is true, it is co-referential with any other true mathematical sentence, such as '$5 = 5$'. These two statements would therefore have to be classified as identical in sense, and so the psychological state of believing the four color theorem would have to be identified with the state of believing that $5 = 5$.

Of course, this interpretation of the distinction between the informative and uninformative truths as a distinction between those that are a posteriori and those that are a priori, along with the accompanying treatment of senses and psychological states, seems problematic for all the familiar reasons. To mention only one of the familiar reasons, the interpretation—based, as it is, on the notion of an ideally intelligent creature—often leaves us at a loss in describing creatures like ourselves, many of whom are less than ideally intelligent, and at least some of whom once seemed to understand the four color theorem without

---

[2]There is really nothing to prevent us from stipulating that certain a posteriori statements also should be classified as self-evident; we might decide that they express truths so fundamental that a speaker could not be said to understand these statements without knowing that they are true. However, this possibility leads to unrelated complications, and I ignore it.

knowing that it was true.  Apparently, we are left with only two options for describing this kind of situation.  We could claim that these individuals did, in some sense, know that the theorem was true, contrary to their impressions; this option appeals to a new concept of knowledge, divorced from its usual role in psychological explanation.  Or we could claim that, contrary to their impressions, these individuals did not really understand the statement of the theorem; this option appeals to a new concept of understanding, again divorced from our usual standards.  Each of these options forces a revision in our ordinary point of view, and neither is particularly satisfying, at least from a contemporary perspective.

But Frege was not necessarily driven by our concerns.  Although it seems problematic for us, it is conceivable that Frege, like some of the logical positivists, might have been willing to accept both the picture of a priori truths as uninformative and the revisions that this picture forces in our ordinary ideas of knowledge and understanding.  In fact, his contrast between the informative and the uninformative statements is often interpreted in this way, as a contrast between a posteriori and a priori truths.[3]  Could the interpretation be correct?

Well, simple common sense suggests that it would have been odd for Frege to adopt anything like this picture, with its consequence that a priori equivalent expressions should carry the same sense.  After all, though he did write extensively about the semantics of empirical languages, his primary concern was always the language of mathematics, where he continued to believe that co-referential expressions were a priori equivalent.  Therefore, if Frege had accepted the view of a priori truths as uninformative, along with its attendant standards for sense identity, he would have been unable to draw a distinction in his primary area of concern between identity of sense and co-referentiality.  It would be hard, then, to understand his preoccupation with the notion of sense, and even harder to see why he would bother to discuss it in the context of his explicitly mathematical works, such as the *Grundgesetze der Arithmetik*.

In spite of this, there is some evidence in Frege's published writings that his notion of sense was, in fact, based on an identification of the uninformative with the a priori truths.  This evidence occurs in an unfortunately prominent position, in the very first paragraph of (1892b), where Frege contrasts an a priori truth with those that may "contain very valuable extensions of our knowledge"— suggesting that any truth with the potential to extend our knowledge, any informative truth, must be a posteriori.  But this evidence is overridden at

---

[3]See, for example, Salmon (1986, p. 57).

once: at the end of the same paragraph, he describes another a priori truth, a statement of geometry, as one that does contain "actual knowledge."[4] And throughout the rest of his work, he provides a number of examples even of very simple a priori equivalent expressions that he describes as differing in sense. In the *Grundgesetze*, for instance, which must be taken to reflect Frege's considered opinion, we learn that '$2^2$' and '$2+2$' carry different senses (1893, p. 7); we learn in (1914, p. 224) that '$2 + 3$' does not share its sense with '5'. Peano is told in (XIV11, p. 128) that '$5 + 2$' differs in sense from '$4 + 3$'. And Russell is told once in (XV14, p. 152) that the sense of '$2^3 + 1$' is different from that of '$3^2$', and then reminded again, two years later in (XV18, p. 163), that '7' and '$4 + 3$' must differ in sense.

It is clear from passages like these that Frege could not have accepted a view that classifies all a priori truths as uninformative. Plainly, then, the distinction between informative and uninformative truths that underlies his notion of sense could not have been based on a model of speakers as the kind of perfect intellects described by Ayer and Hahn; he must have been relying, instead, on a conception of speakers with more limited intellectual resources.

### 2.1.2   Limited intellects

One natural way of developing an interpretation along these lines would be to suppose that the distinction between informative and uninformative truths is based on a view of speakers as a creature more or less like ourselves, subject to our own intellectual limitations and judged by our own standards. According to this interpretation, a true statement '$S$' could be classified as informative, possessing real cognitive value, whenever a speaker judged by our own standards could be said to understand '$S$' without knowing that $S$; the statement would not have to be classified as uninformative, or self-evident, unless our own standards hold that understanding '$S$' implies knowing that $S$. Even on this view, it seems that some statements—such as '$5 = 5$', for example—would still have to count as uninformative: if a speaker, judged by the standards we apply to

---

[4]Additional evidence for the idea that Frege might have taken a priori equivalent expressions as identical in sense can be found in a letter to Husserl (VII4), where he suggests that, under certain circumstances, logically interderivable sentences should be assigned the same sense. This suggestion, however, is so strikingly out of key with Frege's other writings, even of the same period, that it is hard to know what to make of it. My own view, based on Frege's earlier review of Husserl's *Philosophie der Arithmetik*, as well as the arc of their later correspondence, is that Frege had been driven by what he thought of as Husserl's excessive psychologism into trying to formulate an unimpeachably objective notion of sense identity, and had simply gone too far.

ourselves, were actually to doubt that $5 = 5$, we would be inclined to say that the speaker simply did not understand this statement. But not all the a priori truths would have to be classified as uninformative. Some, such as the four color theorem, could now be said to possess real cognitive value, since according to the standards we apply to ourselves, a speaker does not have to know that this theorem is true simply to understand it.

The notion of sense resulting from this interpretation would allow for standards of identity between the senses of individual expressions more like our ordinary standards for synonymy, and for a view of psychological states more like that involved in our everyday reasoning about ourselves. In particular, since the interpretation does not force us to assign the same sense to two expressions just because they are a priori equivalent, it would allow for the possibility of distinctions in sense among co-referential mathematical expressions, and among the psychological states defined in relation to those senses. We would be able to distinguish the sense of the four color theorem from that of '$5 = 5$', for example, and so, to distinguish the psychological state of believing the four color theorem from that of believing that $5 = 5$. Again, we would no longer be forced to agree with Ayer that '7189' expresses the same sense as '$91 \times 75$'; and indeed we could not agree, since people like ourselves, judged by our own standards, can be said to understand the statement '$91 \times 78 = 7189$' without knowing that $91 \times 78 = 7189$.

But what about the variety of intermediate cases, such as Hahn's claim that '5' expresses the same sense as '$2 + 3$'? Could a speaker, judged even by a very liberal version of the standards we apply to ourselves, really be said to understand the statement '$2 + 3 = 5$' without knowing that $2 + 3 = 5$? This question introduces an issue that did not even arise on the previous interpretation, where the distinction between informative and uninformative truths was identified with that between a posteriori and a priori truths. However poorly understood the idea of an a priori truth may be, the line between the a priori and the a posteriori truths is usually thought of as a sharp line, at least; and so the line between the informative and uninformative truths, on this interpretation, was equally sharp. If the distinction is grounded in a conception of speakers like ourselves, however, it may then appear that the line between informative and uninformative truths—and likewise, our standards for sense identity and for the identity of psychological states—may involve a certain amount of vagueness. There will be clear instances of informative truths, such as the four color theorem, or even the statement '$91 \times 78 = 7189$', and clear instances of uninformative truths, such as '$5 = 5$'. But according to the standards we apply to ourselves, there could well be borderline cases, and the statement '$2 + 3 = 5$' might lie among these.

From a contemporary perspective, in fact, we may have good reason to allow for a degree of vagueness in the classification of statements as informative or uninformative, and for a corresponding degree of vagueness in our criteria for identity among the senses of distinct expressions, and among psychological states. It is possible to argue, for example, that an analysis of meaning as correlative with psychological states should not issue in a rigid criterion of synonymy at all, but that it should exhibit a degree of flexibility—perhaps allowing different expressions to be classified as synonymous in different circumstances. For our own purposes, then, we would not necessarily object to a view that grounds the notion of sense in a conception of speakers as creatures like ourselves even if this view does turn out to introduce a measure of vagueness. When it comes to interpreting Frege, however, this kind of vagueness would have to be counted as a fatal defect. Throughout his career, Frege was constantly concerned to eliminate the vagueness found in our ordinary concepts, and he would not have been content to base his notion of sense on a contrast between the informative and uninformative truths if he had thought that this contrast might itself be vague.[5]

It is possible, however, to avoid this kind of vagueness while still adhering to the view that the notion of sense should be grounded in a conception of speakers as less than ideal reasoners. Frege surely believed that reflection on our everyday standards of judgment would lead to a precise distinction between the informative and uninformative truths, and so a precise notion of sense. And in fact, far from supposing that this distinction should be identified with that between the a posteriori and a priori truths, he even seems, at times, to have adopted an extreme position at the other end of the spectrum. Frege tells us that statements of the form '$a = a$' are uninformative, and it is natural to assume by analogy that any statement of the form '$\forall x(Fx = Fx)$' should be classified as uninformative as well.[6] Let us now consider an interpretation according to which, apart from some individual axioms, perhaps, these are the *only* state-

---

[5] As early as (1879, p. 62), Frege had objected to the vagueness of certain natural language expressions, such as 'heap'. It is evident from what he says there that these expressions are to have no place in a properly regimented language, and this consequence is later drawn explicitly, when he writes, for example, that "we have to throw aside concept-words that do not have a referent," explaining that he means by this those concept-words that have "vague boundaries" (1895a, p. 122; see also XIV7, pp. 114–115).

[6] I adopt Frege's notation, according to which the identity sign works like a biconditional when it stands between formulas.

ments that can count as uninformative, or self-evident—that statements of any other form must be classified as informative, possessing cognitive value.

I will refer to this way of understanding the ideas underlying Frege's notion of sense as the *strict interpretation*, since it forces the strictest possible standards for sense identity. By Frege's criterion, two expressions must be assigned distinct senses if their exchange in some sentential context transforms an uninformative statement into one that is informative. But given any pair of distinct expressions, it is always possible, by exchanging one for the other, to transform a statement either of the form '$a = a$' or of the form '$\forall x(Fx = Fx)$' into a statement exhibiting neither form; and so it is a consequence of this strict interpretation that no two distinct expressions could be assigned the same sense.[7] Of course, it follows from this also that the standards for identity among psychological states would have to be equally strict. The same psychological state could not be described in two ways: whenever '$S_1$' and '$S_2$' are different sentences, the psychological state of believing that $S_1$ would have to be classified as distinct from the state of believing that $S_2$.

These consequences of the strict interpretation really are very strange; in many ways, the resulting picture of meaning and psychology is as odd as that derived from the conception of speakers as Ayer-Hahn monsters. Nevertheless, although the matter is complicated, there is strong evidence, some of it deeply rooted in Frege's thought, that this strict interpretation—with its consequence that distinct expressions should be assigned distinct senses—best describes his own views. I turn now to the issues involved.

## 2.2   The strict interpretation

### 2.2.1   Arguments for the strict interpretation

It may seem obvious that Frege could not have adopted any view according to which distinct expressions must be assigned distinct senses. After all, he simply says in a number of places that distinct expressions can agree in sense, as in (1897, p. 143), for example, where he asks that we "never forget that two different sentences can express the same thought." And his writings throughout his career contain a variety of examples: a sentence and its passive form (1897, p. 141); words such as 'dog' and 'cur' (1897, p. 140), or 'steed' and 'nag' (1918, p. 63), that differ only in "shading" or "poetic eloquence" (1892b, p. 31);

---

[7]Linsky (1967, p. 34) also arrives at the conclusion that Frege could not have allowed distinct terms to express the same sense, but by a different route.

and sentences such as '5 is a prime number' and 'The thought that 5 is a prime number is true' (1892b, p. 34).

However, we must consider the problem more closely. Each of these examples involves expressions drawn from natural language, and in Frege's eyes, natural languages were terribly defective instruments: even apart from their vagueness and ambiguity, he believed they were incapable of expressing thoughts in a manner suitable for a precise specification of their inferential relations. In his preface to the *Begriffsschrift*, Frege explains how frustration with the flaws he saw in natural languages led him to develop his alternative formalism, writing that, in attempting to codify these inferential relations:

> I found the inadequacy of language to be an obstacle; no matter how unwieldy the expressions I was ready to accept, I was less and less able ... to attain the precision that my purpose required. This deficiency led me to the idea of the present concept-script. (Frege, 1879, p. 6)

Frege goes on to recall Leibniz's goal of a general reasoning tool, a *calculus ratiocinator*, which, as he notes elsewhere (1881, p. 9), was supposed to rely on the prior design of a *lingua characterica*, an ideal language capable of providing an accurate portrayal of thoughts and concepts. He mentions several specialized languages—for arithmetic, geometry, chemistry—as partial realizations of Leibniz's general goal; and he offers his own formalism as another, more "central" example through which we should be able to "fill the gaps in the existing formula languages" (1879, p. 7). His hope was that the formalism could be used "whenever special value must be placed on the validity of proofs"—not just in mathematics and the more formal sciences, but also in philosophy, where, as he writes, it might help to "break the domination of the word over the human spirit."

Frege never tired of calling attention to the flaws of natural languages for serious conceptual work—the various ways in which the word might mislead and confuse, at least, if not actually dominate the human spirit. At one point, for example, he characterizes the business of a logician as an "unceasing struggle against ... those parts of language and grammar that fail to give clear expression to what is logical" (1879 to 91, pp. 6–7); he even goes so far as to suggest that learning a foreign tongue might form a useful part of our logical education, in order to diminish the impact of the particular distortions in thought introduced by any single natural language (1897, p. 142; see also 1879 to 91, p. 6). And throughout his life, Frege concentrated on the design of an alternative formalism that he hoped to be free of these distortions, an ideal instrument for scientific investigation. The importance of this project can be seen from a brief retrospective fragment—entitled "What may I regard as the result of my work?"—which he begins, simply: "It is almost all tied up with the concept-script" (1906b, p. 184).

It is not really significant, therefore, that Frege recognized distinct expressions of natural languages as carrying the same sense; this may have been merely one of their many deficiencies. The important question is whether he could have allowed that the same phenomenon might occur also in an ideal formal language, such as his own *Begriffsschrift*. And here, as it turns out, the matter is more complicated. There are, to begin with, conclusive reasons for thinking that Frege could not possibly have allowed expressions of different syntactic structure to share the same sense; and there are also powerful, though not quite conclusive, reasons for thinking that he would not have allowed any distinct expressions to share the same sense, even if they happened to agree in syntactic structure.

Let us start by considering structurally distinct expressions. One of Frege's chief objections to natural languages as a vehicle for scientific investigation was the lack of structural correspondence between expressions drawn from these languages and their contents. This concern is especially evident in (1881), an article that Frege wrote in an effort to distinguish the goals and methods of his *Begriffsschrift* from those of Boole's logical calculus, as well as several other formalisms of his day (the article was submitted to three separate journals but in each case rejected). Here, we find that Frege's interest in a structural correspondence between linguistic items and their contents extended to include, not only the composition of more complex phrases from lexical items, but even the topic of lexical compounding itself, a matter that is still not well understood today:

> There is only an imperfect correspondence between the way words are concatenated and the structure of the concepts. The words 'lifeboat' and 'deathbed' are similarly constructed though the logical relations of the constituents are different. So the latter isn't expressed at all, but is left to guesswork. (Frege, 1881, pp. 12–13)

Frege's overall goal in his philosophical logic was to remedy this defect by constructing a formalism capable of representing, through its syntax, those logical relations among the constituents of content that are left to guesswork in natural languages, and in which, therefore, "content is rendered more exactly than is done by verbal language."

In his early work, as we have seen, Frege motivates this goal through a comparison to Leibniz's ideal of a *lingua characterica*, "a system of notation directly appropriate to objects themselves" (1879, p. 6; see also 1881, p. 9).[8] Later, after drawing a distinction between sense and reference, he is able to describe the goal more exactly. The "objects themselves" to which the system of notation is supposed to be directly appropriate are senses, not referents. Frege viewed the sense of a linguistic expression as itself possessing a determinate structure, and one of the ways in which an expression from an ideal language is supposed to be "directly appropriate" to its sense is by exhibiting that structure. He writes in one unpublished essay, for example, that: "As the thought is the sense of the whole sentence, so a part of the thought is the sense of part of the sentence" (1906a, p. 192). And in the *Grundgesetze*: "If a name is part of the name of a truth-value, then the sense of the former name is part of the thought expressed by the latter name" (1893, p. 51).[9] Strictly speaking, these remarks tell us only that, whenever a sentence expresses a thought, each part of that thought will be the sense of some part of the sentence, and also that the sense of each part of the sentence will be part of the thought, not that the sentence and the thought should actually be isomorphic. But the idea of an isomorphism is clearly implicit even in these remarks, and elsewhere he brings it out explicitly:

> We can regard a sentence as a mapping of a thought: correspond-
> ing to the whole-part relation of a thought and its parts we have,
> by and large, the same relation for the sentence and its parts.
> (Frege, 1919, p. 255)

We will return later to a more detailed consideration of the structural correspondences that might be expected between expressions and their senses, but even from these few passages, we should now be able to see why it would have been hard for Frege to allow structurally distinct expressions from an ideal language to share the same sense. If the language is really ideal, the syntactic structure of its expressions should correspond to the structure of their senses.

---

[8]Sluga (1980) traces Frege's concern with this Leibnizian ideal, and even his use of the term '*Begriffsschrift*', to an essay by the nineteenth-century philosopher Adolf Trendelenburg, who used the term to describe a language which brings "the shape of the sign in direct contact with the content of the concept" (see pp. 49–50, and the references provided there; see also pp. 93–94 for further discussion of this ideal).

[9]Frege's syntactic category of "names" is a catch-all category for a variety of meaningful expressions; it includes what we would think of as terms, predicates, function symbols, connectives, and sentences, which he viewed as denoting truth values.

But how could there possibly be such a correspondence if two expressions with different syntactic structures might share the same sense?

These considerations seem, then, to provide firm support for the view that structurally distinct expressions from an ideal language must have different senses. But they do not rule out the possibility that, even within an ideal language, the same sense might be carried by distinct but structurally isomorphic expressions. In fact, it is much harder to locate any conclusive evidence to exclude this latter possibility, but there are, nevertheless, a number of persuasive arguments against the idea, of which I consider two here.

The first of these arguments can be found by reflecting on some of Frege's decisions underlying the design of his logical formalism. As he tells us in the preface to *Begriffsschrift*, the formalism is supposed to represent only those aspects of meaning relevant to determining an expression's inferential role; he has decided to "forgo expressing anything that is without significance for the *inferential sequence*" (1879, p. 6). This decision is illustrated a few pages into the text with his discussion of two sentences, 'The Greeks defeated the Persians at Plataea' and 'The Persians were defeated by the Greeks at Plataea' (p. 12). Frege says that, although we might be able to detect a "slight difference" in meaning between these two sentences, their agreement outweighs it. The difference in meaning between sentences like these is what he will later refer to as shading, or tone. What they have in common, the aspect of meaning that determines their inferential role, he describes as their "conceptual content," and he goes on to argue that, since "*it alone* is of significance for our concept-script, we need not introduce any distinction between propositions having the same conceptual content." Now, admittedly, Frege says here only that his formalism need not distinguish between expressions with the same conceptual content; he does not say that it cannot do so. But if it need not draw such a distinction, why should it? Since the formalism is supposed to forgo expressing those aspects of meaning that are without significance for conceptual content, a syntactic distinction between two expressions carrying the same conceptual content would surely suggest a difference where there is none.

These passages from the *Begriffsschrift* were written, of course, before Frege had replaced his early notion of conceptual content with the sense/reference pair. However, it does seem that the views expressed here survive that transformation; and in particular, that Frege's early idea that his logical formalism should represent only distinctions relevant to conceptual content carries over into the idea that it should register syntactically only those distinctions that represent a real difference in sense. In one later essay, for example, after noting that the same thought can be expressed in natural languages by a number of different sentences, Frege writes that the differences among them concern only the "shading or coloring of the thought, and is irrelevant for logic" (1892a, p. 196, n. 7)—strongly suggesting, at least, that these differences should not be registered by a logic. And he is even more emphatic about the matter in a letter to Husserl, written several years later. Once more, he points out that natural languages are full of "equipollent" sentences (those carrying the same sense, expressing the same thought), but he writes here that, after the kind of logical analysis that forms the background to formalization, we would need only "a single standard proposition for each system of equipollent propositions, and any thought could be communicated by such a standard proposition" (VII3, p. 67). Again, this remark suggests that, in an ideal language, distinct but equipollent sentences should be represented by a single syntactic item.

The second argument supporting the strict view that distinct expressions from an ideal language cannot carry the same sense derives from a different source—not from general reflections about the design of a logical formalism, but from some of Frege's remarks about what it means for a statement to be uninformative, or self-evident. The remarks occur in a passage from (1914), an unpublished monograph, most likely a set of lecture notes, that will occupy a good deal of our attention throughout the next several chapters. Here, Frege argues as follows that the terms '5' and '2 + 3' must be assigned different senses:

> We might say: if we designated the same number by '2 + 3' and by '5' then surely we would have to know that $5 = 2 + 3$ straightoff, and not need first to work it out. It is clearer if we take the case of larger numbers. It is surely not self-evident that $137 + 469 = 606$; on the contrary, we only come to see this as the result of first working it out. This sentence says much more than the sentence '$606 = 606$'; the former increases our knowledge, not so the latter. (Frege, 1914, p. 224)

Although the argument from this passage conforms to the standard pattern, familiar from (1892b) and elsewhere, there is one new twist. What makes the passage especially interesting is that it shows Frege struggling to establish his idea of self-evidence as an idealization—which can then be used to define a precise standard of sense identity in a way that does not depend on what is, in fact, immediately apparent to actual people. He anticipates the objection that most of us do know "straightoff," or very nearly so, that $5 = 2 + 3$: it is surely a fact, which could be verified in the laboratory, that most actual speakers would assent to the sentence '5 = 2 + 3' more quickly than they would assent to a sentence like '379256481 = 379256481', for example. In specifying his idealized concepts of the informative and uninformative statements, Frege means to ignore whatever aspects of our actual performance lead to this difference in response time. To show that the statement '5 = 2 + 3' is informative in this idealized sense, then, he devises an argument by analogy. Actual speakers will notice that they have to work out the sum in order to see that 137 + 469 = 606. But the statements '5 = 2 + 3' and '137 + 469 = 606' are of essentially the same kind, he suggests, except that latter deals with larger numbers; and so he concludes that we must work out the sum also in order to see that 5 = 3 + 2—though in this case, apparently, we are able to work out the sum so quickly that we might not even notice ourselves doing it.[10]

If Frege's distinction between the informative and uninformative statements is an idealization, if it cannot be specified in the laboratory, through something like reaction time measures of actual speakers, then how can it be specified? As far as I can tell, the only answer available to Frege is that the uninformative statements coincide with those that follow from what he calls the "general principle of identity," while the informative statements do not. This answer is suggested in a passage just before that under consideration, where he notes that the sentence '5 = 5' is an "immediate consequence of the general principle of identity," but that '5 = 3 + 3' is not (1914, p. 224). And it is also suggested earlier, and more clearly, in a letter to Russell, where Frege writes that a statement lacks self-evidence, or possesses cognitive value, whenever a "special act of recognition" is required to see that it is true, after explaining that such a special act of recognition is necessary for seeing that a statement is true just in case it "cannot simply by inferred from the principle of identity" (XV14, p. 152). Only statements of the form '$a = a$', and perhaps also of the form '$\forall x(Fx = Fx)$', can plausibly be thought of as following simply from the principle of identity. On the view hinted at in these passages, then, only statements exhibiting this form could be classified as uninformative, or self-evident. It would take a special act

---

[10]Frege describes another kind of case in which we mistake rapid calculation for immediate insight in the *Grundlagen*. Speaking of mathematical inferences that appear obvious, though they do not exhibit the form of simple logical inferences, he writes: "A single such step is really a whole compendium, equivalent to several simple inferences ... Often, nevertheless, the correctness of such a transition is immediately [apparent] to us, without our even becoming conscious of the subordinate steps condensed within it ..." (1884, p. 102). (In order to avoid further confusion I have replaced 'self-evident', which is what appears in Austin's translation, by '[apparent]', since Frege is not speaking of self-evidence in the technical sense under investigation here.)

of recognition—an act either of empirical investigation or logical calculation—to determine the truth of any other statement; and so any other statement would have to be classified as informative, possessing cognitive value.

### 2.2.2   Problems with the strict interpretation

I have belabored these arguments to such an extent in order to show that the reasons for attributing something like the strict interpretation to Frege are not just incidental, or isolated, but in fact flow from a variety of different considerations. For Frege, the space of expressions in an ideal language really was supposed to correspond in a very strong way to the space of senses. There is firm evidence that he was committed to the view that structurally distinct expressions from an ideal language could not share the same sense; and there is also strong, though not conclusive, evidence that he may have thought no distinct expressions from such a language should share the same sense, even if structurally isomorphic.

Unfortunately, however, although these arguments thus support the attribution to Frege of a very strict view of the distinction between informative and uninformative statements, along with equally strict standards for sense identity, we cannot rest with this strict interpretation; for there are several cases in which Frege does seem to allow, even to insist, that distinct expressions from an ideal language—even structurally distinct expressions—should share the same sense.

For our purposes, the most important of these cases, and the only one we consider here, concerns expressions introduced through definition.[11] As Frege explains in the *Grundgesetze* (1893, pp. 44–45), new expressions can be introduced into the language described there through the use of his double-stroke notation for definitions: where '$P$' is some expression belonging to the language already, it is possible to introduce a new primitive expression—say, '$Q$'—simply by writing

$$\Vdash P = Q.$$

---

[11] The other two primary cases involve, first, the discussion of Frege's notorious Basic Law V, in which he claims that, even in an ideal language, expressions of the form $\hat{\epsilon}f(\epsilon) = \hat{\alpha}g(\alpha)$ share their sense with structurally distinct expressions of form $\forall x(f(x) = g(x))$, and second, some remarks from Frege's last published article in which he explicitly claims that expressions with quite different structures, such as 'Neither A nor B' and '(not A) and (not B)', share the same sense (1923, p. 41). I will not consider these two cases here, but for reasons detailed in Horty (1987), I believe that neither can be taken to provide firm evidence against Frege's deeply rooted conception of an ideal language as one whose expressions mirror the structure of thoughts; see also Dummett (1981, pp. 329–336).

Of course, '*P*' and '*Q*' will have to be distinct expressions, since '*Q*' must be new to the language; and they will typically be structurally distinct as well, since '*Q*' must be simple, but '*P*' will typically be complex. In spite of these differences, however, Frege claims that the two expressions should carry exactly the same sense:

> We introduce a new name by means of a *definition* by stipulating that it is to have the same sense and the same denotation as some name composed of signs that are familiar. (Frege, 1893, p. 82)

In this situation, then, we do seem to have a case of agreement in sense, even in an ideal language, between structurally distinct expressions: if '*Q*', a meaningless symbol, is *stipulated* to mean exactly what '*P*' does, then how could it possibly mean anything else?

However, even though the language of the *Grundgesetze* is supposed to be an ideal formal language, and even though it does contain a facility for introducing defined expressions, one might still object to this kind of example on the grounds that this definitional facility is, somehow, not an essential part of the language—that it is present only as a matter of notational convenience. This is, in fact, a standard view of definitions, endorsed by a number of writers, such as Whitehead and Russell, for example, who write in *Principia Mathematica* that "definitions are no part of our subject, but are, strictly speaking, mere typographical conveniences," and that "theoretically, all definitions are superfluous" (1910, p. 11). At times, this view is attributed also to Frege. To select an example almost at random, consider this remark from a paper by Sören Stenlund:

> According to the Frege-Russell tradition a definition is merely a convention of notational abbreviation ... From this point of view, a definition plays no essential role within a theory; its only role is within the linguistic description of the theory. (Stenlund, 1974, p. 202)

In fact, there is much in Frege to support the idea that he should be linked with this "Frege-Russell tradition." In the *Begriffsschrift*, for example, just after first presenting his double-stroke notation for definitions, he writes that the "sole purpose" for introducing defined symbols is to bring about an "extrinsic simplification by stipulating an abbreviation" (1879, p. 55). This attitude is reaffirmed at various points throughout his career, until we find him writing, even late in life, that:

Definitions are not absolutely essential to a system. We could make
do with the original group of signs. The introduction of a simple sign
adds nothing to the content; it only makes for ease and simplicity of
expression. (Frege, 1914, p. 208)

But for Frege, as I will now try to show, this simple picture of definition as no
more than notational convenience is badly misleading.

# Chapter 3

# Definitions

## 3.1 Analyticity

The best way to see the importance of definitions for Frege is to look at his work from a broader perspective, focusing on the notion of *analyticity* in his philosophy of mathematics. One of the first things we learn when we study Frege is that he hoped to show, contrary to Kant, that the truths of arithmetic are analytic. But what does this mean: what is it that Frege hoped to show, exactly, about the truths of arithmetic?

In his canonical characterization of the analytic truths, Kant, writing in the *Critique of Pure Reason*, described them as those subject-predicate statements in which the predicate concept "belongs to the subject [concept], as something which is (covertly) contained in this concept" (1781, A6/B10). And from this description, he was able to derive certain other traits of these statements. He concluded, for instance, that the analytic truths are a priori—or in the language of the previous chapter, that they would be uninformative to an ideal intellect, such as the Ayer-Hahn monster. The reason is simple: since these statements are true solely in virtue of relations among concepts, they can be discovered through conceptual analysis alone, apart from experience. More important for our purposes, Kant seemed to conclude also that the analytically true statements would be uninformative even to more limited intellects, such as our own; even creatures like ourselves, just by understanding the analytic truths, bringing to mind the concepts on which they are based, would have to know that they are true. And again, the reason for this conclusion is easy to understand: concepts, for Kant, were supposed to be such simple things that any statement whose truth could be discovered through conceptual analysis alone would have to be obvious, or very nearly so.

Consider an example.  According to Kant, the statement 'Bodies are extended' is analytic; and that is because the concept of body contains "extension, unpenetrability, figure, etc., all of which are thought in the concept" (A8/B12). Suppose, then, that an individual who understands this statement wants to learn whether it is true.  Because he understands the statement, he must possess the concept of body.  So he brings this concept to mind and begins to examine it, in order to see whether it contains the concept of extension; but since the concept is so very simple, he is able to see at once that it does.  The individual has only to think of a body, simply bringing the concept to mind, in order to see that bodies are extended; and so in a way, there is really nothing for him to learn. Just in virtue of possessing the concept of body, he already knows that bodies are extended.

Of course, Kant hedged just a bit.  An individual who possesses the concept of body already knows that bodies are extended—but he might know this only "covertly" (A6/B10), or "confusedly" (A7/B11); and the analytic judgment might bring him to a clearer realization of the fact.  Kant recognized the importance of this "clearness in concepts," but he was still able to view analytic truths as uninformative, without any real cognitive value; he contrasts the kind of conceptual clarity thus obtained to the "genuinely new addition" to our knowledge provided by synthetic judgments (A10/B14).

Now does any of this show us how to understand *Frege's* claim that arithmetic is analytic?  Does he mean that the truths of arithmetic are analytic in Kant's sense?  Not exactly—for in the *Grundlagen*, he denies that these statements possess either of the two features that Kant takes as distinguishing traits of the analytic truths.  He denies that they are statements whose subject concepts contain their predicate concepts: most, he says, are not even statements of subject-predicate form (1884, pp. 99–100).  And he denies that, for creatures like ourselves, these statements must be uninformative: "propositions which extend our knowledge can have analytic judgments for their content" (p. 104).[1]  Of course, Kant also believed that we could learn something we did

---

[1]Frege is still committed, of course, to the idea that the analytic propositions are a priori, uninformative for an Ayer-Hahn monster; but that is not a distinguishing trait of the analytic truths—not all a priori truths are analytic. It might seem odd, by the way, that I refer to the property of being uninformative for speakers like ourselves as one of Kant's distinguishing traits of the analytic truths. As I described it in the text, their uninformative nature is simply a consequence of Kant's official criterion for analyticity, the grammatical criterion. This is indeed how it appears in the *Critique*, but Kant seems to take another approach in the *Prolegomena to Any Future Metaphysics*. Here, he introduces the analytic/synthetic distinction by noting first that: "there is a distinction in judgments, as to their content, according to

not already know through arithmetic, that arithmetic could be informative; but he and Frege draw radically different conclusions from this fact. Since Kant thought we could gain no real knowledge through conceptual analysis alone, he was forced to conclude that the truths of arithmetic could not be analytic, but must be grounded in synthetic intuition. Frege, on the other hand, concludes that we must be able to gain knowledge through conceptual analysis—and he argues that Kant was led to his view of arithmetic as synthetic only because, "as a result, no doubt, of defining them too narrowly, [he] underestimated the value of analytic judgments" (p. 99).

Evidently, Frege had shifted away from Kant's account of analyticity, and his alternative characterization is not hard to find: he describes the analytic propositions as those that can be derived from general laws of logic and definitions alone (p. 4). In claiming that arithmetic is analytic, then, Frege does not mean either that we think the predicate concept of an arithmetical truth whenever we think its subject concept, or that all of arithmetic is uninformative. What he means is that the truths of arithmetic can be derived in his formal system of logic (or in the right logic, anyway), supplemented only with definitions.

Now, this new criterion of analyticity does represent a real change from Kant's.[2] It is important to see this change, but it is important, also, not to overestimate its significance. Certainly Frege thought of himself as working in the *Grundlagen* with Kant's original notion; he says that his new characterization of the analytic truths is intended "only to state accurately what earlier writers, Kant in particular, have meant" (p. 3). And there is a good deal of continuity between Kant's account of analyticity and Frege's. Put roughly, both view the analytic statements as those whose truth can be discovered entirely through conceptual analysis. In the case of Kant, this is obvious. To see that it is true also for Frege, we must see that he treats definition—the introduction of

---

which [judgments] are either merely *explicative*, adding nothing to our knowledge, or *expansive*, increasing the given knowledge. The former may be called *analytic*, the latter *synthetic*, judgments" (1783, p. 14). And then he continues—as if to explain how it could be that these analytic judgments add nothing to our knowledge—by writing: "Analytic judgments express nothing in the predicate but what has already actually been thought in the concept of the subject, though not so distinctly or with the same (full) consciousness" (p. 14). What this suggests is that the Kant of the *Prolegomena* approaches the notion of analyticity by a somewhat different route: rather than *defining* the analytic propositions as those whose subject concepts contain their predicate concepts and then *deriving* their uninformative nature from this characterization, as he does in the *Critique*, he seems here to define the analytic propositions directly as those that are uninformative and then to arrive at his grammatical characterization of these propositions as a way of *explaining* their uninformative nature.

[2]As emphasized by Benacerraf (1981, p. 26).

a defined expression into a language—as a kind of concept formation, and deduction as an analogue to Kant's process of rendering explicit what is contained in a concept.

## 3.2   Concept formation

Frege's most extensive discussion of concept formation occurs in (1881), a paper we considered earlier in connection with his idea of an ideal language, but which is primarily devoted to an extensive comparison between Boole's logical notation and deductive machinery and his own concept-script. Here, Frege argues for the superiority of his own language, not only because it allows for a more accurate representation of existing concepts, but also, and more significantly, because it allows for the formation of more complex and scientifically fruitful concepts than Boole's. The concept-script, he says, "is in a position to represent the formations of the concepts actually needed in science, in contrast to the relatively sterile multiplicative and additive combinations we find in Boole" (1881, p. 46).

Working within Boole's language, Frege writes, we can form new concepts only by taking the logical sums, products, and complements of concepts that already exist. He explains, for example, how to form the concept *homo* as the product of the already existing concepts *rationale* and *animal* (p. 33). He illustrates the familiar way in which, if these two already-existing concepts are represented by regions in a plane, the new concept can be represented by their intersection. And then, alluding to the illustration, he describes the sterility of these Boolean techniques for the formation of new concepts:

> In this sort of concept formation, one must assume as given a system
> of concepts, or speaking metaphorically, a network of lines. These
> really already contain the new concepts: all one has to do is to use
> the lines that are already there to demarcate complete surface areas
> in a new way. It is the fact that attention is primarily given to
> this sort of formation of new concepts from old ones, while other
> more fruitful ones are neglected, which surely is responsible for the
> impression one easily gets in logic that for all our to-ing and fro-ing
> we never really leave the same spot. (Frege, 1881, p. 34)

In Frege's formalism also, new concepts are supposed to be constructed by definition out of old ones, but they are constructed by means of a richer set of definitional techniques. These techniques play an essential role in allowing him to define such fruitful concepts as that of a continuous function, for example

(p. 24). And when we compare the concepts defined through these new techniques with those that can be constructed using Boolean methods alone, Frege writes, we find that in the new case:

> there is no question of using the boundary lines of concepts we already have to form the boundaries of the new ones. Rather, totally new boundary lines are drawn by such definitions—and these are the scientifically fruitful ones. (Frege, 1881, p. 34)

Although this discussion is concerned with Boole alone, what Frege says here about the limitations inherent in the Boolean techniques for concept formation should apply also to Kant's—even more strongly, it would seem, since he believed that Kant recognized only one operation for forming new concepts out of old ones, a compounding operation analogous to Boole's logical multiplication. And in fact, Frege's later comparison, in the *Grundlagen*, between Kant's view of concept formation and his own is closely parallel to his treatment of Boole from (1881). He begins with the claim that Kant "seems to think of concepts as defined by giving a simple list of characteristics in no special order; but of all ways of forming concepts, that is one of the least fruitful" (1884, p. 100). By contrast, Frege writes:

> If we look through the definitions given in the course of this book, we shall scarcely find one that is of this description. The same is true of the really fruitful definitions in mathematics, such as that of the continuity of a function. What we find in these is not a simple list of characteristics; every element in the definition is intimately, I might almost say organically, connected with the others. (Frege, 1884, p. 100)

And he goes on to describe the difference between Kant's view of definitions and his own through the same geometrical metaphor that occurs in his earlier treatment of Boole: if we think of concepts as figures on a plane, then Kant's techniques allow us to construct new concepts only by using the boundary lines of those already given in a new way; but with his own techniques, it is as if we could draw "boundary lines that were not previously given at all."

At this point, however, Frege's discussion of Kant moves beyond his earlier discussion of Boole: he draws a new conclusion, and one that I want to emphasize. As we have seen, Kant was led to view the truths arrived at through conceptual analysis alone as uninformative, without cognitive value, because of his very simple picture of concepts. But Frege, in presenting us with a more

complicated picture of concepts, also revises Kant's verdict about the truths
that can be discovered through their analysis. Once we have defined such a
complex, scientifically fruitful concept, he says:

> What we shall be able to infer from it, cannot be inspected in ad-
> vance; here, we are not simply taking out of the box again what we
> have just put into it. (Frege, 1884, pp. 100–101)

And he continues by drawing an explicit contrast between his own classification
of the truths that can be discovered through conceptual analysis and Kant's:

> The conclusions we draw from it extend our knowledge, and ought
> therefore, on Kant's view, to be regarded as synthetic; and yet
> they can be proved by purely logical means, and are thus analytic.
> (Frege, 1884, p. 101)

As an example of what Frege has in mind, it might help to consider a particular theorem of the kind that occupied his attention—say, the theorem that a
bounded, nondecreasing sequence of real numbers has a limit point. Each of the
concepts involved in this theorem—the concept of a bounded sequence, a nondecreasing sequence, and a limit point—are definable in Frege's language. And
once they have been defined, the theorem can be established through the analysis of these concepts alone, by drawing conclusions from the definitions using
only the logical techniques he provides. The theorem, therefore, is an analytic
proposition, but also an informative one, capable of extending our knowledge.
Although the concept of a sequence with a limit point is, in a way, contained
within the concept of a bounded, nondecreasing sequence, seeing that this is so
may require a considerable degree of intellectual effort. Frege turns to a new
metaphor to describe the situation: the theorem, he says, is indeed "contained
in the definitions, but as plants are contained in their seeds, not as beams are
contained in a house" (p. 101).[3]

## 3.3   Fruitfulness and eliminability

I hope that what I have said here is enough to show why it is mistaken to think of
definitions, for Frege, as nothing but notational conventions. They play a much
more important role in his thought than that. Frege claims that arithmetic is

---

[3]The most thorough discussion I have seen of concept formation and fruitfulness in Frege
can be found in Tappenden (1995), which draws on some of the same passages considered
here, but goes well beyond these brief remarks.

analytic, characterizing the analytic truths as those that follow from general laws of logic and definitions alone. And it is in part his view of definitions that enables him both to see a connection between his characterization of analyticity and Kant's, but also to break the connection Kant sees between the analytic and the uninformative truths. For Frege, the truths of arithmetic are analytic because they can be discovered through conceptual analysis alone; but his more sophisticated definitional techniques allow us to construct concepts complex enough that their analysis is genuinely informative, extending our knowledge.

This picture of definition as a means of building complex, valuable concepts suggests a certain requirement on a semantic theory of definition, which I will call the requirement of *fruitfulness*: an adequate account must allow for the possibility that some definitions, at least, are worthwhile—that the introduction of defined expressions can make new discoveries, new proofs, possible. We have seen the suggestion of this requirement in Frege's images of boundary lines, boxes, and seeds; and at times, he spells it out directly:

> Definitions show their worth by proving fruitful. Those that could just as well be omitted and leave no link missing in the chain of our proofs should be rejected as completely worthless. (Frege, 1884, p. 81)

But even if definitions are not just notational conventions, even if they play some more important role, they are at least notational conventions, they play this role at least. And so it seems that a theory of definition should be subject also to the requirement of *eliminability*: the theory should represent an expression containing defined symbols as identical in sense with the expression that results when each defined symbol is eliminated in favor of its defining phrase. The remarks cited earlier, just at the end of the previous chapter, provide evidence enough for attributing this requirement to Frege, and he is even more explicit about the matter in the following passage, which expands upon some of these earlier remarks:

> In fact it is not possible to prove something new from a definition alone that would be unprovable without it. When something that looks like a definition really makes it possible to prove something which could not be proved before, then it is no mere definition but must conceal something which would have either to be proved as a theorem or accepted as an axiom. Of course it may look as if a definition makes it possible to give a new proof. But here we have to distinguish between a sentence and the thought it expresses. If the

*definiens* occurs in a sentence and we replace it by the *definiendum*,
this does not affect the thought at all. It is true we get a different
sentence if we do this, but we do not get a different thought. Of
course we need the definition if, in the proof of this thought, we want
it to assume the form of the second sentence. But if the thought can
be proved at all, it can also be proved in such a way that it assumes
the form of the first sentence, and in that case we have no need of
the definition. (Frege, 1914, p. 208)[4]

Now evidently, these two requirements of Frege's—fruitfulness and
eliminability—stand in at least an apparent conflict. According to the fruitfulness requirement, definitions should make new proofs possible; but according
to the requirement of eliminability, "mere" definitions cannot really make it
possible to prove "something which could not be proved before." My goal here
is to explore this apparent conflict between fruitfulness and eliminability in the
treatment of definitions: to see if, in fact, Frege really does endorse conflicting
views on this topic, and if so, what can be done to reconcile them.

In thinking through these issues, it is important to maintain a sharp distinction between *stipulative* and *explicative* definitions. By a stipulative definition,
I mean one that introduces some new expression into a language. I am less sure
of what I mean, exactly, by an explicative definition, but it is something like

---

[4]This passage shows Frege anticipating both of the two criteria of the modern theory of
definition, *eliminability* and *conservativeness*. Suppose a base language is extended by the
introduction of a defined symbol. Then eliminability requires that any sentence in the extended language, containing the defined symbol, must be equivalent to some sentence from
the base language, while conservativeness requires that we should not be able to establish in
the extended language any sentence from the base language that could not already have been
established in the base language. In this passage, then, when Frege objects to a candidate
definition that "makes it possible to prove something which could not be proved before," he
is, in effect, arguing that the candidate fails to satisfy the criterion of conservativeness, and
so cannot be accepted as a correct definition, but must instead be "proved as a theorem or
accepted as an axiom." And he is appealing to the criterion of eliminability when he argues
that the thought expressed by any new sentence from the extended language must already
be expressed by some sentence from the base language—that replacement of *definiens* by
*definiendum* does not "affect the thought at all." In fact, Frege never sets out the technical
criteria of eliminability and conservativeness in any detail; their explicit formulation is generally credited to Leśniewski. But it is clear that he means to abide by these two criteria, and
the principles of definition he describes in the *Grundgesetze* (1893, pp. 51–52) guarantee that
his definitions will be satisfy them. I know of no complete history of the modern theory of
definition, but some historical remarks can be found in Belnap (1993), which also provides a
useful philosophical discussion of both the theory and its limitations, as well as some recent
variants.

this: a reconstruction of the meaning of some expression already in use in terms of others that are better understood, or in some other way less problematic.[5]

Although the distinction between these two kinds of definition is plain and familiar, it is easy to miss in practice, because they often occur together, as parts of the same enterprise: a theorist might introduce some new expression through a stipulative definition, and then claim that this new expression, with its meaning so stipulated, explicates the meaning of another, more problematic expression already in use. Imagine, for example, that an instructor teaching elementary logic has decided, for some odd reason, to work with a formal language containing only the tilde and wedge as primitive. The instructor might then introduce the horseshoe into this formal language, through a stipulative definition in terms of a tilde/wedge combination, and at the same time, present this new expression to the class as an explication of the English 'implies'. This close conjunction of stipulative and explicative definitions is useful, and also harmless as long as we do not lose track of the distinction, remembering that the way in which the tilde/wedge combination is supposed to give the meaning of the horseshoe is different, and subject to different standards of evaluation, from the way in which the horseshoe is supposed to represent the meaning of 'implies'. Since the horseshoe is new to the formal language, a stipulative definition introducing this symbol can be required to satisfy only certain standards of formal correctness; but if we are to view the symbol also as explicating the meaning of an expression already in use, the definition must then meet various standards of material adequacy as well.

It is important, then, to maintain this sharp distinction between stipulative and explicative definitions, but as long as we are able to maintain the distinction in our minds, there is no particular point in trying to enforce it with our notation. As a matter of convenience, it is often easier to act as if we were stipulating directly the meanings of the expressions we wish to explicate. Suppose, as a second example, that we are engaged in the project of "reconstructing" arithmetic within some standard set theory, with epsilon as its only non-logical primitive. Among the expressions of arithmetic whose meanings we will want to explicate are the numerals, such as '5', for instance. Now it is possible to proceed as above, introducing into the formal language of set theory an expression that is type-distinct from '5', and then claiming that the new term, with its meaning so stipulated, explicates the meaning of this numeral. But there

---

[5]Alan Anderson is credited with suggesting that what explicating the meaning of an expression amounts to is proposing "a good thing to mean by" that expression; see Belnap (1993, p. 117).

are a lot of numerals and a lot of other expressions in arithmetic, and even if we did not try to explicate the meanings of all of them, it would be a chore to keep track of which newly defined expressions were supposed to explicate the meanings of which expressions already in use.

It would be easier, as well as standard practice, simply to introduce into our set theoretical language, through stipulative definitions, expressions that happen to be type-identical with those whose meanings we wish to explicate. Following this standard practice, we would introduce the term '5', for instance, directly into the language of the set theory, allowing our notation to carry the claim that this term is supposed to explicate the meaning of the term '5' as it is used. And again, this practice is perfectly harmless as long as we remember that we are really offering two definitions at once, which must, again, be evaluated by different standards: a stipulative definition of an expression new to the language of set theory, and an explicative definition of an expression already in use in the language of arithmetic.

Let us now turn to the topic before us—whether definitions preserve sense, how they might be fruitful—with this distinction between stipulative and explicative definitions born firmly in mind. Since these two kinds of definition are evaluated by different standards, we will consider the cases separately.

### 3.3.1   Explicative definitions

In the case of explicative definitions, as it turns out, there really is no conflict between fruitfulness and eliminability at all; for here, at least according to Frege's mature view of explication, the requirement of eliminability simply does not apply.

This can be seen most clearly by considering a passage from (1914) in which Frege focuses directly on the problem of deciding whether an explicative definition (he calls it an "analytic definition") is correct, whether the defining phrase accurately captures the sense of the defined symbol. He imagines that we have provided an explicative definition of a "word or sign that has been in use over a long period of time" (p. 210). What we have as a definition is a "complex expression the sense of whose parts is known to us," and since the sense of the complex expression "must be yielded by that of its parts," it is known to us as well. Now Frege asks, concerning the sense of this complex expression, "does it coincide with the sense of the word with the long established use?" And in considering how to answer this question, he goes on to point out a difficulty that can be seen as a version of the paradox of analysis, the problem of explaining how a correct philosophical explication, or analysis—which is, after all, simply supposed to reveal the sense of the expression being analyzed—could possibly be informative, how it could have any cognitive value at all.[6]

If the expression in use and its explicative definition turn out to have the same sense, then by Frege's technical standards, the identity between the two should be uninformative, self-evident, or as he says a bit later, "recognized by an immediate insight." It follows, then, just as in the standard version of the paradox of analysis, that in this case—the case in which the explication is surely correct—it can have no cognitive value whatsoever. Frege's way of putting this is to say that what we had thought of as an explicative definition turns out instead to be a mere "axiom," the expression of a self-evident truth. But what about the other case, the case in which the identity between the expression in use and its proposed explicative definition seems to be informative? Even here, Frege is not willing to conclude at once that the two expressions are *not* identical in sense, since, by the time he wrote (1914), he had come to realize explicitly that a speaker might grasp a sense without grasping it clearly. It is only when we have a "clear grasp" of the senses of two expressions that we must know at once whether or not they share the same sense, and so it may be that the informative nature of the attempted explication results only from our unclear, or incomplete, understanding of the symbol whose meaning we were originally trying to explicate:

> If [their agreement in sense] is open to question although we can clearly recognize the sense of the complex expression from the way it is put together, then the reason must lie in the fact that we do not have a clear grasp of the sense of the simple sign, but that its outlines are confused, as if we saw it through a mist. (Frege, 1914, p. 211)

This is, in fact, the kind of situation in which explication will be most useful, since its purpose is "to articulate the sense clearly."

But how, exactly, are we supposed to proceed? Imagine, for example, that 'A' is the expression in use. Its sense is not quite clear to us, and so we have offered the complex expression 'B' as its explicative definition. Now suppose it is not self-evident that the definition is correct, but that, as we realize, this may be due only to our original failure to grasp the sense of 'A' with sufficient clarity. If our understanding of 'A' were clear enough that we could trust this lack of self-evidence as an indication that its definitional link with 'B' is incorrect,

---

[6]Frege's understanding of the problem of analysis, and his response to it, have been described in detail by Resnik (1980, pp. 39–47 and 180–185); see also Dummett (1991b).

there would then be no point in explicating its sense to begin with. There is
a reason to explicate the sense of '$A$' only if we do not already have a clear
grasp of its sense; but then, precisely because our grasp of its sense is unclear,
we cannot necessarily tell whether it shares its sense with '$B$'. So how do we
decide in this case—the only case in which an explicative definition might have
some point—whether or not the definition we have provided is correct?

Frege's strategy—not without its virtues—is simply to ignore the issue:

> we can bypass this question altogether if we are constructing a new
> system from the bottom up; in that case we shall make no further use
> of the sign ['$A$']—we shall only use ['$B$']. (Frege, 1914, pp. 210–211)

Faced with an expression whose sense is not quite clear to us, we first do the best
we can to construct an expression that matches its sense, as we understand it,
in a logically perspicuous language; but once such an expression has been found,
we then simply throw away the original expression and carry on our scientific
work using the new expression alone.

This, then, is Frege's *official* response to the paradox of analysis, but of
course, for anyone actually engaged in the project of reconstructing a science,
it would be very difficult to follow this official policy in practice. Each philosophical analysis would have to be accompanied by the abandonment of some
familiar expression, until, eventually, the whole of the original vocabulary had
been disposed of. Frege realizes the practical inconvenience involved, and he
relaxes his official policy in practice: we may find it "expedient," he says, to
continue working with an old symbol. But this relaxation is only expedience,
not a shift in principle. If we do continue to work with an old symbol, Frege
warns us:

> we must treat it as an entirely new sign which had no sense prior to
> the definition. We must therefore explain that the sense in which this
> sign was used before the new system was constructed is no longer of
> any concern to us ... (Frege, 1914, p. 211)

As this passage shows, correct explicative definitions, for Frege, are not
subject to the requirement of eliminability at all: there is no requirement that
symbols analyzed through explicative definitions must share the sense of their
defining phrases, or that sentences containing these defined symbols must agree
in sense with the sentences that result when these symbols are eliminated in
favor of their explications. Once we explicate the meaning of an expression in
use, we either drop it from our vocabulary, or, even if we retain the expression

to carry the sense provided by our explication, we are no longer concerned with its original sense.[7] Moreover, Frege's discussion here begins to show *why* he did not require explicative definitions to preserve sense: if he had embraced this requirement, his view that an identity between expressions sharing the same sense must be uninformative would have led him into something like the paradox of analysis.

On the other hand, in the case of explicative, or analytic definitions, there is a straightforward way of understanding the fruitfulness requirement—a straightforward way of seeing how such definitions could allow us to establish new truths, which we could not have proved without them. As Frege explains:

> By means of such an analysis, we may hope to reduce the number
> of axioms; for it may not be possible to prove a truth containing a
> complex constituent so long as that constituent remains unanalysed;
> but it may be possible, given an analysis, to prove it from truths in
> which the elements of the analysis occur. (Frege, 1914, p. 209)

And the kind of thing he has in mind here is well illustrated in his own work on arithmetic. If we do not bother to analyze the constituents of the arithmetical truths—the senses of 'Number', the individual numerals, or of the basic predicate and function symbols—then we are forced to take certain arithmetical truths, such as the Peano postulates, for example, as axioms; we cannot prove them. But if we do manage to provide proper explicative definitions of these expressions, such as Frege's own, there is no longer any need to treat these arithmetical truths as axioms; they can be derived instead from other more fundamental assumptions concerning elements of the explication (sets, or courses-of-values). Explicative definitions allow us to prove certain propositions

---

[7]At this point it is worth asking: what *is* the original sense of some expression in use, prior to its explication—what does the expression in use actually mean? The best answer, I think, is that the expression in use should not be taken as carrying any precise sense at all, but only as approximating the sense that a correct explication will eventually assign to it. This reading is supported, for example, by Frege's remarks about Weierstrass at (1914, p. 222), whom he describes as having a "sound intuition of what a number is," but whose precise definitions involve him in contradictions. Still, Frege writes: Weierstrass "arrives at true thoughts, which, one must admit, come into his mind in a purely haphazard way. His sentences express true thoughts, if they are rightly understood. But if one tried to understand them in accordance with his own definitions, one would go astray." Here, Frege seems to be arguing that the "true thoughts" that Weierstrass's sentences should be taken to express are not those provided by his own explications of numerical terms—which themselves lead to contradictions—but those thoughts that would be assigned to these sentences once they are "rightly understood," that is, once the numerical terms and all other problematic items are correctly explicated.

that would otherwise have to be taken as axioms; and so in this way, they allow us to prove things that could not have been proved without them.

### 3.3.2 Stipulative definitions

So explicative definitions, in Frege, are not subject to the requirement of eliminability, but there is a way of seeing how they could be fruitful. In this case, then, since the definitions are not subject to both of these requirements—fruitfulness and eliminability—there can be no conflict between them. But what about the case of stipulative definition? It might seem that there cannot really be a conflict here either. It is very tempting, in fact, to suppose that the whole appearance of conflict in Frege's treatment of definitions results from taking together two requirements that are supposed to apply only separately, to two different kinds of definition. Just as explicative definitions can be fruitful, but are not required to preserve sense, one might suppose that, although stipulative definitions must satisfy the requirement of eliminability, there is no reasonable way of seeing how they could be fruitful.[8]

Such a reading would be mistaken, however. Within Frege's framework, there are, in fact, two distinct ways in which stipulative definitions could be said to be fruitful. The first, which has been explored by Michael Dummett, involves a very robust understanding of fruitfulness, according to which the introduction of defined symbols actually alters the structure of thoughts expressible in a language, so that the possibility of fruitfulness must then be seen as inconsistent with Frege's requirement of eliminability. This kind of fruitfulness is still frequently misunderstood, and has never been developed within the context of a formal semantic theory; we will return to consider the topic in detail in the latter part of this book. The second way of understanding fruitfulness for stipulative definitions is by means of a weak, psychological interpretation, according to which definitions are supposed to be fruitful only by aiding our thinking. This version of fruitfulness is often thought of as unimportant, even by Dummett (1991b, p. 23; see also 1990, p. 275). And in a well-known paper, Paul Benacerraf also dismisses the weak interpretation as follows:

> Definitions are not *simply* conventions of abbreviation; for if they
> were, the requirement of fruitfulness cited above would make lit-
> tle sense. The fruitfulness would be a matter only of psychological

---

[8]Weiner, for example, argues (1984, pp. 66–68; see also 1990, pp. 89–91) that there can be no non-trivial requirement of fruitfulness for stipulative definitions (which she refers to as "mathematical" definitions).

heuristic and not something to which Frege would attach much importance. (Benacerraf, 1981, p. 28)

Benacerraf's gloss on the notion of fruitfulness is very much like that presented here: a definition is fruitful, he says, if "we can prove things with it that we could not have proved without it." He does not explicitly formulate a version of the eliminability requirement, but his idea that definitions are simply conventions of abbreviation is close enough. Taken in its context, then, this passage of Benacerraf's seems to suggest two things: first, that for Frege to care about it, fruitfulness would have to be more than a matter of psychological heuristic; and second, that if fruitfulness were merely psychological, there would be little theoretical difficulty reconciling it with the requirement of eliminability, viewing definitions simply as conventions of abbreviation.

These are, in any case, the two theses I want to discuss in developing the weak interpretation of fruitfulness, whether or not they accurately capture Benacerraf's view. I will argue that both are mistaken. The remainder of this chapter deals with the first of these theses, establishing Frege's concern; the following chapter shows that, even on the weak, psychological interpretation, there is still a conflict between fruitfulness and eliminability.

The evidence that Frege would be concerned with fruitfulness even if it were only a matter of psychological heuristic occurs in yet another passage from (1914), in which he discusses the point of stipulative definitions. Just after the very strong statement cited earlier of his eliminability requirement, according to which stipulative definitions are simply abbreviations, allowing us in principle neither to express nor to prove any new thoughts, he writes:

> It appears from this that definition is, after all, quite inessential. In fact considered from a logical point of view it stands out as something wholly inessential and dispensable. (Frege, 1914, p. 208)

But he continues:

> I want to stress the following point. To be without logical significance is by no means to be without psychological significance. (Frege, 1914, p. 209)

And he then goes on to provide a detailed description of the psychological significance of stipulative definitions in a passage that will occupy our attention throughout the remainder of this chapter. Frege imagines a situation in which, through a series of definitions, perhaps, we have managed to introduce into some formal language a simple expression with a very complex sense; he takes as his example the expression 'integral'—defined, say, in pure set theory, or pure course-of-values theory—and writes:

> If we tried to call to mind everything appertaining to the sense of this word, we should make no headway. Our minds are simply not comprehensive enough. We often need to use a sign with which we associate a very complex sense. Such a sign seems, so to speak, a receptacle for the sense, so that we can carry it with us, while being always aware that we can open this receptacle should we have need of what it contains. It follows from this that a thought, as I understand the word, is in no way to be identified with a content of my consciousness. If therefore we need such signs—signs in which, as it were, we conceal a very complex sense as in a receptacle— we also need definitions so that we can cram this sense into the receptacle and take it out again. So if from a logical point of view definitions are at bottom quite inessential, they are nevertheless of great importance for thinking as it actually takes place in human beings. (Frege, 1914, p. 209)

I will separate my discussion of this passage—our *central passage*—into two parts, first placing Frege's remarks here against the background of his over-all philosophical perspective, and then offering a detailed interpretation of the passage itself.

## The central passage in perspective

As we saw in our earlier discussion of explicative definitions, Frege had come to realize by the time he wrote (1914) that a speaker might grasp a sense without grasping it clearly, in all its parts; and he had begun to adjust his outlook to accommodate this possibility. Many of the adjustments involved are straightfor-ward and predictable, giving his overall theoretical framework a more realistic cast. For example, he exploits the possibility of imperfectly grasped senses in describing the process of mathematical education: even the simplest expressions of arithmetic are supposed to have complicated senses, and a student "in the third or fourth forms" can hope to achieve a clear grasp of these senses only by moving first through an incomplete and imperfect understanding; in the initial stages, for "didactic reasons, . . . sharp logical edges are rounded off" (pp. 221– 222). This application of the possibility of grasping senses imperfectly to the topic of mathematical education might not seem too surprising. What is almost astonishing, however, is Frege's further suggestion that it is also appropriate at times, not just for an elementary student, but also for a working scientist to possess less than a perfectly clear grasp of the senses of certain mathematical expressions.

This is the kind of attitude one might have thought would provoke Frege's violent ridicule. After all, as far back as the *Grundlagen* he had declared it a "scandal" that his fellow mathematicians could be "so unclear about" the most basic concepts and objects of their science (1884, p. ii); and the avowed aim of that work was to enable us to attain a "sharp grasp" of these basic concepts and objects, particularly the "concept of Number" and the individual numbers (pp. 1–2). Although Frege had not yet drawn his distinction between senses and referents, these concerns with sharpness and clarity are so central to his philosophical outlook that one would expect them to survive that distinction, reemerging in an insistence that we should strive for a clear grasp of the senses of mathematical expressions. And indeed, he does return to these familiar themes in (1914). He criticizes our tendency to rest content once we grasp the sense of an arithmetical expression just well enough to get by, as if it would not befit a "serious thinker" to devote any further attention to these "matters of the schoolroom" (p. 222). By succumbing to this tendency, he says, we miss the "full educational value" to be gained through the study of mathematics, and worse, we inhibit our own capacity for research:

> how, it may be asked, can a man do effective work in a science when he is completely unclear about one of its basic concepts? The concept of a positive integer is indeed fundamental for the whole arithmetical part of mathematics. Any unclarity about this must spread throughout the whole of arithmetic. This is obviously a serious defect and one would imagine that it could not but prevent a man from doing any effective work whatsoever in this science. Surely no arithmetical sentence can have a completely clear sense to someone who is in the dark about what a number is. (Frege, 1914, p. 222)[9]

---

[9]When Frege speaks here of "concepts," he takes this word to have the more ordinary meaning he favored prior to 1891, not the technical meaning he conferred upon it later, according to which concepts are the referents of predicates. The passage, then, recapitulates and develops his *Grundlagen* view that we should aim to become "clear about" mathematical concepts; and Frege's easy transition in its final sentence from talk of concepts to talk of senses shows that his later concern with the importance of attaining a clear grasp of senses has its roots in the earlier position. The continuity between Frege's early concern with attaining a

But, surprisingly, Frege goes on to undermine this long-standing position with his very next breath, maintaining both that, as a matter of psychological fact, we are not able to grasp the senses of certain mathematical expressions with perfect clarity, and that, even so, our ability to reason with these expressions need not be hampered. The senses of mathematical expressions can be terribly complicated, and, as he writes:

> We simply do not have the mental capacity to hold before our minds a very complex logical structure so that it is equally clear to us in every detail. For instance, what man, when he uses the word 'integral' in a proof, ever has clearly before him everything which appertains to the sense of this word! And yet we can still draw correct inferences, even though in doing so there is always a part of the sense in penumbra. (Frege, 1914, p. 222)

Certainly, this remark seems to sound a new note. It may be tempting, in some ways, to read it only as a sober recognition of our limitations, not a shift in principle: one might expect to find Frege insisting, even as he recognizes our psychological limitations, that we should strive to grasp the senses of mathematical expressions with as much clarity as these limitations allow. What our central passage from (1914, p. 209) shows, however, is that this is not his attitude at all. On the contrary, we find him suggesting in this passage, not only that we may be unable to grasp the senses of mathematical expressions with perfect clarity, but that we should not always try to—that "we should make no headway" if we actually tried to grasp their senses in full detail, and that we are often better off if we "conceal" certain aspects of their senses from ourselves, "as in a receptacle."

When Frege questions the idea that we are best off grasping senses as clearly as possible, then, he questions a view that goes back at least as far as the *Grundlagen*, occupying a fundamental position in his early philosophy of mathematics. His later standpoint, set out in (1914), and particularly in our central passage, does indeed indicate a real shift in principle, not just a concession to our practical limitations. Let us now return to consider this passage in more detail in order to see what might have led him to such a radical change of outlook.

---

"sharp grasp" of mathematical concepts and his later emphasis on the importance of grasping senses clearly has been described in detail by Burge (1984, particularly pp. 6–12).

### Interpreting the central passage

Frege seems to be concerned in this passage chiefly with limitations on the complexity of thoughts capable even of being grasped, or entertained, by creatures like ourselves. These limitations are supposed to result from the fact that, as he says here, our minds are not sufficiently "comprehensive," or elsewhere, as we have just seen, that we "simply do not have the mental capacity to hold before our minds a very complex logical structure so that it is equally clear to us in every detail" (p. 222). Although this kind of observation is very reasonable, and certainly conforms to our everyday intuitions, it is not easy to see how it can be accommodated within Frege's framework, since prior to this discussion, at least, he tells us so little about the mechanism through which we are supposed to grasp thoughts that it is hard to locate any source at all for constraints on the complexity of the thoughts we might be able to grasp. In fact, even in this manuscript, Frege presents his point about our mental limitations by appeal to metaphors of containment, suggesting that very complicated thoughts are somehow just too "large" to fit directly into our minds. And it may seem that these metaphors are particularly inappropriate, since it is so central to his philosophy that thoughts (and senses generally) are not supposed to be contained *in* our minds at all.

One of the most interesting things to notice about our central passage, however, is that it shows Frege exploring, at least in a tentative way, the consequences of a *representationalist* view of thinking—a view according to which we are supposed to grasp thoughts and other senses, not directly, but rather through the mediation of linguistic items with which they are associated. Of course, this kind of view is popular today, but it is not necessarily something one would have expected to find in Frege. Still, strictly speaking, the representationalist idea is not even new to (1914). Frege had remarked on several earlier occasions, such as (1882, p. 84) and (1897, pp. 142–143), simply that we do think in language; but these remarks have the character of asides, and it is not until his later work that he seems to have reflected on the consequences of this idea in any detail. His concern with the role of language in our grasp of senses is especially evident in (1918), where he says at one point that thoughts become graspable by being "clothed in the perceptible garb of a sentence" (p. 61), and elsewhere apologizes to the reader for not being able to exhibit a thought directly, but only "wrapped up in a perceptible linguistic form" (p. 66, n. 6). He returns to the idea again in one of his very last manuscripts, writing that it is necessary for human beings that any thought of which we are conscious should

be "connected in our mind with some sentence or another" (1925, p. 269).[10]
And it seems that the idea is at work also in our central passage, where he
speaks, for example, of linguistic expressions as "receptacles" for senses.

I believe that it is by taking seriously this representational idea of Frege's—as
he himself did in his later works—that we can best understand both the source
of the constraints he recognized in (1914) on our ability to grasp and reason with
complex senses, and also the way in which definitions are supposed to help us
get around these constraints. Against the background of this representational
picture, it is natural to interpret Frege's metaphors of containment as applying,
not exactly to thoughts themselves, but instead, to the linguistic items through
which these thoughts are presented to us. It is these items that can reasonably
be described as contained in the mind, subject to the limitations on our mental
capacity. If we tried to grasp a very complicated thought by presenting ourselves
with a sentence that faithfully encoded each of its structural details, we might
find that this sentence exhausted our limited mental capacity. Definitions enable
us to get around the problem, then, by giving us the means to present such a
thought to ourselves through an expression that conceals some of these details—
allowing us, presumably, both to grasp and to establish thoughts that would
have been inaccessible to us otherwise.

This interpretation of fruitfulness can be illustrated by elaborating Frege's
own example, the concept of an integral. Let us suppose that, along with some
numerals and terms denoting certain functions, the conventional symbol for an
integral has been properly introduced into a pure set theory, or a pure course-
of-values theory. Now consider even a simple sentence containing these new
expressions—a sentence of the sort that might appear in an introductory calculus text, such as '$\int_0^3 x^2 dx = 9$'. Since the defined expressions in this sentence
have been properly introduced, they will be eliminable in favor of their defining
phrases; and the result of eliminating them will be some sentence from the base
language—'$P$', say—that is provable in principle just in case '$\int_0^3 x^2 dx = 9$' is
provable in the extended language. However, '$P$' will be a very complicated
sentence, expressing a correspondingly complicated thought. And what Frege
seems to believe, quite sensibly, is that creatures like ourselves, with our psychological limitations, would either be unable to think such a complex thought
by presenting ourselves with the sentence '$P$', or even if we were able to do so,
that merely attending to this sentence, which represents the thought in complete detail, would exhaust so much of our mental capacity that we would find

---

[10]Although Frege admits the possibility of creatures who could grasp thoughts without the
aid of some linguistic, or at least perceptible, medium, he says that we are not like that.

it impossible to hold this thought in mind along with others, or to manipulate its representation in the ways that constitute reasoning. For most ordinary purposes, much of the structure contained in the thought that $P$ will be irrelevant anyway; definitions are helpful because they allow us to pack away this irrelevant structure, representing to ourselves only the complexity called for by the purposes at hand, and so conserving our limited mental capacity.

This emphasis on metaphors of mental capacity might suggest that the sheer "size" of a representation is the only issue, and that definitions aid our thinking only by allowing us to represent a complex thought to ourselves more compactly. But there is more to it than that. In general, definitions allow us, not only to suppress structure in our representation of thoughts, but also to modify that structure. The sentences '$\int_0^3 x^2 dx = 9$' and '$P$' will not share a common structure even at the highest level of syntactic analysis. We cannot expect to find constituents of '$P$' corresponding to the grammatical constituents of '$\int_0^3 x^2 dx = 9$'. There will be no single, isolable constituent of '$P$' corresponding to the occurrence in this sentence of the function symbol '$\int$', for example, or even to the occurrence of '9'. When we present the thought that $P$ to ourselves through the sentence '$\int_0^3 x^2 dx = 9$', then, we are representing this thought in a way that is not only more compact than its representation as '$P$', but also essentially different—through a sentence with a different logical form, constructed from new constituents, in a new manner. And for creatures like ourselves, representing the same thoughts through sentences with essentially different structures may aid our thinking in a way that goes beyond conservation of mental capacity; for it may be that certain logical linkages among thoughts are more easily noticeable depending on the structure of the sentences through which they are represented.

As an example, consider now the sentences '$9 = 2 + 7$' and '$\int_0^3 x^2 dx = 2 + 7$', belonging, again, to the definitional extension of our base language. Just as the sentence '$\int_0^3 x^2 dx = 9$' reduces to the base language sentence '$P$', the defined symbols in these other sentences will also be eliminable, resulting again in sentences from the base language—say, '$Q$' and '$R$'. And of course, there will be logical linkages among the thoughts expressed by these three sentences from the base language, the thoughts that $P$, $Q$, and $R$: any two of them will entail the third. Now let us, for a moment, put aside any worries about our limited mental capacity; suppose we did have the mental capacity to represent these three thoughts to ourselves directly, through the sentences '$P$', '$Q$', and '$R$'. We might *still* have a hard time establishing the logical linkages among these thoughts when they are represented in this way. Even apart from the advantages gained through compactness of presentation, even if this were not an issue, we might still be able to discover the connections among these three thoughts much more easily if we represented them to ourselves, respectively, through the sentences '$\int_0^3 x^2 dx = 9$', '$9 = 2 + 7$', and '$\int_0^3 x^2 dx = 2 + 7$'.

It is easiest to understand why this should be so if we examine the issue using the model of thinking as the manipulation of mental symbols—the manipulation, then, not of thoughts themselves, but of the linguistic items through which they are presented to us, a process analogous to the manipulation of logical formulas through ordinary rules of inference. If they are anything like their proof-theoretic counterparts, the mental manipulations involved in establishing linkages among the thoughts that $P$, $Q$, and $R$ when they are presented directly—that is, through the sentences '$P$', '$Q$', and '$R$'—would be very complicated. Even if we did have the capacity simply to *entertain* these thoughts in this way, we might still find it difficult to carry out the complicated manipulations necessary for discovering their logical connections. On the other hand, if we were to represent these thoughts to ourselves with the alternative structures proposed above, the mental manipulations necessary for discovering their logical linkages—again, if they are anything like their proof theoretic counterparts—would be simple, easy to perform. When they are represented through the sentences '$\int_0^3 x^2 dx = 9$', '$9 = 2 + 7$', and '$\int_0^3 x^2 dx = 2 + 7$', any two of these three thoughts are cast as containing a common constituent, flanking the thought-constituent corresponding to the identity sign. It is precisely by recognizing these common constituents, which do not appear on the other representation, that we are able to see logical linkages among these thoughts so easily: it is because of the common grammatical constituents of these sentences that the mental manipulations involved in establishing the connections among the thoughts they represent can be so simple.

Of course, in the passage I have cited from (1914), Frege does not discuss *this* particular way in which definitions can be helpful—by allowing us to represent thoughts to ourselves through sentences with different structures, so that we can see the linkages among them more easily. He speaks instead only about conservation of mental capacity, and no wonder; the idea that thoughts might be represented through sentences with essentially different (as opposed to simply: less) structure clashes much more severely with his view that sentences from an ideal language should mirror in their structure the thoughts they express. Other writers, however, have noted the possible benefits of allowing structurally distinct representations of the same thought. To take a single illustration, this is surely the kind of thing that Wittgenstein (1956, pp. 84–88) has in mind, for example, when he argues that definitions are primarily useful, not simply for providing us with a "shortened" notation (p. 86), but for facilitating the kind of conceptual advance that he describes as discovering a new aspect:

> It might be called "finding a new aspect," if someone writes '$a(f)$' instead of '$f(a)$'; one might say: "He *looks* at the function as an argument of its argument." Or if someone wrote '$\times(a)$' instead of '$a \times a$' one could say: "he looks at what was previously regarded as a special case of a function with two argument places as a function with *one* argument place."
>
> If anyone does this he has certainly altered the aspect in a sense, he has for example classified *this* expression with others, compared it with others, with which it was not compared before. (Wittgenstein, 1956, p. 87)[11]

In any case, whether we are concerned only with the conservation of mental capacity, or also with the advantages to be gained through the choice of structurally distinct representations, the example set out here illustrates one important way in which stipulative definitions might be fruitful, enabling us to overcome some of our mental limitation, and so to discover thoughts that we could not have discovered without them. It is perfectly reasonable to suppose that—purely as a matter of psychological fact—a creature with our cognitive restrictions would never have been able to discover the thought that $P$ working only in the base language of set theory, where this thought could be presented only through the sentence '$P$'. It is at least in part because the introduction of defined expressions allows us to present this thought to ourselves through the sentence '$\int_0^3 x^2 dx = 9$', therefore, that we are able to discover its truth.

---

[11] A useful discussion of "seeing a new aspect," deriving from but also building on Wittgenstein's views, can be found in Waismann (1956, pp. 377–379).

# Chapter 4

# Sense and meaning

Let us review. As we saw in Chapter 1, Frege was committed through his treatment of indirect discourse to the idea that sentential senses, or thoughts, should correlate with psychological states—that statements such as 'Susan believes that $S_1$' and 'Susan believes that $S_2$' should agree in truth value whenever '$S_1$' and '$S_2$' express the same sense. And as we saw in Chapter 2, Frege's notion of sense itself was closely bound up with a conception of speakers as creatures subject to psychological limitations. He did not classify expressions as identical in sense simply on the basis of a priori equivalence, as he would have if the notion had been grounded in a conception of speakers as ideal reasoners. Instead, his writings suggest a view of sense identity at least as strong as our ordinary concept of synonymy, and very much stronger, as we have seen, in the case of an ideal language.

In Chapter 3, we turned our attention to Frege's theory of definition, focusing on an apparent conflict between two of its central tenets. The first was the requirement of fruitfulness: the idea that definitions should make it possible to prove things that we could not have proved without them. The second was the requirement of eliminability: the idea that an expression containing defined symbols should share its sense with the expression that results when those symbols have been eliminated. In interpreting Frege's notion of fruitfulness, we have concentrated thus far on a weak, psychological reading, according to which definitions are supposed to be fruitful simply because they aid the thinking of creatures like ourselves, enabling us to overcome some of our psychological limitations.

Now it may seem, as it has to several writers, that this weak interpretation of the fruitfulness requirement is theoretically uninteresting, and in particular, that there should be no difficulty reconciling the requirement taken in this way with Frege's requirement of eliminability. My goal in the present chapter is to show that this is not so.[1] Even on the weak, psychological interpretation, it turns out that there is still a tension between these two requirements: once the idea of fruitfulness is taken into account, Frege cannot maintain both his requirement of eliminability and the correlation he sought between senses and psychological states. After describing this conflict, I explore one way in which Frege might have resolved it, and I compare that method of resolution with some similar themes in more recent work.

## 4.1 The conflict

It is easiest to see how fruitfulness forces a conflict between Frege's requirement of eliminability and his correlation of senses with psychological states by focusing on a particular example; so let us return to the situation described earlier, toward the end of the previous chapter. We supposed there that the language of pure set theory, or pure course-of-values theory, had been definitionally enriched with the conventional symbols for the numbers and certain functions, including the definite integral. The enriched language contained the sentence '$\int_0^3 x^2 dx = 9$', whose definitional reduction into the base language, we assumed, was the sentence '$P$'. And we supposed that, as a matter of psychological fact, a creature with our cognitive limitations might be able to establish the sentence '$\int_0^3 x^2 dx = 9$' in the enriched language, though not able to establish the sentence '$P$' working in the base language alone.

Now imagine that Susan is such a creature, and that—working in the extended language, using the appropriate proof or calculational techniques introduced along with the defined expressions—she does manage to establish the sentence '$\int_0^3 x^2 dx = 9$'. Does Susan then believe that $\int_0^3 x^2 dx = 9$? Well, we can suppose that, as a result of having established this sentence, she is now willing to assent to it, write it in an exam booklet during a calculus test, perhaps even place bets on its truth. In that case, it seems that our ordinary standards would force us to the conclusion that Susan believes that $\int_0^3 x^2 dx = 9$, and therefore, that the sentence 'Susan believes that $\int_0^3 x^2 dx = 9$' is true.

But must we conclude also that Susan believes that $P$? Since the sentence '$P$' follows by definitional reduction alone from one that Susan has already accepted, we can assume that she possesses a procedure for discovering its truth: applying the appropriate definitional reductions. But our ordinary standards

---

[1]This chapter is based on an argument presented in Horty (1993).

allow a distinction between possessing a procedure, even an effective procedure, for discovering the truth of some sentence and actually believing the proposition it expresses. Once Susan has learned grade school arithmetic, she can be said to possess an effective procedure for discovering the truth of the sentence '$91 \times 79 = 7189$', for example; but our ordinary standards do not force us to conclude that Susan believes that $91 \times 79 = 7189$, just because she knows how to do column multiplication. The definitional reductions involved in arriving at '$P$' from the sentence '$\int_0^3 x^2 dx = 9$' are considerably more complex than the procedure for calculating that $91 \times 79 = 7189$. Susan may not have bothered to carry out these reductions, or she may have tried to but carried them out incorrectly. In either case, she might reasonably withhold assent from '$P$', refuse to write it in the exam booklet, or decline to place bets on its truth. And it would then seem to accord most closely with our ordinary standards to describe the situation as one in which Susan simply does not believe that $P$, and so, in which the sentence 'Susan believes that $P$' is false.

If this story is coherent, our ordinary standards for judging such things seem to allow for a situation in which 'Susan believes that $\int_0^3 x^2 dx = 9$' is true while 'Susan believes that $P$' is false. Susan might be in a psychological state properly characterized as believing that $\int_0^3 x^2 dx = 9$ without also being in a state that could be characterized as believing that $P$. Because of the correlation that Frege sought between senses and psychological states, we would then have to conclude that the two sentences '$\int_0^3 x^2 dx = 9$' and '$P$' possess distinct senses. But of course, this conclusion clashes with his requirement of eliminability for defined expressions, since the second of these sentences is a definitional reduction of the first. Even the weak, psychological aspect of fruitfulness leads, therefore, to a conflict with Frege's requirement of eliminability: it forces a clash between eliminability and the idea that senses should correlate with psychological states.[2]

---

[2]Readers familiar with Kripke (1979) will recognize that our argument appeals to something like the principles of disquotation formulated there. If Susan assents to '$\int_0^3 x^2 dx = 9$', we can conclude that she believes that $\int_0^3 x^2 dx = 9$ using the simple principle of disquotation (p. 248); but to conclude that Susan does not believe that $P$ from his refusal to assent to '$P$' we must appeal to the strengthened principle (p. 249). In fact, if we are able to view definitional reduction as a *translation* from a language containing defined expressions into its base fragment—a view that seems very sensible—then a conflict similar to that set out here could be derived from Kripke's principles rather than Frege's. Because Susan assents to the sentence '$\int_0^3 x^2 dx = 9$', simple disquotation tells us that 'Susan believes that $\int_0^3 x^2 dx = 9$' is true. From this, Kripke's additional principle of translation (p. 250) would allow us to conclude that 'Susan believes that $P$' is true as well; but we must also conclude from strengthened disquotation that 'Susan believes that $P$' is false, since she will not assent to '$P$'.

In a way, this kind of conflict should really come as no surprise. To say that definitions are psychologically fruitful, that their fruitfulness is due only to our psychological limitations, is simply to say that a creature without these limitations, such as the Ayer-Hahn monster, would not find the introduction of defined expressions helpful in the way that we do. When we present the thought that $P$ to ourselves through the sentence '$\int_0^3 x^2 dx = 9$', we are—precisely because of our cognitive limitations—in a psychological state significantly different from that in which we present this thought to ourselves through the sentence '$P$'. More of our cognitive capacity remains free, and we are more likely to see certain connections between this thought and others; different predictions are warranted about the sentences we will assent to, and about other aspects of our behavior as well. Because of this, there seems to be a legitimate distinction, for us, between the psychological state characterized as believing that $\int_0^3 x^2 dx = 9$ and the state characterized as believing that $P$.

Since there are no bounds on the cognitive capacity of the Ayer-Hahn monster, which in any case sees all logical connections instantaneously, such a creature would be in exactly the same psychological state no matter how it was presented with the thought that $P$; and so, for a creature like this, there would be no point in drawing a distinction between the state of believing that $\int_0^3 x^2 dx = 9$ and the state of believing that $P$. But as we saw earlier, the Ayer-Hahn monster would be in the same state also, and for exactly the same reasons, whether it was presented with the sentence '$2 + 3 = 5$', the sentence '$91 \times 79 = 7189$', or even a sentence expressing the four color theorem. It is just because of our cognitive limitations that we find ourselves in different psychological states when we are presented with these different sentences; so it is just because of these limitations that Frege's principles force us to assign them distinct senses. And likewise, if our cognitive limitations place us in different psychological states when we are presented with the sentences '$\int_0^3 x^2 dx = 9$' and '$P$', then it would seem—as long as sentential senses are to correspond to our own psychological states, not those of the Ayer-Hahn monster—that Frege's principles should force us to assign these two sentences distinct senses as well.

## 4.2 Resolving the conflict

Frege was committed to the idea that sentential senses, or thoughts, should correlate with psychological states—so that sentences like 'Susan believes that $S_1$' and 'Susan believes that $S_2$', for example, should agree in truth value whenever '$S_1$' and '$S_2$' express the same sense. In addition, he explicitly endorsed a requirement of eliminability for stipulative definitions, according to which a sentence containing defined expressions should share its sense with the sentence that results when those expressions are eliminated. But if the state of believing that $\int_0^3 x^2 dx = 9$ is to be distinguished from the state of believing that $P$—if 'Susan believes that $\int_0^3 x^2 dx = 9$' can be true while 'Susan believes that $P$' is false—then Frege cannot maintain both of these two things. Which should he give up?

In the previous section, we saw how retaining the correlation between senses and psychological states might force us to abandon the requirement of eliminability, allowing a sentence containing defined symbols to be assigned a distinct sense from the sentence that results when those symbols are eliminated. However, in some very interesting remarks, Frege suggests that he prefers to take the other route: maintaining eliminability, the requirement that a sentence containing defined symbols and the sentence resulting from their elimination must express the same thought, but allowing that this thought might not entirely determine the psychological state of a speaker who entertains it.

The first of these remarks sets the stage for our central passage from (1914), which was discussed in the previous chapter:

> When we examine what actually goes on in our mind when we are doing intellectual work, we find that it is by no means always the case that a thought is present to our consciousness which is clear in all its parts. For example, when we use the word 'integral', are we always conscious of everything appertaining to its sense? I believe that this is only very seldom the case. Usually just the word is present to our consciousness, allied no doubt with a more or less dim awareness that this word is a sign which has a sense, and that we can, if we wish, call this sense to mind. (Frege, 1914, p. 209)

The second occurs within this central passage, but I will repeat it here, for convenience. Right in the midst of his argument, in the course of explaining how definitions can be useful for thinking as it actually takes place in human beings, Frege writes:

> It follows from this that a thought, as I understand the word, is in no way to be identified with a content of my consciousness. (Frege, 1914, p. 209).

Now, most often when he contrasts thoughts with "contents of consciousness," as at (1918, pp. 68–75), for example, Frege intends to make his familiar

point that thoughts are objective, external to the mind. But the context shows
that this cannot be what he means here, in the second of these remarks, since
the observation is supposed to be justified by the preceding discussion ("It follows from this that ..."), and he is not even talking about objectivity; he is
talking, instead, about the usefulness of being able to present thoughts to ourselves in different ways, by means of more compact formulas. Throughout this
passage, Frege seems to be describing contents of consciousness in much the
same way that we would characterize psychological states; it is the contents of
our consciousness, for example, that help to explain the inferential connections
we will recognize in our mathematical research. Evidently, the contents of our
consciousness are supposed to be determined by what is "present to our consciousness," and this, as Frege says in the first of these remarks, need not be a
thought, but might be only a linguistic expression ("the word"). What Frege
seems to mean, then, when he claims that thoughts are not to be identified
with contents of consciousness is simply that we can be in different psychological states while presenting the same thought to ourselves—as we are when we
present the thought that $P$ to ourselves, first, through the sentence '$P$' itself,
and then again, through the sentence '$\int_0^3 x^2 dx = 9$'. Our psychological states
are determined, not only by the thoughts we entertain, but also by the particular ways in which we entertain them, the particular expressions we use to
present these thoughts to ourselves.

As far as I can tell, the passage we have been studying from (1914) is the
only place in which Frege considers the idea that, because of defined expressions,
sentential senses, or thoughts, might not correlate with psychological states; and
of course, he does not really explore it in any detail here. If he had explored it, I
think that he would have been forced to restructure some important components
of his overall semantic theory. For example, if Frege had explicitly admitted
that 'Susan believes that $\int_0^3 x^2 dx = 9$' might be true while 'Susan believes
that $P$' is false, even though '$\int_0^3 x^2 dx = 9$' and '$P$' express the same sense, he
would have been forced to conclude either that the referent, or truth value, of
a sentence is not determined compositionally from the referents of its parts, or
more likely, that the referent of an expression standing in an indirect context is
something other than its sense, perhaps its psychological significance. I think it
is not inconceivable also that Frege might have come to view a statement like
'$(\int_0^3 x^2 dx = 9) = P$' as informative, even though it is an identity between two
expressions with the same sense, since these expressions differ in psychological
significance.

On such a picture, some of the functions assigned to sense would have to be allocated instead to a separate notion of psychological significance, much as Frege had divided his earlier notion of "conceptual content" in arriving at the distinction between senses and referents. It would be the psychological significance of a sentence that determines its informativeness, and also acts as its indirect referent at least in propositional attitude contexts. It would be the sense of an expression—still a more fine-grained aspect of meaning than its referent—that is preserved by definitional reduction, and perhaps also, that determines the ideal route to its referent. The requirement of a correspondence in structure between expressions and their senses would have to be dropped; but it would be plausible to impose a similar requirement for psychological significance.

Rather than speculating further, however, on what the resulting theory—which Frege did not develop—would have been like if he had developed it, I now want to consider two connections between the picture suggested here, in these remarks from (1914), and some more recent work in the philosophy of language and the philosophy of mind.

### 4.2.1   Indexicals

I have been arguing that reflection on the role of stipulative definitions shows that Frege's notion of sense should be factored into two components, with one of these components corresponding more closely than the other to the psychological states of language users. But of course, arguments like this are not new. As long ago as the 1970s, it had been pointed out by David Kaplan (1989) and John Perry (1977) that the presence of demonstratives and other indexicals in a language forces a similar bifurcation in Frege's notion of sense.

To illustrate, imagine that I introduce the proper name 'Lucky' to refer to the winner, whoever that might be, of last night's Pennsylvania State Lottery; and suppose I am the winner, but that I do not know this yet. If I then say to myself, 'Lucky is fortunate', there is a sense in which I am saying exactly what I would have said by uttering the sentence 'I am fortunate'. We can capture this particular dimension of equivalence by introducing the concept of a proposition, defined as a function from possible worlds into truth values. Both of these utterances, then, would express the same proposition—one that holds in any particular world just in case that world is one in which I am fortunate. Still, even though both express the same proposition, my sincere utterance of the sentence 'Lucky is fortunate' indicates a different psychological state than a sincere utterance of the sentence 'I am fortunate' would have; indeed, I might be depressed over my lack of fortune, and envious of Lucky.

So utterances that express the same proposition need not indicate the same psychological state. To see the converse, that utterances signaling the same psychological state need not express the same proposition, imagine that both you and I say to ourselves, both believing it, 'I am fortunate'. Then we are, in the relevant sense, both in the same psychological state, since we both believe that we are fortunate. But we are entertaining different propositions. The proposition I am entertaining (true in any world just in case I am fortunate in that world) is true, since I just won the lottery; the proposition you are entertaining (true in any world just in case you are fortunate in that world) may not be true.

Although Frege did consider indexicals at various points, most extensively in (1918), he continued to work with a unitary notion of sense, rather than separating this idea into the two components alluded to here, one leading to the notion of a proposition and one corresponding more closely to our psychological states. We should therefore expect to find some tension and some confusion in his discussion of indexicals. Perry documents it. Kaplan provides an elegant formal semantics in which the cognitive significance of an expression is more accurately represented by its "character"—in the case of sentences, a function from contexts of utterance into propositions, which he refers to as "contents."[3]

Both Kaplan and Perry agree, then, that indexicals force a break in Frege's unitary notion of sense. At times, however, both seem to suggest that this kind of separation is necessary *only* to account for indexicality. Kaplan writes, for example: "So long as Frege confined his attention to indexical free expressions . . . it is not surprising that he did not distinguish objects of thought (content) from cognitive significance (character), for that is the realm of *fixed* character and thus . . . there is a natural identification of character with content" (1989, p. 533). And Perry: "There will be no conflict, when one is dealing with eternal sentences . . . The need for distinguishing [two components] will not be forced to

---

[3]This literature in this area presents the reader with some badly conflicting vocabulary. The aspect of a sentence's meaning that is supposed to represent its cognitive significance, which Kaplan calls "character," Perry refers to as its "sense." The aspect of a sentence's meaning that determines its truth value in a possible world, which Kaplan calls its "content," Perry refers to as the "thought" expressed by that sentence. Burge (1979, p. 401, n. 1) criticizes Perry's vocabulary—in particular, his use of "sense"—as suggesting that Frege's primary concern lay with ordinary linguistic meaning. Accordingly, he refers to a sentence's cognitive significance as its "conventional usage," or simply its "meaning" (p. 409), reserving the term "sense" for the thought expressed by that sentence.

our attention, so long as we concentrate on such cases" (1977, p. 495).[4] I do not know how seriously to take these remarks; but even if they are interpreted very broadly, so that "indexicality" is supposed to encompass all the various ways in which environmental contingencies might affect sense, they are surely mistaken. The presence of a facility for introducing defined expressions forces a break between the sense of an expression and its psychological significance even in languages containing only indexical-free, eternal sentences; this is what Frege recognized in (1914).

Nevertheless, it would be a mistake to overemphasize the similarity of the distinction between sense and psychological significance that is forced by index-icals with that resulting from the presence of defined expressions. There are at least two important differences. The first concerns structural features of the phenomena. Indexicals allow a two-way slippage between the different aspects of content: not only can sentences distinct in psychological significance express the same proposition, but as we have seen, expressions identical in psychological significance can be used to express different propositions. In the case of definitions, however—at least on the account sketched here—the slippage works only one way: the same sense can be carried by expressions distinct in psychological significance, but expressions identical in psychological significance must agree also in sense. The second difference concerns the overall character of the two phenomena, and the appropriate mode of analysis in each case. Kaplan's work shows that there is a plausible model theoretic explication of the distinction between sense and psychological significance that is introduced by indexicals. However, it is hard to see how the distinction introduced by defined expressions could be accommodated within a model theoretic framework, since this distinction depends upon exactly those syntactic features of expressions that model theory is designed to ignore.

### 4.2.2   Language learning

The second connection to be considered here between Frege's theory of definition and the more recent philosophical literature is deeper and more extensive. I suggested earlier that Frege, at least in some of his later works, was tentatively exploring a representationalist picture of thinking, according to which we are supposed to grasp senses through the mediation of linguistic items. As

---

[4]See also Burge (1979), who writes: "Frege would perhaps have granted that meaning and sense are identical in a 'perfect' context-free language. But this would be because such a language would be perfectly fitted to express thought contents" (p. 409).

mentioned there, this view is popular today; and it has been developed with particular force in the work of Jerry Fodor. Although Fodor is best known for advocating a philosophy of mind that centers around the role of an internal language in our cognitive processes, his overall position is actually very close to that being ascribed to Frege; this is clear from the discussion in (1978a, pp. 200–202), for example, where Fodor imagines that our relations to "propositions" much like Frege's senses might be mediated by items of an internal language.[5] Working against the background of this shared position, my purpose here is to trace the manner in which the theory of language learning developed by Fodor in his early monograph (1975) runs into problems very much like those we have already seen in Frege's treatment of defined expressions.

I begin by reviewing two of Fodor's central ideas, in order to arrive at a simplified version of his theory that will concern us here.

The first is his treatment of those psychological states that can be characterized as propositional attitudes. On Fodor's view, these are analyzed as involving relations to sentences. For each individual propositional attitude—believing, hoping, and so on—there is supposed to be a particular relation between speakers and sentences; the speaker is then thought to bear that attitude toward a proposition just in case he stands in that relation to some sentence expressing the proposition (1975, pp. 75–77; see also 1987, p. 17). As an example, suppose that $R_{Bel}$ is the relation corresponding to the attitude of belief. The account then tells us that:

($*$) A speaker believes that $S_1$ if and only if there is some sentence '$S_2$' such that (i) the speaker stands in the relation $R_{Bel}$ to '$S_2$', and (ii) '$S_2$' means that $S_1$.

Of course, there is much more to Fodor's account than this: he emphasizes, for example, that the sentence '$S_2$' in this schema is supposed to belong to the speaker's internal language, and also that the relation $R_{Bel}$ is supposed to be a computational relation. But there is no need to consider these additional

---

[5] And the idea is spelled out in more detail in (1981a), where Fodor writes that it is possible "to run [the internal language theory] on a Fregean line," and then illustrates the idea as follows (where uppercase expressions indicate "concepts," items from the internal language): "the word 'dog' expresses the concept DOG; the concept DOG expresses the sense *dog* (i.e., expresses a certain Fregean concept); the relation *expresses* is transitive. On this account (to which I am, in fact, partial) expressing a Fregean concept is a semantic property par excellence and the formulae of natural language inherit their semantic properties from those of mental representations" (p. 260).

aspects of the theory, since they do not affect the phenomena we are concerned
with here.

The second of Fodor's ideas that we need to review is the particular picture
of language learning set out in (1975), according to which a speaker can arrive at
an understanding of a new predicate, incorporating it into its language, only by
learning some generalization that determines its extension (p. 59). For Fodor,
this involves mastering what he calls a "truth rule" for the new predicate. If
the new predicate is '$F$', for example, the appropriate truth rule would have the
form

'$Fx$' is true if and only if $Gx$,

where '$G$' is some (possibly complex) predicate already understood by the
speaker. It is important that the speaker should already understand '$G$', since
otherwise, the truth rule cannot convey what it needs to about the new predicate
'$F$'.

From this simple picture of language learning, Fodor draws some notorious
conclusions. He observes that, because the speaker can learn new predicates only
through truth rules linking them to predicates that are already understood, the
speaker must already know a language "rich enough to express the extension"
of any learnable predicate; the observation is then paraphrased as follows:

> To put it tendentiously, one can learn what the semantic properties
> of a term are only if one already knows a language which contains
> terms having the same semantic properties. (1975, p. 80)

This paraphrase seems to involve a kind of slide—from the assumption that
the language already known by the speaker must be rich enough to express the
extension of any predicate he can learn, to the conclusion that it must contain
also a predicate having the same "semantic properties." It may appear that
this slide is unwarranted, since there is more to meaning than extensionality.
However, although Fodor is explicitly discussing only extensions in this passage,
he notes earlier that his conclusions should hold also for intensional aspects of
meaning (p. 60); and he reemphasizes this point in the present setting, writing
that "intentionalist theories lead to precisely the same conclusions as I have just
drawn, and do so by precisely the same route" (p. 82, n. 19; see also p. 80, n. 18).
So it seems that we are to take the paraphrase literally, as applying to *all*
semantic properties, intensional as well as extensional. Fodor means to claim,
not only that the speaker cannot learn a predicate unless he already knows one

with the same extension, but also that the speaker cannot learn a new predicate unless he already knows one with the same meaning.

Now the picture at work here of the way in which we are supposed to extend our language through truth rules is, of course, very close to a definitional picture. Rather than moving through truth, explicitly specifying the truth conditions for sentences of the form '$Fx$' using portions of the language he already knows, the speaker could just as easily have introduced the predicate '$F$' into his language through a stipulative definition. From this perspective, it is natural to view Fodor's idea that a speaker cannot learn a new expression unless he already knows one with the same semantic properties as an analog to Frege's principle of eliminability, according to which defined expressions must inherit the semantic properties of their defining phrases. And in fact, Fodor then goes on (pp. 82–84) to describe an apparent "paradox" in his account of language learning that is very much like the conflict we have already seen between fruitfulness and eliminability in Frege's theory of definition.

Fodor considers a situation in which a speaker learns a new language, or systematically extends a language he already knows. Of course, Fodor himself is primarily interested in the special case of a speaker who originally knows only his internal language of thought, and is learning some natural language; but nothing depends on that. We could just as well suppose that the original language is a natural language and the speaker extends it by learning some specialized subject, such as chemistry or tax law; or that the original language is set theory and the speaker extends it by introducing symbols appropriate for number theory and real analysis. Now Fodor admits that there is "*some* sense" in which, as a result of extending the original language in this way, incorporating within it a new conceptual system, the speaker is able to think thoughts that he "could not otherwise entertain" (p. 84). But he notes that his own picture of language learning seems to rule out this possibility, since according to this picture, "nothing can be expressed" in the definitionally enriched language that cannot already be expressed in the original.

At this point, the parallels should be clear between the problem confronting Fodor's view of language learning and the conflict in Frege's treatment of definitions. Fodor's idea that any expression a speaker can learn must share its semantic properties with one he already knows is like Frege's requirement of eliminability. His observation that learning new expressions seems to allow speakers to think thoughts they could not otherwise have entertained is like Frege's principle of fruitfulness. And Fodor—like Frege—must find some way of explaining how enriching a language in this way could actually enable speakers to entertain these new thoughts, given that any proposition that can be expressed in the enriched language could just as well have been expressed in the original.

In fact, after setting out such a similar problem, Fodor then goes on to propose a solution very much along the lines of that attributed here to Frege. Although the enriched language can be no more expressive than the original in principle, for an ideal reasoner, Fodor suggests that it might nevertheless allow speakers like ourselves to entertain new thoughts precisely because we are not ideal reasoners. This suggestion can be seen in the following passage, which again focuses on the special case of a speaker extending his language of thought to incorporate items from some natural language:

> True for every predicate in the natural language it must be possible to express a coextensive predicate in the internal code. It does not follow that for every natural language predicate *that can be entertained* there is an *entertainable* predicate of the internal code. It is no news that single items in the vocabulary of a natural language may encode concepts of extreme sophistication and complexity. If terms of the natural language can become incorporated into the computational system by something like a process of abbreviatory definition, then it is quite conceivable that learning a natural language may increase the complexity of the thoughts that we can think. (Fodor, 1975, p. 85)

Fodor's explanation of the utility of defined expressions for speakers like ourselves, like Frege's, relies crucially upon the consideration of our psychological limitations, what he calls our "performance parameters" (p. 86). And just as we highlighted the role of these considerations in Frege's account by emphasizing the worthlessness of definitions for speakers without such psychological limitations, such as our Ayer-Hahn monsters, Fodor also reinforces his point by focusing on another kind of ideal reasoner:

> If an angel is a device with infinite memory and omnipresent attention—a device for which the performance/competence distinction is vacuous—then, on my view, there's no point in angels learning Latin; the conceptual system available to them by virtue of having done so can be no more powerful than the one they started out with. (Fodor, 1975, p. 86)

So both the tension in Fodor's account of language learning and his way of resolving it are similar to what we have already seen in Frege: the introduction of new symbols into a language allows us to entertain new thoughts only in a weak, psychological sense, by enabling us to overcome some of our cognitive limitations.

Now in the case of Frege, we saw that even this weak notion of fruitfulness forced a conflict between his requirement of eliminability for defined expressions and the idea that senses should correlate with psychological states. And in fact, Fodor is likewise committed to something like Frege's idea of a correlation between senses and psychological states; this comes about through his treatment of propositional attitudes, such as the analysis of belief presented earlier in (∗), which relies in its second clause on a notion of meaning. It should come as no surprise, then, that Fodor's theory also harbors a conflict like that found in Frege. Fodor wants to require that any predicate the speaker can learn must share, not only its extension, but all of its semantic properties, intensional as well as extensional, with some predicate that is already known. But it turns out that he cannot maintain this strong claim along with his treatment of the propositional attitudes; and in particular, he cannot include among these shared semantic properties the very aspects of meaning that are supposed to figure in his analysis of the propositional attitudes.

Again, the conflict between these two aspects of Fodor's theory is best seen through an example, so let us return yet again to the case of Susan, a creature who shares our psychological limitations. As before, we suppose that Susan has enriched her base language of set theory with numerals and symbols from analysis—allowing her to form, for example, the sentence '$\int_0^3 x^2 dx = 9$', which reduces to '$P$' in his base language. And let us suppose now simply that Susan believes that $\int_0^3 x^2 dx = 9$.

Then, according to the analysis of belief put forth in (∗), there must therefore be some sentence '$Q$' such that

(i) Susan bears the relation $R_{Bel}$ to '$Q$', and
(ii) '$Q$' means that $\int_0^3 x^2 dx = 9$.[6]

But suppose we agree with Fodor that each expression in Susan's enriched language really does share all of its semantic properties with some expression from the base language—and in particular, that '$P$' is the sentence from the base language that shares the semantic properties of the sentence '$\int_0^3 x^2 dx = 9$' from the enriched language. Then from (ii) we must therefore conclude that

---

[6]Of course, the most plausible candidate for the sentence '$Q$' is '$\int_0^3 x^2 dx = 9$' itself, but this particular substitution is not required by the analysis.

'$Q$' means that $P$,

which along with (i) forces the conclusion that Susan believes that $P$. As we have seen earlier, however, there are situations in which, at least for speakers like ourselves, a notion of belief suitable for a role in psychological explanation should allow us to distinguish the state of believing that $\int_0^3 x^2 dx = 9$ from the state of believing that $P$.

Fodor's theory thus seems to contain a conflict, much like that found in Frege, between the ideas that, on the one hand, meanings correlate with propositional attitudes and, on the other, that any expression a speaker can learn must share its semantic properties with some expression that the speaker already knows. There are, of course, several options for restructuring Fodor's overall theory to avoid this conflict; but the one that seems most promising follows the line explored earlier with Frege. Fodor must weaken his claim that new expressions share *all* of their semantic properties with expressions from the original language. They may be required to share extensional properties, and even some properties commonly regarded as intensional, just as Frege requires defined symbols to share the senses of their defining expressions. But there must be some aspects of meaning—and aspects relevant to our characterization of propositional attitudes—that the new expressions a speaker learns cannot be required to share with expressions that the speaker already knows.

# Chapter 5

# A simple semantic model

Earlier, in Chapter 3, we distinguished two distinct ways in which stipulative definitions could be thought of as fruitful—a robust interpretation, according to which the introduction of defined symbols actually alters the structure of thoughts capable of being expressed, and a weak, psychological interpretation. We have now seen that even this weak interpretation leads to a clash between the requirements of fruitfulness and eliminability for defined expressions, and suggests certain modifications in Frege's overall account of sense.

At this point, I want to change gears entirely and focus on the more objective, robust interpretation of fruitfulness, not only for defined expressions, but also for the "incomplete" expressions that play such an important role in Frege's thinking. The present chapter contains preliminary material. In order to explore this objective interpretation of fruitfulness, according to which the presence of defined and incomplete expressions actually alters the structure of expressible senses, it will be helpful to work with a precise semantic framework in which senses are assigned definite structures. This chapter develops such a framework. The framework is explicitly procedural, with the sense of an expression interpreted as a procedure for determining its referent. Since this kind of framework is not a standard choice in formal semantics, we begin with a few words about the interpretation itself.[1]

---

[1] Although the procedural treatment of meaning is not standard, it is not unheard of either. The idea has, from time to time, been either hinted or explicitly proposed by a number of philosophers, linguists, psychologists, and computer scientists, including: Davies and Isard (1972), Johnson-Laird (1977), Moschovakis (1994), Partee (1982), Suppes (1980, 1982), Woods (1975, 1981), and van Heijenoort (1977). Some of these formulations have been incautious, inviting the kind of criticisms directed by Fodor (1978b) against Woods and Johnson-Laird; but others, such as that of Moschovakis, are detailed and sophisticated.

## 5.1   Senses as procedures

Frege's idea that senses determine referents is presented only through a series
of metaphors. It is hard to base any definite interpretation on these metaphors,
and not just because they are metaphors, but because they are metaphors of
different kinds, suggesting broadly conflicting points of view. Some give the
impression that a sense determines a referent by depicting it, as a portrait
depicts its subject, or as a description might be said to depict an object satisfying
it. Frege frequently writes that the sense of an expression contains a "mode of
presentation" of its referent, as in (1892b, pp. 26–30), for example, where he
offers the description "the pupil of Plato and the teacher of Alexander the Great"
as the kind of thing we might take to be the sense of the name 'Aristotle', and
draws a careful analogy likening the relation between a sense and its referent to
the relation between an image of the moon projected onto the object lens of a
telescope and the moon itself.

Metaphors like these, which guide several well-known interpretations of senses
as descriptions, are prevalent throughout Frege's work. The suggestion that
senses depict, or describe, referents is noticeably absent, however, from some of
his other metaphors, where referents are instead cast as destinations, and senses
as routes to these destinations. An early example can be found in (1891b, p.85),
where Frege says, first, that different signs for the same thing are inevitable
"since there are different possible ways of arriving at it," and then illustrates
the point in a footnote: " '4', '$2^2$', '$(-2)^2$' are simply different signs for the
same thing and their differences simply indicate the different ways in which it is
possible for us to arrive at the same thing." Although Frege is speaking here in
terms of his early distinction between sign and content, rather than the latter
distinction between sense and referent, the two distinctions are closely related.
And in any case, he later makes the same point explicitly in terms of senses
and referents when he tries to explain, in a letter to Russell (XV14, p. 152),
how two signs with different senses can "determine the same object in different
ways" by writing: "it could be said that they lead to it from different directions." An image of the same kind occurs later still in a draft letter to Jourdain
(VIII12, p. 80), where Frege describes a hypothetical situation in which the
senses of two terms referring to the same mountain, 'Aphla' and 'Ateb', correspond to different routes leading to that mountain.

Although less common than the descriptive metaphors, Frege's allusions to
senses as routes to referents suggest a procedural interpretation that has been
explored, most notably, by Dummett, who views the sense of a word as "some

means by which a reference of the appropriate kind is determined for that word," and treats understanding—grasping a sense—as a certain kind of knowledge of this means, or method.[2] The account of senses to be developed here follows the general pattern of Dummett's procedural interpretation, but differs in two important ways, both of which involve separating out from Dummett's over-all treatment only certain aspects that represent his own views, rather than those that he attributes to Frege. Both of these differences, furthermore, reflect high-level, strategic decisions about the appropriate direction of philosophical explanation, which I cannot possibly defend here. I mention them, therefore, not in an attempt to justify the present approach, but only to position it properly.

To begin with, then, it is really the notion of understanding, grasping a sense, that is at issue for Dummett, and that needs to be explicated. He does not proceed by asking, first, what senses are, and then what it could mean to grasp them. Instead, he adopts the broadly pragmatist strategy of attempting to explicate the idea of grasping a sense directly, without providing any inde-pendent treatment of the senses themselves that are supposed to be grasped. The account developed here takes the opposite, broadly platonist approach, by focusing first on senses as independent entities. These senses—procedures for determining referents—are reified as set-theoretic constructs, much as certain semantic theories reify propositions as sets of possible worlds, for example. The benefit of this platonist approach is that it enables us to formulate much more detailed hypotheses about the precise structure of senses. The cost, of course, is that it defers a number of crucial questions concerning the role of these senses in the explanation of human understanding; but this cost was accepted by Frege himself, who never attempted to formulate any careful account of what it might mean to grasp a sense, and it is accepted also by those contemporary semantic theorists who are willing to assign entities of various kinds to expressions as their meanings.

The second difference between Dummett's procedural account and that pre-sented here, like the first, also reflects the pragmatist orientation of his thought. In Dummett's view, the knowledge involved in grasping a sense, a procedure for determining a referent, is to be analyzed as a particular kind of practical ability—the ability, at least in principle, to carry out that procedure. But if grasping a sense requires an ability to carry out the relevant procedure, then, he feels, this places a very strong constraint on the kinds of procedures that

---

[2]Dummett's interpretation of senses as procedures ("means" or "methods") for determining referents, and of understanding as knowledge of these procedures, is developed throughout his (1973), particularly in Chapters 5 through 7; the phrase quoted in the text occurs on p. 93.

might act as senses: they must be *effective procedures*. And from this, Dummett reaches his notorious conclusion that—at least given the usual treatment of reference and truth—we simply cannot understand a variety of languages we are generally thought to understand. First order arithmetic provides an example. Suppose the predicate '$P$' holds of an integer just in case that integer is the Gödel number of an arithmetical truth, so that the sense of '$P$' is a procedure for deciding, for any given integer, whether or not it represents an arithmetical truth. Then if understanding '$P$' requires the ability in principle to carry out the procedure that constitutes its sense, and it is agreed that any procedure we have the ability to carry out must be effective, it follows that we simply cannot understand the predicate '$P$', since there is no effective procedure for recognizing arithmetical truth.

From a general perspective, Dummett's interpretation of senses as procedures for determining referents can be seen as forcing a clash between two ideas. The first is the standard treatment of reference and truth for languages such as that of arithmetic; the second is the requirement that the procedures that constitute senses should be effective, which is itself driven by the pragmatist view that understanding is to be analyzed as the practical ability to carry out these procedures. In his own work, Dummett chooses to abandon the first of these ideas, the standard treatment of reference and truth. He is drawn, instead, to the idea that a sentence should be associated with verification conditions, rather than truth conditions—or in the special case of mathematical languages, with proof conditions, since the relation between a mathematical sentence and a proof that justifies it is generally taken to be an effectively decidable relation. This choice then forms the stepping-off point for Dummett's sophisticated defense of constructive reasoning in mathematics, and of an anti-realistic metaphysics more generally.

The account set out here, by contrast, is driven by the opposite choice. It maintains the first of these two conflicting ideas, the standard treatment of reference and truth, but abandons the second, the idea that senses must be effective procedures, along with its motivating view that we can grasp senses only by possessing the ability to carry out these procedures. This account is based, instead, on a picture of senses as *ideal procedures* for determining referents—procedures that need not be effective, or indeed, executable by a speaker at all. Although this view of senses as ideal procedures allows us to preserve a realistic metaphysics, with a standard treatment of reference and truth, the degree of idealization involved, as before, carries a significant cost, since it separates the notion of sense from at least one plausible account of what it might mean to grasp a sense. Again, however, it is common to accept a fairly high level of idealization in the initial stages of semantic theory, with the hope that the entities introduced as meanings can later be related in some systematic way to human understanding. The picture of senses as ideal procedures would have been, I believe, congenial to Frege, and it is at least no worse off from the standpoint of idealization than other similarly abstract approaches.

The purpose of this chapter is to develop this kind of abstract procedural picture, by setting out a particular semantic theory in which referents of the usual sort are assigned to expressions, and senses are then cast as ideal procedures for determining these referents. Although the procedural approach can be applied more widely—and would need to be applied more widely in order to justify any general claim to plausibility—it is developed here only for a very simple arithmetical language, containing numerals, predicates, function symbols, and connectives, but no quantifiers or higher-order features at all. These features are omitted here only for the sake of simplicity, allowing us to explore defined and incomplete expressions without being distracted by unrelated complications, not because the procedural framework rules out an adequate treatment. On the contrary, the framework is sufficiently abstract to allow for a number of different approaches to quantification or higher-order predication, for example; but this is not the place to describe these different approaches or decide among them.

Both the syntax and the semantics for our simple arithmetical language are set out in some detail. The point of this is not just fussiness, but that our study of defined and incomplete expressions in the next several chapters will require careful attention to the interplay between syntactic and semantic rules.

## 5.2 Syntax

The syntactic analysis of our simple arithmetical language is presented in a familiar style, pioneered by Frege himself, that involves specifying the set of expressions belonging to each of a number of syntactic categories. The *categories* themselves are defined as follows: both $e$ and $t$ are categories; if each of $\alpha_1, \ldots, \alpha_n$, and $\beta$ is either $e$ or $t$, then $\langle \alpha_1, \ldots, \alpha_n : \beta \rangle$ is a category; and those are the only categories.[3] Frege classifies expressions as *complete* or *incomplete*, where the complete expressions are terms and sentences, and the incomplete

---

[3]This system of categories restricts the standard treatment, which allows $\langle \alpha_1, \ldots, \alpha_n : \beta \rangle$ as a category whenever $\alpha_1, \ldots, \alpha_n$, and $\beta$ are arbitrary categories, basic or derived; the restriction limits consideration to a first order fragment.

expressions are those that must be combined with other expressions to form complete expressions—typically, predicates, function symbols, and connectives. In the current framework, $e$ and $t$ are the categories of complete expressions: $e$ is the category of terms, $t$ the category of sentences. All other syntactic categories contain only incomplete expressions, with a category of the form $\langle \alpha_1, \ldots, \alpha_n : \beta \rangle$ containing those incomplete expressions that combine with complete expressions from the categories $\alpha_1, \ldots, \alpha_n$ to form complete expressions belonging to the category $\beta$. The category $\langle e, e : t \rangle$, for instance, is the category of two-place predicates, each of which combines with a pair of terms to form a sentence; the category $\langle t : t \rangle$ is the category of one-place connectives, which combine with single sentences to form sentences.

To arrive at a concrete instance of this kind of categorical language, we first specify the *basic expressions* contained in particular categories. In the case of our arithmetical language, let us suppose that: the category $e$ of terms contains the numerals ('0', '1', '2', ...) as basic expressions; the category $\langle e, e : e \rangle$ of two-place function symbols contains the basic expression '+'; the category $\langle e, e : t \rangle$ of two-place predicates contains the basic expressions '=' and '>'; the category $\langle t : t \rangle$ of one-place connectives contains the basic expression '¬'; and the category $\langle t, t : t \rangle$ of two-place connectives contains the basic expression '∧'. The five categories listed will be the only ones containing basic expressions, and the basic expressions listed the only ones contained in these categories.

The *expressions* belonging to a category will then include its basic expressions, together with those *complex expressions* assigned to that category by the syntactic rules, where a *syntactic rule* tells us, in general, how to combine expressions from particular categories to form an expression belonging to a particular category. From this description, it is clear that a syntactic rule must carry at least three items of information: first, the categories to which its input expressions belong; second, the category to which its output expression belongs; and third, the way in which these inputs are combined to form the output—the structural operation through which the output expression is constructed from the input expressions.[4]

In general, syntactic rules can be very complicated, as anyone studying natural languages can attest, but our arithmetical language is simple enough that the relevant syntactic information can be presented very easily, through a uniform family of rules—one, in fact, corresponding to each incomplete category, of

---

[4]This conception of a syntactic rule is developed by Montague (1970), where rules are represented explicitly as triples containing input categories, output categories, and structural operations; a careful discussion is provided by Thomason (1974, pp. 6–11).

the form $\langle \alpha_1, \ldots, \alpha_n : \beta \rangle$. For each such category, then, we will let $P_{\langle \alpha_1, \ldots, \alpha_n : \beta \rangle}$ be the syntactic rule according to which: if $\pi$ is an expression belonging to the category $\langle \alpha_1, \ldots, \alpha_n : \beta \rangle$, and each $\tau_i$ is an expression belonging to the category $\alpha_i$, then $\pi(\tau_1, \ldots, \tau_n)$ is an expression belonging to the category $\beta$. The syntactic rules belonging to this family will be referred to as *P-rules*, or *predication rules*, though of course, the family also contains among its members the rules governing the application of function symbols and connectives, as well as a number of crossbreeds. To illustrate: the rule $P_{\langle e,e:e \rangle}$ tells us that '$+(3,2)$' is an expression belonging to the category $e$, since '$+$' belongs to the category $\langle e, e : e \rangle$ and both '3' and '2' belong to the category $e$; the rule $P_{\langle e,e:t \rangle}$ then tells us that '$= (+(3,2), 5)$' is an expression belonging to the category $t$, since '$=$' belongs to $\langle e, e : t \rangle$ and both '$+(3,2)$' and '5' belong to $e$.

A couple of conventions will help to simplify the presentation of expressions and their syntactic analyses. First, when the rule $P_{\langle \alpha_1, \ldots, \alpha_n : \beta \rangle}$ tells us that the expression $\pi(\tau_1, \ldots, \tau_n)$ belongs to the category $\beta$, we will present this fact by saying that

$$P_{\langle \alpha_1, \ldots, \alpha_n : \beta \rangle}(\pi, \tau_1, \ldots, \tau_n) = \pi(\tau_1, \ldots, \tau_n).$$

And second, since our output expressions can be odd to look at, we will often write them more naturally, using infix notation where it seems right and omitting unnecessary parentheses. Together, these two conventions allow us to rephrase our example from the preceding paragraph by saying that

$$P_{\langle e,e:t \rangle}(` = ', P_{\langle e,e:e \rangle}(` + ', `3', `2'), `5') \ = \ `3 + 2 = 5'.$$

In addition to the expressions, just defined, we also introduce a broader class of *open expressions*, formed by applying the same syntactic rules to the same set of basic expressions, except that the basic expressions belonging to the categories $e$ and $t$ are supplemented with additional sets of *term variables* ('$x$', '$y$', '$x_1$', '$y_1$', ...) and *sentence variables* ('$u$', '$v$', '$u_1$', '$v_1$', ...), respectively. All expressions are therefore classified as open expressions, but the open expressions also include formulas containing variables—such as '$x + 2 = 5$', for example—that are not expressions; these open expressions are not part of our language, strictly speaking, but play an auxiliary role to be described shortly.

## 5.3  Semantics

The semantic interpretation for this simple language follows Frege's pattern: we define two functions, $\rho$ and $\sigma$, mapping expressions into their referents and senses, with the provision that an expression's sense is to be interpreted as a procedure for determining its referent.

### 5.3.1   Referents

As emphasized earlier, our semantic interpretation is based on the standard assignment of referents to expressions, which we review here only briefly.

First, for each syntactic category $\alpha$, a domain of objects $D_\alpha$ is specified to serve as referents for expressions belonging to that category, as follows: $D_e$ is the set of positive integers; $D_t$ is the set containing the two truth values, Truth and Falsity; and for any category of the form $\langle \alpha_1, \ldots, \alpha_n : \beta \rangle$, the set $D_{\langle \alpha_1, \ldots, \alpha_n : \beta \rangle}$ contains those functions mapping $n$-tuples belonging to the Cartesian product $D_{\alpha_1} \times \ldots \times D_{\alpha_n}$ into objects belonging to $D_\beta$.

Next, the function $\rho$ is stipulated to assign a referent from the appropriate domain to each basic expression. For basic terms: $\rho['0']$ is 0, $\rho['1']$ is 1, $\rho['2']$ is 2, and so on. For basic function symbols: $\rho['+']$ is the function mapping any pair of numbers $\langle a, b \rangle$ onto the number $a + b$. For basic predicates: $\rho['=']$ is the function mapping any pair of numbers $\langle a, b \rangle$ onto Truth if $a = b$ and Falsity otherwise, and $\rho['>']$ is the function mapping $\langle a, b \rangle$ onto Truth if $a > b$ and Falsity otherwise. And for basic connectives: $\rho['\neg']$ is the function mapping $\langle \text{Truth} \rangle$ onto Falsity and $\langle \text{Falsity} \rangle$ onto Truth, and $\rho['\wedge']$ is the function mapping the pair $\langle \text{Truth, Truth} \rangle$ onto Truth and any other pair of truth values onto Falsity.[5]

Finally, the definition of $\rho$ is extended to include complex as well as basic expressions, in two steps. The first step introduces Frege's principle of *compositionality for referents*, according to which

$$\rho[P_{\langle \alpha_1, \ldots, \alpha_n : \beta \rangle}(\pi, \tau_1, \ldots, \tau_n)] = \rho[P_{\langle \alpha_1, \ldots, \alpha_n : \beta \rangle}](\rho[\pi], \rho[\tau_1], \ldots, \rho[\tau_n]).$$

What this principle tells us is that the referent of any complex formed by an application of the predication rule $P_{\langle \alpha_1, \ldots, \alpha_n : \beta \rangle}$ depends on the referents of its parts in a way determined by the function $\rho[P_{\langle \alpha_1, \ldots, \alpha_n : \beta \rangle}]$, which can be thought of as the referent of the predication rule. The second step defines the function $\rho[P_{\langle \alpha_1, \ldots, \alpha_n : \beta \rangle}]$ itself, by stipulating that

$$\rho[P_{\langle \alpha_1, \ldots, \alpha_n : \beta \rangle}](Y, X_1, \ldots, X_n) = Y(X_1, \ldots, X_n)$$

---

[5]This account simplifies by taking as the referents of incomplete expressions, not the "functions" and "concepts" that Frege viewed as their referents, but rather, objects akin to what Frege would have viewed as the *extensions* of their referents. What might be lost, or gained, through this simplification is a question we do not consider here.

whenever $Y$ belongs to $D_{\langle \alpha_1,\ldots,\alpha_n:\beta \rangle}$ and each $X_i$ belongs to $D_{\alpha_i}$; this definition captures Frege's idea that the referential correlate of predication is nothing but function application.

The workings of these various principles can be illustrated by calculating the referent of the complex expression '$3 + 2 = 5$', as follows:

$$
\begin{aligned}
\rho['3 + 2 = 5'] &= \rho[P_{\langle e,e:t \rangle}('=', P_{\langle e,e:e \rangle}('+', '3', '2'), '5')] \\
&= \rho[P_{\langle e,e:t \rangle}](\rho['='], \rho[P_{\langle e,e:e \rangle}](\rho['+'], \rho['3'], \rho['2']), \rho['5']) \\
&= \rho['='](\rho['+'](\rho['3'], \rho['2']), \rho['5']) \\
&= \text{Truth.}
\end{aligned}
$$

The first of these equations reflects the syntactic fact that the sentence '$3 + 2 = 5$' is analyzed as $P_{\langle e,e:t \rangle}('=', P_{\langle e,e:e \rangle}('+', '3', '2'), '5')$; the second equation then follows by the principle of compositionality for referents; the third through an application of the functions $\rho[P_{\langle e,e:e \rangle}]$ and $\rho[P_{\langle e,e:t \rangle}]$ that interpret the predication rules; and the fourth by applying ordinary functions to ordinary arguments.

### 5.3.2  Senses

Now that we have seen how referents are assigned to the expressions of our simple language, we can turn to the more interesting task of specifying their senses— that is, defining a function $\sigma$ that maps each expression from our language into an ideal procedure for determining its referent. Even though we are working with a broader class of ideal procedures, it will be useful to introduce them just as the effective procedures are often introduced, by first defining a number of basic procedures, and then certain modes of procedural composition, ways of fitting these basic procedures together to form complexes. The senses of basic expressions will be interpreted as basic procedures; the senses of complex expressions will be interpreted as complex procedures; and the syntactic rules will be interpreted as modes of procedural composition.

### Basic procedures

In a straightforward way, procedures can be said to compute functions. Just as a function has arguments and values, a procedure has inputs and outputs; and we can say that a procedure *computes* a function whenever, given that function's arguments as inputs, the procedure yields that function's value as an output. In general, of course, we cannot individuate procedures along with the functions they compute. Procedures are individuated, instead, by the particular *ways* in which they compute functions, the ways in which they arrive at their outputs, given their inputs. Two complex procedures might compute the same function in different ways; they might be constructed from different basic procedures, or from the same basic procedures assembled differently.

Basic procedures themselves, however, are special. There is no particular way in which a basic procedure computes a function—or if there is, we choose to ignore it when we make the decision to regard the procedure as basic. Of course, the procedures we decide to regard as basic might vary from one setting to another: a procedure that is regarded as basic from the standpoint of a high-level programming language, for example, might actually be complex from the standpoint of assembly language; a procedure that is regarded as basic from the standpoint of assembly language might be complex from the standpoint of machine language. At any given level, however, the decision to regard a procedure as basic is the decision to view it as having no internal structure. There is nothing *to* a basic procedure apart from its input/output pattern, the function it computes; once we know what function is computed by a basic procedure, we know all there is to know about it. Unlike more complex procedures, then, basic procedures *can* be individuated on the basis of the functions they compute. We can therefore introduce a class of basic procedures simply by specifying the particular function computed by each procedure in the class.

Let us begin, then, with the basic procedures that might act as senses for incomplete expressions. As we have seen, for each syntactic category $\langle \alpha_1, \ldots, \alpha_n : \beta \rangle$, there is a set of functions $D_{\langle \alpha_1, \ldots, \alpha_n : \beta \rangle}$ to serve as referents for expressions belonging to this category—the set of functions mapping $n$-tuples from the Cartesian product $D_{\alpha_1} \times \ldots \times D_{\alpha_n}$ into members of $D_\beta$. And we can now introduce the appropriate basic procedures simply by stipulating that, for each of these functions belonging to each of these sets, there is some basic procedure that computes it.

Of course, there will be infinitely many of these sets of functions, and all but one of them (the set containing the four functions mapping members of $D_t$ into $D_t$) will itself be either countably infinite or uncountable. So if there is to be a basic procedure computing each function belonging to each set, there will be a lot of basic procedures, only a few of which will correspond to effectively computable functions. For these reasons—because there are so many of these procedures, and because the functions they compute are not effective—it might seem odd to refer to them as *basic*. But remember, we are defining a more general class of ideal procedures, and this oddity indicates the direction of generalization. When one introduces the effective procedures by first identifying a class of basic procedures, these are supposed to be basic in two ways. They are supposed to be metaphysically basic, in the sense that they are not further analyzed within whatever account of the effective procedures is being developed, but they are also supposed to be basic in an epistemic sense: particularly easy to carry out, so simple that their execution is purely mechanical, requiring no intelligence at all.

In the present setting, although we maintain the metaphysical constraint on basic procedures, insisting that they have no internal structure, we drop the epistemic constraint; and once this constraint is gone, there is no reason not to accept as basic a procedure that computes any function at all. After all, from a metaphysical point of view, there is no real difference in kind between, say, the function that maps an integer into 1 if it is even and 0 if it is odd, and the function that maps an integer into 1 if it is the Gödel number of an arithmetical truth and 0 otherwise. Although only one of these functions is effective, and we would be more impressed with the intelligence of a device that could compute one than the other, this is an epistemic matter. From a strictly metaphysical point of view, they are both just functions, and if we can accept as basic a procedure computing one, there is no reason not to accept as basic a procedure computing the other.

These same reasons, which lead us to accept the possibility of basic procedures computing any of these functions, should lead us also to accept the possibility that there might be basic procedures computing all of them. It is more common, of course, to suppose that there should be only a small, finite number of basic procedures, but this is surely an epistemic matter. From a strictly metaphysical point of view, there is no real difference between, say, the numbers 7 and $\aleph_1$. They are both just numbers, and apart from epistemic considerations, it is hard to locate any reason for accepting the possibility that there might be as many as 7 basic procedures while denying that there could be as many as $\aleph_1$.

So much for rhetoric.

And just in case this rhetorical justification for basic procedures is not persuasive, I want to mention the possibility that the basic procedures—since they are both defined by and individuated along with the functions they compute— might simply be identified with these functions. The result would be an *austere version* of the procedural approach, according to which basic procedures are simply functions, and a complex procedure turns out to be nothing but an orderly process of applying these functions to arguments, much like the process of calculating the referent of an expression.

Having introduced the class of basic procedures, we can now begin to specify the $\sigma$ function by assigning such a procedure to each basic incomplete expression as its sense, following the recipe: the sense of a basic expression is the basic procedure computing its referent. Thus, for example, $\sigma['+']$ will be the basic procedure that computes the function $\rho['+']$, yielding $a + b$ as output whenever it is given the pair $\langle a, b \rangle$ as an input; this particular basic procedure can be referred to as plus. And likewise, $\sigma['=']$, $\sigma['<']$, $\sigma['\neg']$, and $\sigma['\wedge']$ will be the basic procedures that compute the functions $\rho['=']$, $\rho['>']$, $\rho['\neg']$, and $\rho['\wedge']$, respectively, which can be referred to as equal, greater, not, and and. It is worth emphasizing again that the basic procedures assigned to basic expressions as their senses are little more than surrogates for their referents—and indeed, if we adopt the austere version of the procedural approach, the senses of basic expressions will then be identified with their referents.[6]

There is a slight wrinkle involved in identifying an appropriate class of basic procedures to serve as the senses of basic complete expressions. Here, we cannot just follow the recipe of assigning to these expressions the basic procedures that compute their referents, since the referents of complete expressions are objects, not functions. Instead, each of these expressions can be associated with the basic procedure yielding that expression's referent as an output when it is given no inputs at all—that is, the basic procedure computing the function that maps the empty sequence $\langle \rangle$ into the expression's referent. Thus, $\sigma['0']$ will be the basic procedure computing the function $\{\langle\langle\rangle, 0\rangle\}$, which maps $\langle\rangle$ into 0; this basic procedure can be referred to as 0. And likewise, $\sigma['1']$, $\sigma['2']$, $\sigma['3']$, ... will be the basic procedures computing the functions $\{\langle\langle\rangle, 1\rangle\}$, $\{\langle\langle\rangle, 2\rangle\}$, $\{\langle\langle\rangle, 3\rangle\}$, ... , which can be referred to as 1, 2, 3 ... .

### Complex procedures

Having defined the basic procedures and assigned them as senses to the basic expressions, the next step is to extend the $\sigma$ function so that it assigns senses to complex expressions as well.

We begin by introducing Frege's principle of *compositionality for senses*,

---

[6]This idea—that the senses and referents of basic expressions might be identified—may seem to run contrary to the grain of Frege's thought, but I am not sure that it does. Frege did, of course, insist that single lexical items from various natural languages might share the same referent while differing in sense, and likewise for complex expressions from his ideal language; but is there any reason to think that he would have wanted to allow basic, or primitive, expressions from an ideal language to share a referent while differing in sense? In any case, we will see later, toward the end of Chapter 8, how the model to be developed here allows for an ideal language in which simple, though not basic, expressions might carry complex senses.

according to which

$$\sigma[P_{\langle\alpha_1,\dots,\alpha_n:\beta\rangle}(\pi,\tau_1,\dots,\tau_n)] \;=\; \sigma[P_{\langle\alpha_1,\dots,\alpha_n:\beta\rangle}](\sigma[\pi],\sigma[\tau_1],\dots,\sigma[\tau_n]).$$

What this principle tells us is that the sense of a complex expression formed by the syntactic rule $P_{\langle\alpha_1,\dots,\alpha_n:\beta\rangle}$ depends on the senses of its parts in a way determined by the function $\sigma[P_{\langle\alpha_1,\dots,\alpha_n:\beta\rangle}]$—some uniform mode of procedural composition that assembles the procedures associated with the parts of this expression into a procedure that can be associated with the whole.

How should such a mode of procedural composition be defined? Consider the sentence '$3+2=5$' as an example. This sentence is formed by an application of the rule $P_{\langle e,e:t\rangle}$ to the expressions '$=$', '5', and '$3+2$', which is itself formed by an application of $P_{\langle e,e:e\rangle}$ to '$+$', '3', and '2'. Its sense will therefore be formed by an application of $\sigma[P_{\langle e,e:t\rangle}]$—the corresponding mode of procedural composition— to the senses of its parts: equal, 5, and the sense of '$3+2$', which will itself be formed by an application of $\sigma[P_{\langle e,e:e\rangle}]$ to plus, 3, and 2. We know that the basic procedures 3, 2, and 5 output the numbers 3, 2, and 5, respectively, given no inputs at all, that plus takes a pair of numbers as input and outputs their sum, and that equal takes a pair of numbers as input and outputs Truth if they are equal. So it is natural to suppose that $\sigma[P_{\langle e,e:e\rangle}]$ should assemble plus, 3, and 2 into the complex procedure of, first, executing 3 and 2, and then executing plus, with the pair of outputs determined by these two initial procedures as its input; and that $\sigma[P_{\langle e,e:t\rangle}]$ should then assemble this complex procedure, along with 5, in such a way that the pair of outputs they determine is taken as an input by equal.

As this example illustrates, the process of executing a complex procedure is nothing but a coordinated process of executing basic procedures, with specified inputs, and then passing their outputs along as inputs to other basic procedures. Such a process is subject to two constraints that do not emerge when we consider basic procedures alone. First, the basic procedures involved in the process must be subject to some particular ordering. And second—the point of the ordering— the interaction among these basic procedures should be organized in such a way that the outputs of some are taken as inputs by others.

There are a number of ways of achieving this kind of coordination among basic procedures, from which we choose one that is simple and natural. Let us begin by introducing an infinite set of registers to act as pick-up and drop-off points for the inputs and outputs of procedures, where each register $\Gamma_i$ has a sequence $i$ of positive integers as its address. These registers can be thought of as arranged in a downward-branching tree, defined as follows. The register $\Gamma_1$

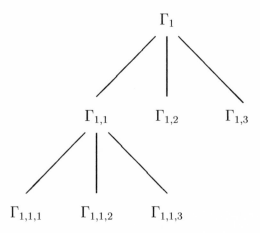

Figure 5.1: Part of a register tree.

is the topmost node in the tree; and where $i$ is a sequence (and $*$ represents concatenation), the registers $\Gamma_{i*1}$, $\Gamma_{i*2}$, $\Gamma_{i*3}$, ... are immediately below $\Gamma_i$, with each register $\Gamma_{i*(n+1)}$ lying immediately to the right of $\Gamma_{i*n}$. A portion of this infinite tree of registers is depicted in Figure 5.1.

Once this tree of registers has been defined, a unique register from the tree can then be associated with each occurrence of each basic procedure contained in a complex, with this association used both to establish an ordering among basic procedures and to organize their inputs and outputs. Very roughly, it works like this. Imagine that the basic procedures assigned to the basic expressions in a syntactic complex are themselves arranged in a tree, corresponding to the syntactic structure of the expression itself. The primary basic procedure—the procedure assigned to the dominant syntactic item—will be at the top of the tree, and then lying immediately below any incomplete procedure, arranged from left to right, will be the procedures whose outputs that incomplete procedure is to take as inputs; the procedure tree associated with the sentence '$3 + 2 = 5$', for example, appears in Figure 5.2.

In general, any such procedure tree will be isomorphic to a unique topmost, leftmost subtree of the tree of registers, and each basic procedure from the procedure tree will then be associated with the corresponding register from the register tree. The basic procedures in the procedure tree will then be executed in an order corresponding to a left branching, depth first traversal of that tree. Each basic procedure will take any necessary inputs from the leftmost registers just below it, and then deposit its output in its own associated register. The

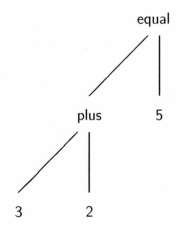

Figure 5.2: A procedure tree.

entire process will terminate when the output of the primary basic procedure—
which will be the referent of the original expression—is finally deposited in the
topmost register of the tree.

In order to describe this kind of process more precisely, we need some way
of representing both the use of registers and the ordering among procedures.
Where $\mathcal{P}$ is a basic procedure, then, let us take

$$[\mathcal{P} \ \langle \Gamma_{i_1}, \ldots, \Gamma_{i_n} \rangle \ \Gamma_j]$$

to represent the action of executing $\mathcal{P}$, with the contents of the registers
$\Gamma_{i_1}, \ldots, \Gamma_{i_n}$ taken as inputs, and with its own output then deposited in $\Gamma_j$.
Such an action—the execution of a basic procedure, with specified pick-up
and drop-off points—will be described as a *basic procedure execution*; and
where $\Sigma_1, \Sigma_2, \ldots, \Sigma_m$ are several of these executions, we define the tuple
$\langle \Sigma_1, \Sigma_2, \ldots, \Sigma_m \rangle$ as an *execution sequence* that represents the process of performing these actions in turn, running from $\Sigma_1$ through $\Sigma_m$.

This notation can be illustrated by returning to the sentence '3 + 2 = 5',
and characterizing its associated procedure more precisely, now, through the
execution sequence

$$\langle \quad [3 \ \langle\rangle \ \Gamma_{1,1,1}],$$
$$[2 \ \langle\rangle \ \Gamma_{1,1,2}],$$
$$(*) \qquad [\text{plus} \ \langle \Gamma_{1,1,1}, \Gamma_{1,1,2} \rangle \ \Gamma_{1,1}],$$
$$[5 \ \langle\rangle \ \Gamma_{1,2}],$$
$$[\text{equal} \ \langle \Gamma_{1,1}, \Gamma_{1,2} \rangle \ \Gamma_1] \ \rangle.$$

As we can see, what this sequence represents is the complex procedure that involves: first, executing the basic procedures 3 and then 2, with their outputs deposited in the registers $\Gamma_{1,1,1}$ and $\Gamma_{1,1,2}$, respectively; then executing plus, with the contents of $\Gamma_{1,1,1}$ and $\Gamma_{1,1,2}$ taken as inputs and its own output deposited in $\Gamma_{1,1}$; then executing 5, with its output deposited in $\Gamma_{1,2}$; and finally executing equal, with the contents of $\Gamma_{1,1}$ and $\Gamma_{1,2}$ taken as inputs and its own output deposited in $\Gamma_1$, the topmost register.

In a way, this is really the right result. It is execution sequences like this that best represent procedures, and that should be associated with expressions as their senses; and it would, in fact, be possible to formulate our modes of procedural composition so that they map expressions into these execution sequences directly. Nevertheless, we will follow a more indirect route here, which relies on an intermediate level of representation. We begin by defining modes of procedural composition in such a way that they assign to complex expressions—as their *senses*—only certain tuples of basic procedures, rather than full execution sequences. Once this definition is in place, we then justify our interpretation of senses as procedures by showing how these tuples can themselves be mapped into execution sequences.

The decision to associate expressions, in the first instance, only with procedure tuples, rather than full execution sequences, makes it very easy to formulate modes of procedural composition, of course. For each predication rule of the form $P_{\langle\alpha_1,...,\alpha_n:\beta\rangle}$, the associated mode of composition $\sigma[P_{\langle\alpha_1,...,\alpha_n:\beta\rangle}]$ can then be defined through the simple stipulation that

$$\sigma[P_{\langle\alpha_1,...,\alpha_n:\beta\rangle}](\mathcal{P}, \mathcal{Q}_1,...,\mathcal{Q}_n) = (\mathcal{P}\ \mathcal{Q}_1\ ...\ \mathcal{Q}_n),$$

whenever $\mathcal{P}, \mathcal{Q}_1,...,\mathcal{Q}_n$ are themselves either basic procedures or tuples built from them.[7] Together with the principle of compositionality for senses, introduced earlier, this definition now leads to a uniform assignment of *complex complete senses* to complex complete expressions, which can be illustrated in the case of '$3+2=5$', for example, as follows:

$$
\begin{aligned}
\sigma['3+2=5'] &= \sigma[P_{\langle e,e:t\rangle}('=', P_{\langle e,e:e\rangle}('+', '3', '2'), '5')]\\
&= \sigma[P_{\langle e,e:t\rangle}](\sigma['='], \sigma[P_{\langle e,e:e\rangle}](\sigma['+'], \sigma['3'], \sigma['2']), \sigma['5'])\\
&= (\sigma['='] (\sigma['+'] \sigma['3'] \sigma['2']) \sigma['5'])\\
&= (\text{equal (plus 3 2) 5}).
\end{aligned}
$$

---

[7]The use of the list notation $(\mathcal{P}\ \mathcal{Q}_1\ ...\ \mathcal{Q}_n)$ to represent tuples, rather than the more familiar $\langle\mathcal{P}, \mathcal{Q}_1,...,\mathcal{Q}_n\rangle$, is supposed to have a procedural flavor, and create pleasant associations in the minds of those readers familiar with the LISP programming language.

Again, the first of these equations reflects the syntactic analysis of '$3 + 2 = 5$'; the second follows by the principle of compositionality for senses; the third from an application of the appropriate modes of procedural composition, $\sigma[P_{\langle e, e:e \rangle}]$ and $\sigma[P_{\langle e, e:t \rangle}]$; and the fourth is nothing but a rewriting of the third in which basic procedures are referred to by their standard names.

Now, how can these senses, as they have been defined here—basic procedures or tuples built from them—be mapped into execution sequences? As a first approximation, we might imagine that a complete sense $\mathcal{P}$ could be interpreted simply as the sequence $\langle [\mathcal{P} \langle \rangle \Gamma_1] \rangle$ containing only a single execution: the action of executing $\mathcal{P}$ itself, with no inputs at all and its own output deposited in $\Gamma_1$. In fact, this suggestion is entirely adequate when $\mathcal{P}$ is a basic procedure, such as 2 or 3, for in this case, the notion of executing a basic procedure can be taken for granted.[8] But the suggestion leads to difficulties when $\mathcal{P}$ is a complex complete sense, such as (equal (plus 3 2) 5), since we do not yet have any notion of what it might mean to execute a complex sense like this.

As it turns out, however, these difficulties can be resolved in a natural way by analyzing the idea of executing a complex sense in terms of executions of the various basic procedures out of which it is constructed. Just as a basic procedure execution is an execution containing the sense of a basic expression, we begin by defining a *complex procedure execution* as an execution containing a complex complete sense. It is easy to see, by reflecting on our formation rules for expressions, as well as the rules through which expressions are mapped into senses, that any complex complete sense $\mathcal{P}$ must be a tuple of the form $(\mathcal{P}' \, \mathcal{Q}_1 \, \ldots \, \mathcal{Q}_n)$, where $\mathcal{Q}_1 \, \ldots \, \mathcal{Q}_n$ are complete and $\mathcal{P}'$ is incomplete. And we can now introduce a rule allowing us to expand any execution containing such a sense—that is, any complex procedure execution—into the particular sequence of executions that constitutes its *immediate expansion*, as follows.[9]

- *Expansion Rule 0:* If $\mathcal{P}$ is a complex complete sense of the form $(\mathcal{P}' \, \mathcal{Q}_1 \, \ldots \, \mathcal{Q}_n)$, then the execution

$$[\mathcal{P} \langle \rangle \Gamma_i]$$

---

[8] If we adopt the austere interpretation, for example, in which basic procedures are identified with the function they compute, executing a basic procedure is nothing more than applying a function.

[9] The peculiar name for this initial expansion rule reflects the fact that it will later, in Chapter 8, be subsumed under another rule, known there as Expansion Rule 1.

has as its immediate expansion the sequence

$$\langle \quad [\mathcal{Q}_1 \ \langle\rangle \ \Gamma_{i*1}],$$

$$\cdot$$

$$\cdot$$

$$\cdot$$

$$[\mathcal{Q}_n \ \langle\rangle \ \Gamma_{i*n}],$$
$$[\mathcal{P}' \ \langle \Gamma_{i*1}, \ldots, \Gamma_{i*n}\rangle \ \Gamma_i] \ \rangle.$$

The immediate expansion of a complex procedure execution can be thought of as a way of implementing that execution. What Expansion Rule 0 tells us, then, is that the execution of the complex sense $\mathcal{P}$ at the register $\Gamma_i$ is implemented through the successive executions of $\mathcal{Q}_1, \ldots, \mathcal{Q}_n$, with their outputs deposited in the registers $\Gamma_{i*1}, \ldots, \Gamma_{i*n}$, followed by an execution of $\mathcal{P}'$, with the values contained in $\Gamma_{i*1}, \ldots, \Gamma_{i*n}$ taken as inputs and its own output deposited in $\Gamma_i$.

This expansion rule allows us to map any complex procedure execution into an execution sequence through which it is implemented—but of course, a single application of the rule may not be enough to eliminate complex executions entirely, since the individual executions belonging to this sequence might themselves be complex. We therefore introduce the notion of a fully expanded sequence, in the following three steps. Let us say, first, that the execution sequence $\langle\Sigma_1, \ldots, \Sigma_{j_1}, \ldots, \Sigma_{j_m}, \ldots, \Sigma_n\rangle$ is an *immediate expansion* of the sequence $\langle\Sigma_1, \ldots, \Sigma_j, \ldots, \Sigma_n\rangle$ whenever $\langle\Sigma_{j_1}, \ldots, \Sigma_{j_m}\rangle$ is an immediate expansion of the complex execution $\Sigma_j$; second, that one execution sequence is an *expansion* of another if it can be reached from that sequence through a series of immediate expansions; and third, that one execution sequence is a *full expansion* of another if it is an expansion of that sequence that contains only basic executions.

With these definitions in place, we can now refine our initial suggestion for mapping a complete sense $\mathcal{P}$ into an execution sequence by defining the *execution sequence associated with* $\mathcal{P}$, not simply as $\langle [\mathcal{P} \ \langle\rangle \ \Gamma_1] \rangle$ itself, but instead, as *the full expansion of* $\langle [\mathcal{P} \ \langle\rangle \ \Gamma_1] \rangle$. The resulting mapping is well-defined, since it is easy to verify that any such sequence has a unique full expansion, which can be arrived at through successive applications of Expansion Rule 0. If $\mathcal{P}$ is itself basic, then of course $\langle [\mathcal{P} \ \langle\rangle \ \Gamma_1] \rangle$ is its own full expansion, containing a single basic procedure execution; otherwise, if $\mathcal{P}$ is a complex complete sense, the full expansion of $\langle [\mathcal{P} \ \langle\rangle \ \Gamma_1] \rangle$ is the sequence of basic procedure executions through which the complex procedure execution is implemented.

The mapping yields, in addition, the desired outcome that the sense of any expression is interpreted as a procedure for determining its referent—literally,

an execution sequence leading to the placement of that expression's referent
in the register $\Gamma_1$. The verification of this fact is omitted, but the outcome
can be illustrated by considering our sample expression '$3 + 2 = 5$', which has
been assigned the complex sense (equal (plus 3 2) 5). The execution sequence
associated with this sense is now defined as the full expansion of

$$\langle\, [(\text{equal (plus 3 2) 5}) \ \langle\rangle \ \Gamma_1]\, \rangle,$$

which is simply the sequence (∗) displayed earlier, a procedure for determining
Truth as the expression's referent.

This mapping of the tuples representing senses into basic execution sequences, then, justifies our interpretation of senses as procedures, but it is worth
asking: what is the point of the indirect approach followed here—why not just
map expressions directly into execution sequences, and ignore the tuples entirely? There are three reasons. The first is simplicity. It is good to be able to
think of senses as procedures, but it is also good to suppress clutter, and the
indirect approach allows us to do both. The second is generality. Any detailed
model of procedures will contain a number of arbitrary features. With suitable
changes elsewhere, our registers, for example, could easily have been arranged
in some other fashion—perhaps in a linear order, like the squares on a Turing
Machine tape. The representation of senses as tuples is an effort to suppress
the arbitrary features involved in our particular model of procedures, while displaying only what is essential: the basic procedures involved in a complex, their
nesting, and order.

The third reason has to do with connections to other proposals in the literature. The conception of senses as procedures that is developed here has much
in common with a number of other accounts that represent meanings, also, as
structured objects of various kinds, though not necessarily as procedures. In
the modern literature, this idea goes back to Rudolph Carnap's (1947) notion
of intensional isomorphism. It was explored in detail by David Lewis (1972),
refined by M. J. Cresswell (1985), and has received considerable attention from
a group of writers, such as Salmon (1986) and Scott Soames (1987), who ad-
vocate a picture of meanings as Russellian propositions.[10] Since the issues to
be considered here concerning incomplete and defined expressions have a bearing on these other accounts as well, it is helpful to be able to display only as
much structure as our senses share with these other treatments of meanings as

---

[10]Much of the recent literature on structured meanings is surveyed by King (2001), whose
own contributions can be found in his (1995) and (1996).

structured entities, allowing any further details necessary for the interpretation of senses as procedures to remain hidden behind the scene.

# Chapter 6

# Removal rules

We now consider how the simple model of senses as procedures set out in the previous chapter can be elaborated to handle two important issues. The account presented there seems to conflict, first of all, with a number of things Frege says about the formation, and the semantic role, of incomplete expressions; and second, it is still necessary to extend this account to accommodate Frege's idea that expressions introduced into a language through stipulative definition should allow us to express genuinely new thoughts—not simply to represent familiar thoughts to ourselves in a new way.

Although these issues are closely related, I begin with the first.

## 6.1 Incomplete expressions

### 6.1.1 The conflict

Frege's writing about senses seems to reflect two different perspectives, which we can characterize as *compositional* and *decompositional*.[1] Each involves two theses: a metaphysical thesis concerning the structure of senses themselves, and an epistemic thesis concerning the relative priority of sentential senses and their parts in an explanation of our understanding.

In the case of the compositional perspective, the metaphysical thesis is simply the idea—considered earlier, in Chapter 2—that thoughts, and senses more generally, possess a determinate structure, which is supposed to be revealed by the grammatical structure of expressions belonging to an ideal language.

---

[1]The issues discussed here are treated at length in Chapter 15 of Dummett (1981). What I call the compositional and decompositional perspectives correspond to Dummett's B-theses and A-theses, respectively.

Although, as we saw in our earlier discussion, this metaphysical thesis is occasionally set out on its own, it is stated most forcefully when it occurs in conjunction with its epistemic counterpart—the idea that we come to understand a complex expression by, first, grasping the senses of its parts, and then assembling these senses in a way that corresponds to the grammatical construction of that expression. This idea is attractive to us because it helps to explain how a speaker could understand an infinite number of expressions without having to memorize the meaning of each one, and it was attractive to Frege for exactly the same reason, as we can see from the opening words of his last published article:

> It is astonishing what language can do. With a few syllables it can
> express an incalculable number of thoughts, so that even if a thought
> has been grasped by an inhabitant of earth for the very first time,
> a form of words can be found in which it will be understood by
> someone else to whom it is entirely new. This would not be possible
> if we could not distinguish parts in the thought corresponding to the
> parts of a sentence, so that the structure of the sentence can serve
> as a picture of the structure of the thought. (Frege, 1923, p. 36)

A similar passage occurs earlier, in (1914), where Frege again tries to explain the possibility of understanding an infinite number of sentences by noting that:

> thoughts have parts out of which they are built up. And these
> parts, these building blocks, correspond to groups of sounds out
> of which the sentence expressing the thought is built up, so that
> the construction of the sentence out of the parts of a sentence
> corresponds to the construction of a thought out of parts of a
> thought. (Frege, 1914, p. 225)

And the same line of reasoning is explored in a draft of a letter to Jourdain, composed during the same period:

> The possibility of our understanding sentences which we have never
> heard before rests evidently on this, that we construct the sense of
> a sentence out of parts that correspond to the words. If we find
> the same word in two sentences, e.g., 'Etna', then we also recognize
> something common to the corresponding thoughts, something cor-
> responding to this word. Without this, language in the proper sense
> would be impossible. (Frege, VIII12, p. 79)

Passages like these seem to establish Frege's compositional picture of senses, and especially its epistemic motivation, beyond any shadow of a doubt. But there are other passages, particularly in his discussion of complex incomplete expressions, in which Frege seems to reject this compositional picture in favor of a view almost directly opposed to it. Rather than treating the meaning of a sentence as built up from the meanings of its parts, he seems to treat the meanings of incomplete expressions, at least, as somehow dependent on the meanings of sentences in which they occur. This alternative, decompositional perspective is also motivated by an epistemic thesis, but one that turns the compositional idea on its head: Frege appears to think that a speaker comes to understand an incomplete expression only by, first, grasping the meaning of some sentence in which it occurs, and then "decomposing" the meaning of that sentence to arrive at the meanings of it parts.

The decompositional strand of thought running through Frege's writings is not incidental, and cannot be dismissed. It reflects, instead, what he took to be one of his major achievements. As we saw earlier, Frege placed particular emphasis on the way in which his formalism was able to account for the formation of interesting and useful concepts, those actually needed in science. Unlike previous logical systems, which seemed to insist that all concepts should be formed either by abstraction from individuals, or else through the sterile techniques of Boolean multiplication and addition (union and intersection), Frege viewed his own logic as the first to supply a formal account of the correct, Kantian view that concepts can actually be derived from judgments. And as it turns out, his idea of decomposition, along with his treatment of incomplete expressions more generally, provides the key to this process.[2]

The precise mechanism through which we are supposed to form concepts from judgments makes its appearance as early as the *Begriffsschrift*, where Frege explains how we can arrive at "functions" by "viewing" sentences in some particular way:

> Let us assume that the circumstance that hydrogen is lighter than carbon dioxide is expressed in our formula language; we can then replace the sign for hydrogen by the sign for oxygen or that for

---

[2]See Sluga (1980, pp. 90–95) for a full discussion of the relation between Frege's views and Kant's doctrine of the priority of judgments over concepts. Note also that, although the German *Begriff* ('concept') is used in Frege's technical vocabulary to designate the referent of a predicate, he often uses the same word more informally—and in a way that corresponds more closely to the English 'concept'—to designate what we would naturally think of as a predicate's sense. It is this usage of the term that concerns us here.

nitrogen. This changes the meaning in such a way that "oxygen" or "nitrogen" enters into the relations in which "hydrogen" stood before. If we imagine that an expression can thus be altered, it decomposes into a stable component, representing the totality of relations, and the sign, regarded as replaceable by others, that denotes the object standing in these relations. The former component I call a function, the latter its argument. The distinction has nothing to do with the conceptual content; it comes about only because we view the expression in a particular way. (Frege, 1879, pp. 21–22)

This passage is a little bit garbled. It runs together what Frege will later distinguish as senses, referents, and expressions; and as a result, it ends up saying that functions are the stable components that remain once we imagine that expressions have been altered in certain ways, which sounds like gibberish.[3] Nevertheless, once these confusions are sorted out, the passage admits a natural interpretation according to which it seems to say something quite sensible: that we form a concept like "being lighter than carbon dioxide" by, first, grasping the meaning of a sentence like 'Hydrogen is lighter than carbon dioxide', and then imagining what this meaning would be like if the part of it corresponding to 'hydrogen' were replaced by a part corresponding to 'oxygen', then by a part corresponding to 'nitrogen', and so on. The stable component—the part of the meaning that remains fixed while these different pieces are being swapped in and out—is the concept "being lighter than carbon dioxide" (here referred to as a function); we come to grasp this concept by decomposing the meaning of a sentence, viewing its meaning in a certain way, with certain parts missing.

Now, although these remarks do clash with the epistemic thesis involved in the compositional perspective—the idea that our understanding of a syntactic complex depends on our understanding of its parts—there is, so far, no clear conflict with the metaphysical thesis. Even if our grasp of a complex sentential sense is somehow epistemically prior to our grasp of its parts, it is still possible

---

[3]At least to our modern ears. It may have sounded better to Frege's mathematical contemporaries, who tended to think of functions as particular kinds of expressions. This is the view that Frege later seeks to overturn in (1891a), where he takes as his starting point the idea that a function of a variable $x$ is "a mathematical expression containing $x$, a formula containing the letter $x$" (and see also (1893, p. 5), where he is still concerned with the possibility that functions might be confused with expressions). The understanding of functions among Frege's contemporaries is discussed in detail by Sluga (1980, pp. 85–87), who describes it as a "peculiar wavering" between syntax and semantics, citing as an example Euler's definition of a function of a variable as "an analytic expression which is composed in a certain way out of the variable quantity and constant numbers or quantities."

that the complex sense should be structured in some unique, determinate way. What Frege goes on to say, however, undermines this metaphysical thesis as well, for he seems to hold that there are, in fact, different ways of viewing the meaning of the same complex expression, different ways of decomposing that meaning into parts, which then lead to different concepts:

> According to the conception sketched above, "hydrogen" was the argument and "being lighter than carbon dioxide" the function; but we can also conceive of the same conceptual content in such a way that "carbon dioxide" becomes the argument and "being heavier than hydrogen" the function. We then need only regard "carbon dioxide" as replaceable by other ideas, such as "hydrochloric acid" or "ammonia" ... The situation is the same for the proposition that Cato killed Cato. If we here think of "Cato" as replaceable at its first occurrence, "to kill Cato" is the function; if we think of "Cato" as replaceable at its second occurrence, "to be killed by Cato" is the function; if, finally, we think of "Cato" as replaceable at both occurrences, "to kill oneself" is the function. (Frege, 1879, p. 22)

Again, we should not let the confusions in this passage obscure its point. If, in the meaning of 'Hydrogen is lighter than carbon dioxide', we now imagine the part corresponding to 'carbon dioxide' as replaceable, we will be led to another concept: "being heavier than hydrogen." And we can likewise form three different concepts from the meaning of 'Cato killed Cato', depending on whether we remove the part corresponding to the first occurrence of 'Cato', the part corresponding to the second occurrence, or both at once. This idea—that there is no single, determinate way of decomposing a complex sense into its parts—is the metaphysical thesis associated with the decompositional perspective.

Both the epistemic priority of sentential meanings over the meanings of their parts and the metaphysical claim that there are different ways of decomposing sentential meanings are again emphasized in (1881), in a passage that is much easier to read, because Frege has dropped the confusing vocabulary used to present these ideas in the *Begriffsschrift*. Instead of referring to the meanings of incomplete expressions, awkwardly, as functions, he now echoes Kant in calling them "concepts," and in calling the meanings of sentences "judgments" (or, better, "contents of possible judgment").

After mentioning the views of Aristotle and Boole, both of whom regarded concepts as epistemically prior to judgments, Frege begins this passage with a clear statement of his own Kantian view that judgments are to have priority:

> As opposed to this, I start out from judgments and their contents,
> and not from concepts ... I only allow the formation of concepts
> to proceed from judgments ... And so instead of putting a judg-
> ment together out of an individual as subject and an already pre-
> viously formed concept as predicate, we do the opposite and ar-
> rive at a concept by splitting up the content of possible judgment.
> (Frege, 1881, pp. 16–17)

And he illustrates:

> If, that is, you imagine the 2 in the content of possible judgment
> $2^4 = 16$ to be replaceable by something else, by $(-2)$ or by 3 say,
> which may be indicated by putting an $x$ in the place of the 2:
> $x^4 = 16$, the content of possible judgment is thus split into a con-
> stant and a variable part. The former, regarded in its own right
> but holding a place open for the latter, gives the concept "4th root
> of 16." (Frege, 1881, p. 16)

This example is especially notable because, for the first time, Frege actually
displays an expression that is supposed to take one of these newly formed concepts as its meaning: the incomplete expression '$x^4 = 16$'. He then goes on,
using this same notation, to describe the other concepts that can be formed,
through decomposition, from the meaning of '$2^4 = 16$', again displaying the incomplete expression associated with each. By treating the part of this meaning
that corresponds to '4' as replaceable, he writes:

> we get the concept "logarithm of 16 to the base 2": $2^x = 16$. The $x$
> indicates here the place to be occupied by the sign for the individual
> falling under the concept. We may now also regard the 16 in $x^4 = 16$
> as replaceable in its turn, which we may represent, say, by $x^4 = y$. In
> this way we arrive at the concept of a relation, namely the relation
> of a number to its 4th power. (Frege, 1881, p. 17)

The two perspectives adopted by Frege in his thinking about senses appear, then, to offer sharply conflicting views concerning both the structure of
senses themselves and the relative epistemic priority of sentential senses and
their parts. According to the compositional perspective, the sense of a complex
expression is supposed to have a determinate structure, corresponding to that of
the expression, and we are supposed to understand such an expression by, first,
grasping the senses of its parts. According to the decompositional perspective,

there are supposed to be a number of different ways in which the sense of a sentence, at least, can be decomposed into its parts, and our grasp of these parts is supposed to depend on a prior understanding of the sentence. How can the conflict between these two perspectives be reconciled?

### 6.1.2  Resolving the conflict

Since the passages supporting the decompositional perspective tend to come early in Frege's career, while those supporting the compositional perspective were written late, it is occasionally suggested that Frege might have adopted these two conflicting perspective at different times—in particular, that he might have abandoned his decompositional ideas about the priority of judgments over concepts, adopting the compositional ideas instead, once he had introduced his distinction between senses and referents. But this suggestion will not work.[4] Although Frege certainly put less emphasis on the decompositional perspective once he had formulated the distinction between senses and referents, he did not abandon the idea. He continues to discuss the many ways in which "a thought can be split up ... so that now one thing, now another, appears as subject or predicate" in (1892a, p. 199), an article in which the distinction between senses and referents is recognized. And we find him still advocating his early views on decompositionality even very late in life: "I do not begin with concepts and put them together to form a thought or judgment; I come by the parts of a thought by decomposition of the thought" (1919, p. 253). We cannot, therefore, explain away the apparent conflict between these two strands in Frege's thought by denying that he maintained them both at once: he did maintain them at once, and so from an interpretive standpoint, we would like to see how he could have.

It may seem that the apparent conflict would pose less of a problem for a contemporary semantic theorist interested only in drawing on Frege's ideas, or providing a reconstruction rather than a strict interpretation—since, in light of the conflict, one or the other of these competing perspectives could then be abandoned. But the matter is not so straightforward. It is not as though one of the two perspectives is simply mistaken, so that the only problem we face is merely deciding which to omit. Both of these ideas—compositionality, of course, but also Frege's logical implementation of Kant's view that complex concepts can be formed by decomposition from judgments—represent important insights in his philosophy, which we would like to preserve. Our task as semantic theorists is therefore similar to the interpretive task: we have to find some way

---

[4]As pointed out by Dummett (1981, pp. 262–263).

of reconciling the apparent conflict between these two perspectives, working out
a semantic theory that is able to accommodate both.

My effort to reconcile these two perspectives will based on a proposal set out
by Dummett in (1981).[5] What Dummett suggests is that, in spite of Frege's
contradictory statements, there was actually no conflict in his thought at all,
since he was describing two different part/whole relations among senses. Of
course, as Dummett says, there may have been some purely verbal confusion,
and like a lot of verbal confusion, it may have led to a bit of real confusion:

> Frege himself never introduced any distinct terminology to differ-
> entiate the two types of [part/whole relation]; hence the apparent
> contradiction between what he says when he has one type in mind
> and what he says when he has in mind the other. It is even pos-
> sible that he did not remain ... vividly aware of the distinction ...
> (Dummett, 1981, p. 271)

But none of this confusion is supposed to be serious; none of it is supposed
to indicate any real conflict among Frege's ideas that could not be sorted out
simply by distinguishing the two different part/whole relations he had in mind.

In order that *we* should remain vividly aware of this distinction, I now introduce some terminology, adopted from Dummett, for describing the two different
kinds of parts to be found in a complex sense, and the two different processes
involved in resolving a complex into parts of these different kinds. According
to the compositional perspective, there is a unique way of resolving the sense
of a complex expression into its parts, corresponding to the construction of
the expression itself, and the parts of the complex sense are epistemically prior
to the whole. Let us refer to the kind of parts of which this is true as "constituents," and to the process of resolving a sentential sense into its constituents
as "analysis." According to the decompositional perspective, there are many
different ways of resolving the sense of a whole sentence, at least, into its parts,
and these parts are epistemically dependent on the whole. Let us refer to the
parts of which this is true as "components," and to the process of resolving a
sentential sense into its components as "decomposition."

Given this vocabulary, we are now able to furnish a verbal resolution to
the conflict, at least. We are no longer forced to say contradictory things about

---

[5]The proposal appears in Chapter 15; it was hinted at it earlier, but not developed, in
Dummett (1973, pp. 28–29), criticized from a textual standpoint by Baker and Hacker (1984),
and defended in Dummett (1984, pp. 221–223). Useful discussions of the issues surrounding
this proposal can also be found in Bell (1987), Dummett (1989), and Bell (1996).

some single relation between a sentential sense and its parts: we can instead say, consistently, that each complex sense has a unique analysis into its constituents, which are epistemically prior to that sense itself, but that it can be decomposed in a variety of different ways into components, which are epistemically dependent on the complex sense.

This is what we can say, but what does it mean? In order to provide real substance to this verbal resolution, we now show how these two perspectives—compositional and decompositional—can be accommodated within the formal semantic framework set out earlier.

**The compositional perspective**

Well, it turns out that the compositional perspective is captured by the account of sense already presented. We need only define the notion of a *constituent* in such a way that each basic sense is a constituent of itself, and the constituents of a complex sense $\sigma[P_{\langle\alpha_1,\ldots,\alpha_n:\beta\rangle}](\mathcal{P}, \mathcal{Q}_1, \ldots, \mathcal{Q}_n)$—that is, a structure of the form $(\mathcal{P}\ \mathcal{Q}_1\ \ldots\ \mathcal{Q}_n)$—include the senses $\mathcal{P}$, $\mathcal{Q}_1$, ..., $\mathcal{Q}_n$, along with any of their constituents. This notion of sense constituency parallels the obvious notion of *grammatical constituency*, according to which the basic expressions are grammatical constituents of themselves, and the grammatical constituents of the complex expression $P_{\langle\alpha_1,\ldots,\alpha_n:\beta\rangle}(\pi, \tau_1, \ldots, \tau_n)$—an expression of the form $\pi(\tau_1, \ldots, \tau_n)$—are $\pi$, $\tau_1$, ..., $\tau_n$, along with their constituents. And the principle of compositionality for senses, formulated earlier, then guarantees that the construction of the sense of a complex expression out of its constituents corresponds to the construction of that expression itself out of its grammatical constituents. To illustrate: the sentence '3 + 2 = 5' takes (equal (plus 3 2) 5) as its sense. The six constituents of this sense will be equal, (plus 3 2), 5, plus, 3, and 2; the six constituents of the sentence will be '=', '3 + 2', '5', '+', '3', and '2'; and the analysis of the sense as $\sigma[P_{\langle e,e:t\rangle}](\text{equal}, \sigma[P_{\langle e,e:e\rangle}](\text{plus}, 3, 2), 5)$ mirrors the analysis of the sentence as $P_{\langle e,e:t\rangle}('=', P_{\langle e,e:e\rangle}('+', '3', '2'), '5')$.

This is enough to establish the metaphysical thesis involved in the compositional perspective. And our current treatment of senses likewise seems to support the epistemic thesis, according to which a speaker comes to grasp the sense of a complex expression by first grasping the constituents of that sense; it seems reasonable to suppose, for example, that a speaker could not understand the sentence '2 + 3 = 5' without first grasping the senses of its grammatical constituents.

Frege's compositional perspective is thus captured perfectly in the framework already presented; the challenge, therefore, is to see how this same syntactic and semantic framework can be extended to accommodate the alternative, and apparently conflicting, point of view.

### The decompositional perspective

Just as the analysis of a complex sense into its constituent senses corresponds to the analysis of a complex expression into its grammatical constituents, there should be some grammatical operation corresponding to whatever act of thought is involved when one forms a new concept by decomposing a complex sense into its component senses. Indeed, as we have seen, Frege first presents this operation of concept formation through a grammatical analogy: we are said to form the concept "4th root of 16," for instance, by doing to the meaning of the sentence '$2^4 = 16$' something like what we do when we pass from this sentence itself to the new expression '$x^4 = 16$'. Rather than trying to study this operation of concept formation directly, then, we follow Frege's strategy of working backward from its linguistic analogue. Our first step will be to augment the simple arithmetical language described so far with a syntactic rule allowing us to decompose complete expressions into their component expressions.

Frege's clearest description of his notion of syntactic decomposition can be found in the *Grundgesetze*:

> If from a proper name we remove a proper name that forms a part of it or coincides with it, at some or all of the places where the constituent proper name occurs—but in such a way that these places remain recognizable as capable of being filled by one and the same arbitrary proper names ... then I call that which we obtain by this means a *name* of a first-level function of one argument. (Frege, 1893, p. 43)[6]

When he speaks of a "proper name," Frege means to include both what we would call terms and sentences, expressions belonging to the categories $e$ or $t$; when he speaks of a "name of a first-level function of one argument," he means to include

---

[6]In the same section, Frege goes on to say that first-level functions of two arguments can then be formed from these first-level functions of one argument by the further removal of another complete expression, but the status of this idea is controversial; Dummett, for example, argues in both (1973, p. 40) and (1981, p. 286) that it clashes with Frege's general grammatical principles, and should be regarded as a lapse. Although I am not entirely convinced by the argument, I ignore this further principle of abstraction in what follows, largely for the sake of simplicity, and treat two-argument functions as formed by the simultaneous removal of two complete expressions from a single complete expression.

both what we would call one-place function symbols and one-place predicates, expressions belonging to the categories $\langle e : e \rangle$ and $\langle e : t \rangle$. This description of Frege's, therefore, already follows the pattern of our syntactic rules, specifying the category of expressions from which it takes its inputs, the category to which it contributes its outputs, and the way in which inputs are modified to yield outputs—roughly, by having certain pieces removed from them. Frege's notation for this kind of removal varied. In his early work, as we have seen, he used Roman italics to mark the places from which pieces of an expression have been removed: the removal of '2' from '$2^4 = 16$' led to '$x^4 = 16$'. He later switched to Greek letters, so that the result of this same removal would be written as '$\xi^4 = 16$'. And we will adopt a different notation still, the standard notation of the $\lambda$-calculus, so that the result of this removal will now turn out to be the predicate '$\lambda x(x^4 = 16)$'.[7]

In order to incorporate Frege's idea of removal into the current syntactic framework, as a new rule of decomposition, we first introduce a common convention according to which the result obtained by substituting the terms $\kappa_1, \ldots, \kappa_n$ for the variables $\xi_1, \ldots, \xi_n$ in the open expression $\psi$ can be referred to as $[\kappa_1, \ldots, \kappa_n/\xi_1, \ldots, \xi_n]\psi$. Thus, for example, $['2'/'x']('3 + x = 5')$ will be the expression that results when the term '2' is substituted for the variable '$x$' in '$3 + x = 5$'—that is, the sentence '$3 + 2 = 5$'.

It is important to note that expressions of the form '$[\kappa_1, \ldots, \kappa_n/\xi_1, \ldots, \xi_n]\psi$' do not actually belong to our object language. They are, instead, metalinguistic devices for presenting a certain canonical description of object language expressions—capturing, in Frege's phrase, a particular way of "viewing" these expressions, as resulting from particular substitutions. To adapt Frege's own example from (1881), when we describe the sentence '$2^4 = 16$' as $['2'/'x']('x^4 = 16')$—that is, as the sentence resulting from '$x^4 = 16$' when '2' is substituted for '$x$'—we capture one particular view of the sentence, which suggests the concept "4th root of 16." But this same sentence could also be described as $['4'/'x']('2^x = 16')$, which presents a different view, suggesting the concept "logarithm of 16 to the base 2." In Frege's eyes, coming to view a

---

[7]The notation for the $\lambda$-calculus, which is all the reader needs to know in order to understand the body of this book, is explained in several introductory texts in logic and semantics, such as Suppes (1957) or Heim and Kratzer (1998). A few footnotes, however, draw on certain elementary concepts from the theory of the $\lambda$-calculus, such as the concepts of *reduction* or *normal form*. These ideas will be explained in any modern text on the $\lambda$-calculus or combinatory logic, such as Hindley, Lercher, and Seldin (1972); an authoritative treatment of great historical interest can be found in Church (1941).

familiar sentence in a new way might well be the foundation of a significant cognitive advance, the discovery of a new concept.

Using our substitution convention, then, let us now introduce a family of syntactic *R-rules*, or *removal rules*, each of the form $R_{\langle \alpha_1,\ldots,\alpha_n : \beta \rangle}$, according to which: if a complete expression $\phi$ from the category $\beta$ can be described as $[\kappa_1,\ldots,\kappa_n / \xi_1,\ldots,\xi_n]\psi$, with $\psi$ an open expression and each $\kappa_i$ belonging to the category $\alpha_i$, then $\lambda\xi_1,\ldots,\lambda\xi_n\psi$ is an expression belonging to the category $\langle \alpha_1,\ldots,\alpha_n : \beta \rangle$. When the expression $\lambda\xi_1,\ldots,\lambda\xi_n\psi$ is introduced in this way, we will say that

$$R_{\langle \alpha_1,\ldots,\alpha_n : \beta \rangle}(\text{`}[\kappa_1,\ldots,\kappa_n / \xi_1,\ldots,\xi_n]\psi\text{'}) = \lambda\xi_1,\ldots,\lambda\xi_n\psi.$$

It is worth noting explicitly that these removal rules, unlike our earlier predication rules, are intensional. They do not simply take object language expressions as their inputs, but instead, certain views of these expressions—canonical descriptions presented in the metalanguage, using the substitution prefix. What the removal rules give us is a way of reflecting these metalinguistic views of object language expressions in new expressions belonging to the object language itself, which we can now refer to as *complex incomplete expressions*.

To illustrate: the rule $R_{\langle e : t \rangle}$ tells us that '$\lambda x(x + 2 = 5)$' is a complex one-place predicate, an expression belonging to the category $\langle e : t \rangle$, since the category $t$ expression '$3 + 2 = 5$', for example, can be described as $['3'/'x']('x + 2 = 5')$ and '3' belongs to the category $e$. We express this fact by saying that

$$R_{\langle e : t \rangle}(\text{`}['3'/'x']('x + 2 = 5')\text{'}) = \text{`}\lambda x(x + 2 = 5)\text{'},$$

where this notation displays, not just the complete expression from which the complex predicate is formed, but the particular substitutional description, or view, of that expression that justifies the application of the removal rule. The sentence '$3 + 2 = 5$' could also be described as $['2'/'x']('3 + x = 5')$, for instance, yet we would have

$$R_{\langle e : t \rangle}(\text{`}['2'/'x']('3 + x = 5')\text{'}) = \text{`}\lambda x(3 + x = 5)\text{'},$$

with the new view of the same sentence leading to a different object language predicate.

I believe that the removal rules set out here provide an accurate representation, in a clear syntactic framework, of Frege's grammatical idea that complex incomplete expressions—predicates, function symbols, or connectives—can be formed through the "removal" of complete expressions from complete expressions.[8] And given these new removal rules, we are now in a position to define what it means for one expression to be a component of another, as follows: a complex incomplete expression $\pi$ is a *syntactic component* of a complete expression $\phi$ just in case $\pi$ can be arrived at from $\phi$ by an application of a removal rule—just in case, that is, there is a description of $\phi$ as $[\kappa_1, \ldots, \kappa_n / \xi_1, \ldots, \xi_n]\psi$ and $\pi$ is the expression $\lambda \xi_1, \ldots, \lambda \xi_n \psi$.[9] To illustrate: the complex predicate '$\lambda x(x + 2 = 5)$' is a syntactic component of the sentence '$3 + 2 = 5$' since this sentence can be described as $['3'/'x']('x + 2 = 5')$.

This definition provides, I believe, exactly what is wanted as an explication of the decompositional perspective in Frege's treatment of sense. It helps us understand, first of all, the metaphysical idea that there are many different ways of decomposing an expression into its components, corresponding to the different way of decomposing a complex sense into concepts. We have already seen, for example, that the sentence '$3 + 2 = 5$' contains, not only the predicate '$\lambda x(x + 2 = 5)$', but also the predicate '$\lambda x(3 + x = 5)$' as a component, leading to the concepts "being two units less than five" and "being three units less than five." There are several other interesting component expressions contained

---

[8]There is one minor point of difference. Our removal rules allow for the formation, through vacuous abstraction, of complex incomplete expressions like '$\lambda x(3 + 2 = 5)$'—as, for example, $R_{\langle \alpha_1, \ldots, \alpha_n : \beta \rangle}('['6'/'x']('3 + 2 = 5')')$—but Frege's own description, cited earlier, requires that one expression can be removed from another only if it actually "forms a part of it." It would be easy enough to restrict the formulation of our removal rules so that they did not allow vacuous abstraction, but here, I think, a slightly revisionist approach is preferable, since this requirement of Frege's is really just an artifact of his notation. We are free to permit vacuous abstraction, because it is possible to distinguish the sentence '$3 + 2 = 5$' from the one-place predicate '$\lambda x(3+2 = 5)$'. Frege was forced to forbid the analogous construction, I believe, only because his removal notation simply did not allow him to distinguish the sentence '$3 + 2 = 5$' itself from the predicate that results from this sentence when the term '6', for example, is removed from it.

[9]The definition is adequate only for first-order languages, which is all that we consider here. For higher-order languages, we would have to appeal to the notion of *reduction* from the $\lambda$-calculus, defining $\pi$ as a *component* of $\phi$ just in case there are expressions $\kappa_1, \ldots, \kappa_n$ such that $\pi \kappa_1, \ldots, \kappa_n$ reduces to $\phi$. In the first-order case, this definition is equivalent to that provided in the text, since $(\lambda \xi_1, \ldots, \xi_n \psi)\kappa_1, \ldots, \kappa_n$ reduces to $\phi$ just in case $\phi$ can be described as $[\kappa_1, \ldots, \kappa_n / \xi_1, \ldots, \xi_n]\psi$; each reduction, in this case, is just a single contraction, which is the idea captured by the definition in the text. In higher-order languages, where reductions might involve several contractions, we would have to move to the more general definition set out in this note. This treatment of the notion of a component for higher-order languages should be compared to the more complicated treatments described by Dummett in (1973, pp. 45–48) and (1981, pp. 275–276), both of which involve, first, defining the conditions under which one expression can be said to "occur" in another, and then defining the components of an expression as what remains when other expressions occurring in it are removed.

within this sentence, such as '$\lambda xy(x + 2 = y)$' ("being two units apart"), and of course, others that are not very interesting.

And second—because each expression contains so many components, most of which it is reasonable to think we have no idea of in advance—this definition also supports the epistemic idea that speakers cannot be expected to grasp the sense of these components prior to understanding the expression from which they are derived.[10] Instead, it seems that epistemic dependence flows in the other direction, from expressions to their components, just as the decompositional strand in Frege's thought suggests. It is entirely reasonable to suppose that a speaker comes to understand a complex predicate or function symbol by, first, understanding some complete expression from which it is derived—that a speaker comes to understand '$\lambda xy(x + 2 = y)$', for example, by first understanding either '$3 + 2 = 5$' or some other sentence containing this complex predicate as a component.

## 6.2   Defined expressions

As I said at the beginning of this chapter, there is a good deal of overlap between the two issues under consideration here, concerning both incomplete and defined expressions. Now that we have set out our syntactic rule for introducing incomplete expressions, I want to consider defined expressions as well, both to justify the claim of overlap, and so that the later, more delicate syntactic and semantic analysis of both kinds of expressions can proceed in parallel.

We will be concerned here, not with abbreviative definitions, which belong to the metalanguage, but with the kind of stipulative definitions that are thought to augment the object language itself. Frege signaled the occurrence of these stipulative definitions through his double-stroke notation, according to which, for example, the definition

$$\Vdash (x + 2 = 5) = Fx,$$

---

[10] This phenomenon—that we need not already know all the components of expressions we understand—is especially evident in higher-order languages, where even the simplest expressions will have infinitely many components, moving all the way up the type hierarchy. Consider, for instance, the sentence '$E6$' ("six is even"). If we were working in a higher-order context, with components defined as in the previous note, this sentence would then have as components, not only '$\lambda x(Ex)$', but also, for example, the type $\langle\langle e:t\rangle:t\rangle$ expression '$\lambda\Phi(\Phi 6)$', since '$(\lambda\Phi.\Phi 6)E$' reduces to '$E6$', the type $\langle\langle\langle e:t\rangle:t\rangle:t\rangle$ expression '$\lambda\Omega(\Omega E)$', since '$[\lambda\Omega(\Omega E)](\lambda\Phi(\Phi 6))$' reduces to '$E6$', the type $\langle\langle\langle\langle e:t\rangle:t\rangle:t\rangle:t\rangle$ expression '$\lambda\Theta(\Theta(\lambda\Phi(\Phi 6)))$', since '$[\lambda\Theta(\Theta(\lambda\Phi(\Phi 6)))](\lambda\Omega(\Omega E))$' reduces to '$E6$', and so on. Dummett discusses a similar phenomenon in (1981, pp. 288–290), under the heading of "degenerate decompositions."

would have the effect of assigning to the new symbol '$F$' the semantic properties— "the same sense and the same reference"—of its defining expression (1893, p. 45).

But how, exactly, are we to understand the introduction of a new symbol like this into the object language from a syntactic perspective? The question is rarely asked. The most common position, I suspect, is that "introducing" a new symbol through a stipulative definition is not, in fact, introducing anything at all, but moving to an entirely new language, just like the old one in both syntax and semantics, except that it contains the new symbol among its basic expressions. An extreme example of this position is adopted by Mark Steiner, who writes:

> "Introduction," here, is something of a metaphor: if the rules for stipulative definitions are set out fully, they fix in advance every such definition possible. Each language that permits stipulations, therefore, is really an infinite set of object languages with a common core, differing only as to how references or extensions are to be assigned via stipulation to the "extra" terms. (Steiner, 1975, p. 59)

Now I do not mean to suggest that there is really anything *wrong* with this standard position, even in its extreme version. But it does tend to obscure certain connections—such as the similarities between expressions like the new symbol '$F$', as defined above, and the complex incomplete expression '$\lambda x(x + 2 = 5)$', which surely is part of the original language. Furthermore, the standard position is a bit complicated as a model of our actual practice. Suppose that we were working in arithmetic, or some other large language, and that we actually did introduce the new symbol '$F$' through the definition set out above. According to this standard position, we would then have two large languages on hand; and, formally, we would have to go through the bother of identifying the whole of the original language with the '$F$'-free fragment of its definitional extension. No one ever does such a thing.

In actual practice, it seems, we really do just introduce defined expressions directly into whatever language we are using, through rules of definition very much like our syntactic rules. As a rough but more accurate model of our practice, then, we now enhance our simple arithmetical language by fashioning rules of definition that conform to our standard pattern for syntactic rules.

We must imagine, to begin with, that our language has been formulated against the background of an infinite set of auxiliary symbols ('$F_1$', '$F_2$', '$F_3$', . . .), which are divided, at any given time, into those that have already been assigned to syntactic categories and those that are still unused; the idea is that the auxiliary symbols assigned to syntactic categories have already been defined, while the unused symbols are available for future definitions. Given this set of auxiliary symbols, our rules of definition can now be introduced as variations of the standard removal rules, in the following way. For each removal rule $R_{\langle \alpha_1,\ldots,\alpha_n:\beta \rangle}$, we postulate a *variant form*—written, $R^*_{\langle \alpha_1,\ldots,\alpha_n:\beta \rangle}$—according to which: if a complete expression $\phi$ from the category $\beta$ can be described as $[\kappa_1,\ldots,\kappa_n/\xi_1,\ldots,\xi_n]\psi$, with $\psi$ a open expression and with each $\kappa_i$ belonging to the category $\alpha_i$, then at any given time, an arbitrary unused auxiliary symbol $\pi$ can be removed from the set of unused symbols and assigned to the syntactic category $\langle \alpha_1,\ldots,\alpha_n:\beta \rangle$. If $\pi$ is assigned to a category through a rule of this kind, we say

$$R^*_{\langle \alpha_1,\ldots,\alpha_n:\beta \rangle}(\text{‘}[\kappa_1,\ldots,\kappa_n/\xi_1,\ldots,\xi_n]\psi\text{’}) = \pi.$$

To illustrate: the sentence '$3 + 2 = 5$' can be described as $['3'/'x']('x + 2 = 5')$, and so we are able, as before, to apply the standard removal rule $R_{\langle e:t \rangle}$ to form the complex predicate '$\lambda x(x + 2 = 5)$'; but in addition, we are now free to apply the new rule $R^*_{\langle e:t \rangle}$, the variant form of the standard removal rule, to classify some unused auxiliary symbol—say, '$F_7$'—as an expression belonging to the category $\langle e:t \rangle$, in which case we say that

$$R^*_{\langle e:t \rangle}(\text{‘}['3'/'x']('x + 2 = 5')\text{’}) = \text{‘}F_7\text{’}.$$

These variant form $R^*$-rules exhibit some peculiar properties. Standard syntactic rules, we recall, specify both the categories of input and output expressions, as well as the way in which the inputs are modified or combined to form outputs. These variant form rules also specify the categories of inputs and outputs, but in this case, the outputs do not result from any sort of modification or combination of the inputs. They are, instead, simply selected from a pool of unused auxiliary symbols; the sole syntactic effect of a variant form rule is that one of these symbols is now assigned to a particular syntactic category. This feature, although peculiar from a syntactic standpoint, seems to be necessary in any model of our actual practice, since stipulative definitions do involve arbitrary symbols, subject only to the constraint that they have not already been defined. And in any case, the idea that the outputs of these new rules are independent of their inputs holds only from the syntactic standpoint. It remains necessary to consider the inputs of these rules in order to establish the semantic properties of their outputs, the defined expressions; and in fact, the reason these definitional rules are classified as variant forms of our standard removal rules is simply that, semantically, the outputs of these two kinds of rules—complex incomplete and defined expressions—depend upon their inputs in exactly the same way.

# Chapter 7

# Syntactic and semantic options

We now turn our attention explicitly to the semantics of these complex incomplete and defined expressions: our task is to extend the $\rho$ and $\sigma$ functions, mapping expressions into their referents and senses, to apply also to the syntactic outputs of our new removal rules.

## 7.1 Referents

The reference function $\rho$ can again be handled in a standard fashion, which can be presented in three steps, the first two of which are preliminary and notational.

We begin by assigning referents to the open expressions defined earlier, containing variables, as well as to ordinary expressions with no variables—that is, to open expressions such as '$x + 2 = 5$' as well as ordinary expressions such as '$3 + 2 = 5$'. For this, it suffices to let the reference function $\rho$ map each term variable into an arbitrary member of $D_e$ and each sentence variable into an arbitrary member of $D_t$; the reference function can then be extended to arbitrary open expressions through the principles of compositionality and function application set out earlier. To illustrate: it is easy to see through an application of these principles that $\rho['x + 2 = 5']$ is Truth if $\rho$ maps the variable '$x$' into the object 3, but Falsity if $\rho$ maps '$x$' into 4.

Next, where each $\xi_i$ is a variable belonging to the category $\alpha_i$ and each $o_i$ is an object from the set $D_{\alpha_i}$, we let the reference function $\rho^{o_1/\xi_1,\ldots,o_n/\xi_n}$ mirror the behavior of the function $\rho$ in its application to basic expressions, except that it assigns to each variable $\xi_i$ the object $o_i$. Of course, $\rho^{o_1/\xi_1,\ldots,o_n/\xi_n}$ can itself then be extended to the entire language through the principles of compositionality and function application. To illustrate: the reference function $\rho^{4/'x'}$ will assign the object 4 to the variable '$x$', no matter how this variable is treated by $\rho$ itself, and so $\rho^{4/'x'}['x + 2 = 5']$ will be Falsity.

Finally, with these preliminaries behind us, let us suppose that $\pi$ is either the incomplete expression $\lambda\xi_1, \ldots, \xi_n\psi$, with the syntactic analysis

$$R_{\langle\alpha_1,\ldots,\alpha_n:\beta\rangle}('[\kappa_1, \ldots, \kappa_n/\xi_1, \ldots, \xi_n]\psi'),$$

or else a defined expression introduced through the variant form rule $R^*_{\langle\alpha_1,\ldots,\alpha_n:\beta\rangle}$ and analyzed in the same way. The standard idea, then, is to define $\rho[\pi]$ as the particular function $f$ belonging to $D_{\langle\alpha_1,\ldots,\alpha_n:\beta\rangle}$ such that, whenever $\langle o_1, \ldots, o_n\rangle$ is a tuple belonging to the Cartesian product $D_{\alpha_1} \times \ldots \times D_{\alpha_n}$, we have

$$f(o_1, \ldots, o_n) = \rho^{o_1/\xi_1,\ldots,o_n/\xi_n}[\psi].$$

To illustrate: suppose, as in the previous chapter, that the complex predicate '$\lambda x(x + 2 = 5)$' has the syntactic analysis

$$R_{\langle e:t\rangle}('['3'/'x']('x + 2 = 5')')$$

and that the new symbol '$F_7$' is introduced through the variant form rule $R^*_{\langle e:t\rangle}$, and analyzed in the same way. Then both of these expressions will take as their referents the function $f$ from $D_{\langle e:t\rangle}$ such that, for any object $o$ from $D_e$, we have

$$f(o) = \rho^{o/'x'}['x + 2 = 5'];$$

this is, of course, precisely the function that maps the number 3 into Truth and any other number into Falsity.[1]

Although somewhat complicated from a notational standpoint, this treatment of reference for complex incomplete and defined expressions is, again, entirely standard, involving familiar ideas and techniques.[2]

---

[1] All of this can be put a bit more simply if we allow lambda abstraction in our metalanguage. We can then simply stipulate, in the general case, that $\rho[R_{\langle\alpha_1,\ldots,\alpha_n:\beta\rangle}('[\kappa_1, \ldots, \kappa_n/\xi_1, \ldots, \xi_n]\psi')] = \lambda o_1, \ldots, o_n(\rho^{o_1/\xi_1,\ldots,o_n/\xi_n}[\psi])$, or in the case of our example, that $\rho[R_{\langle e:t\rangle}('['3'/'x']('x + 2 = 5')')] = \lambda o(\rho^{o/'x'}['x + 2 = 5'])$.

[2] It is worth noting only that these ideas and techniques are not found in Frege, but had to await Tarski, and also that, contrary to what we are often told, this treatment of reference is not, strictly speaking, compositional: the value assigned by the reference function $\rho$ to a complex incomplete or defined expression does not depend on the values assigned to the constituents of that expression by $\rho$, but instead, in the general case, on the values assigned to these constituents by $\rho^{o_1/\xi_1, \ldots, o_n/\xi_n}$, an entirely different function.

## 7.2    Senses

The problem of extending the notion of sense to these new expressions, by
contrast, has rarely been considered in any detail, and raises a number of difficult
issues. These issues, moreover, are not entirely semantic; particularly in the case
of complex incomplete expressions, they involve the interplay between syntactic
rules and the rules governing semantic evaluation. We begin by considering some
purely syntactic matters, concerning the proper formulation of predication rules
for a language containing complex incomplete expressions.

### 7.2.1    Syntactic options

Previously, when all of our incomplete expressions were basic, there was really
only one way for predication rules to combine them with complete expressions—
through concatenation, or anyway something very similar. Accordingly, these
rules were formulated so that $P_{\langle \alpha_1,\ldots,\alpha_n:\beta \rangle}(\pi, \tau_1, \ldots, \tau_n)$—that is, the result of
assembling the incomplete expression $\pi$ with the complete expressions $\tau_1, \ldots, \tau_n$
through a predication rule—turned out to be, simply: $\pi(\tau_1, \ldots, \tau_n)$. Now
that the rules of decomposition allow us to form complex incomplete expressions, however, another quite reasonable syntactic option presents itself:
we could suppose that predication rules operate on complex expressions, at
least, not just by concatenating them with complete expressions, but instead, by fitting complete expressions into the "vacancies" left in these complex incomplete expressions by the removal rules. That is, we could modify our predication rules in such a way that, whenever $\pi$ can be analyzed
as $R_{\langle \alpha_1,\ldots,\alpha_n:\beta \rangle}(\text{‘}[\kappa_1, \ldots, \kappa_n/\xi_1, \ldots, \xi_n]\psi\text{’})$—that is, whenever $\pi$ is an expression of the form $\lambda\xi_1, \ldots, \xi_n\psi$—then $P_{\langle \alpha_1,\ldots,\alpha_n:\beta \rangle}(\pi, \tau_1, \ldots, \tau_n)$ turns out to be
$[\tau_1, \ldots, \tau_n/\xi_1, \ldots, \xi_n]\psi$, rather than simply $\pi(\tau_1, \ldots, \tau_n)$.

We are faced, then, with two options: either to stick with our original
predication rules, which combine incomplete and complete expressions always
through simple concatenation, or to modify these rules so that their application to complex incomplete expressions, at least, involves a more complicated
substitutional operation. Let us refer to these two options, respectively, as
Option 1 and Option 2. And just to have a simple illustration at hand, we
consider how each of these options would handle the predication involved in the
construction of a sentence from the complex predicate '$\lambda x(3 > x)$'—analyzed,
say, as $R_{\langle e:t \rangle}(\text{‘}[\text{‘}1\text{’}/\text{‘}x\text{’}](\text{‘}3 > x\text{’})\text{’})$—and the term '2'. According to the familiar

Option 1, we would have

$$P_{\langle e:t\rangle}(`\lambda x(3 > x)\text{'}, `2\text{'}) \ = \ `\lambda x(3 > x)\, 2\text{'};$$

that is, the result of predicating '$\lambda x(3 > x)$' of the term '2' is realized simply by concatenating the two expressions. But our new contender, Option 2, would tell us that

$$\begin{aligned} P_{\langle e:t\rangle}(`\lambda x(3 > x)\text{'}, `2\text{'}) \ &= \ [`2\text{'}/`x\text{'}](`3 > x\text{'}) \\ &= \ `3 > 2\text{'}, \end{aligned}$$

so that the result of this predication is achieved through a much more complicated structural operation—in effect, fitting the term '2' directly into the vacancy that was left in the incomplete predicate '$\lambda x(3 > x)$' when it was formed through the application of a removal rule.

Now we must ask: does it *matter* which of the two options we choose; and if it does, which option did Frege select, and which is the right choice? I will argue that it matters, that Frege selected Option 2, but that the right choice is Option 1.

We begin with the textual point, concerning Frege's own selection of Option 2. Not surprisingly, Frege never discusses this particular issue—the relative merits of Option 1 and Option 2—but I feel confident in ascribing Option 2 to him both because it is suggested by various things he does say, and because his practice conforms to this choice.

The closest thing in Frege to a statement of our predication rules occurs in a grammatical section of the *Grundgesetze*, where, speaking of the formation of a "proper name ... from a proper name and a name of a first-level function," he writes:

> This formation is carried out in this way: a name fills the argument
> places of another name that are fitting for it. (Frege, 1893, p. 46)

Recall that "proper names" include both terms and sentences, and that "names of first-level functions" include predicates, function symbols, and connectives. So this statement describes, among other things, the formation of a sentence from a term and a predicate; and what Frege says is that the sentence results when the term *fills* the argument place of the predicate. This syntactic construction is illustrated toward the end of the same section, where he says that "we can form, from the proper name '$\Delta$' and the function name '$\xi = \zeta$', the function-name '$\Delta = \zeta$', and further from the latter name and '$\Delta$', the proper name '$\Delta = \Delta$'." What Frege gets here, when he combines the function name

'$\xi = \zeta$' with the proper names '$\Delta$' and '$\Delta$', is the expression '$\Delta = \Delta$'—that is, the Option 2 result, not something like '$(\xi = \zeta)\Delta\Delta$', which is what Option 1 would yield.

Of course, this example is not quite conclusive, since Frege tended to blur the distinction between certain basic expressions, such as the basic predicate '$=$', and the corresponding complex incomplete expressions, such as the complex predicate '$\lambda xy(x = y)$'.[3] It may be that Frege intended the expression '$\xi = \zeta$' here as something more like a basic expression, our '$=$', in which case the example would lose its force, since even according to Option 1, the result of combining the basic expression '$=$' with '$\Delta$' and '$\Delta$' would be '$\Delta = \Delta$'. However, another example of Option 2 at work occurs just at the beginning of the book, and this one does seem to be conclusive. Writing of functions and arguments, Frege says:

> we obtain a name of the value of a function for an argument, if we
> fill the argument places in the name of the function with the name
> of the argument. In this way, for example, '$(2 + 3 \cdot 1^2) \cdot 1)$' is a name
> of the number 5, composed of the function-name '$(2 + 3 \cdot \xi^2) \cdot \xi)$'
> and '1'. (Frege, 1893, p. 6)

Surely no one could think of '$(2 + 3 \cdot \xi^2) \cdot \xi)$' as a basic predicate; "composed," here, has to mean composed in accord with the syntactic rule of predication, and what Frege gives us, again, is the Option 2 result.

Passages like these show conclusively that Frege's own treatment of predication conformed to our syntactic Option 2: rather than simply being concatenated with complex incomplete expressions, terms and sentences were placed directly into the vacancies formed in these expressions by the removal rules.[4]

---

[3]See Dummett (1973, pp. 27–33) for a discussion.

[4]In the case of higher-order complex expressions, Option 2 generalizes to the idea that the syntactic result of applying, say, the expression $\pi$ to $\tau$ through a higher-order predication rule is not simply the concatenated expression $\pi\tau$, but what is known in the *normal form* of this expression—that is, the expression that results when all $\lambda$-expressions have been eliminated through the operation of *reduction*. Here the Option 2 idea is that predication should be analyzed syntactically as, first, performing simple concatenation—which leads to the Option 1 outcome—and then reducing the resulting expression to its normal form by performing as many reductions as necessary; this idea generalizes the statement of Option 2 for the first-order case that is provided in the text. In fact, we can find evidence that Frege abides by this higher-order generalization of Option 2 as well. In (1893 p. 36), for example, he tells us (translating into modern notation and using $\lambda$-abstraction in place of Frege's notation for removal) that the sentence '$\neg\forall x\neg\neg(x > 0 \supset x^2 = 1)$' can be "obtained"—obviously, through a rule of predication—from the expressions '$\lambda\Phi\neg\forall x\neg\Phi(x)$' and '$\lambda y\neg(y > 0 \supset y^2 = 1)$'. Again, then,

And it is this aspect of Frege's syntax, I think, that has led a number of commentators, beginning with Peter Geach (1961, p. 143ff.), to suggest that Frege's incomplete expressions are best regarded only as *patterns*, or features, of complete expressions, rather than actual *parts* . This view of incomplete expressions as patterns or features, rather than parts, is also endorsed by Dummett, who explains it as follows:

> There is no part in common to the sentences 'Brutus killed Brutus' and 'Cassius killed Cassius' which is not also part of the sentence 'Brutus killed Caesar': yet the predicate '$\xi$ killed $\xi$' is said to occur in the first two and not in the third. Such a complex predicate is, rather, to be regarded as a *feature* in common to the two sentences, the feature, namely, that in both the simple relational expression '... killed ... ' occurs with the same name in both of its argument-places. (Dummett, 1973, p. 31)

Now it seems reasonable to suppose, no matter which of our two syntactic options is selected, that complex incomplete expressions should be viewed only as patterns of the terms and sentences in which they occur as components, and from which they are formed through decomposition, a process represented by our removal rules. It is in part the recognition of these patterns that constitutes the creative act of concept formation.

But what about the terms and sentences that are then formed from these complex incomplete expressions, once they have been recognized and isolated, through predication rules, and in which these expressions therefore occur as constituents? Here, the correct view—whether complex incomplete expressions are actual parts, or only patterns—does depend on the choice between our syntactic options. According to Option 1, the result of predicating, say, '$\lambda x(x$ killed $x)$' of 'Brutus' would lead to the sentence '$\lambda x(x$ killed $x)$Brutus', in which the expression '$\lambda x(x$ killed $x)$' occurs as a syntactically distinguishable part. But according to Option 2, the result of applying the same predicate to the same term would lead instead to the sentence 'Brutus killed Brutus', in which, again, '$\lambda x(x$ killed $x)$' seems to occur only as a pattern.

The syntactic Option 2 thus has the consequence that complex incomplete expressions cannot ever occur in a complete expression as distinguishable parts:

---

Frege favors the syntactic Option 2. The Option 1 result would have been the concatenated expression '$[\lambda\Phi\neg\forall x\neg\Phi(x)](\lambda y\neg(y > 0 \supset y^2 = 1))$'. But what Frege gives us instead is the normal form of this expression, which can be arrived at from the Option 1 candidate through two reductions, the first leading to '$\neg\forall x\neg(\lambda y\neg(y > 0 \supset y^2 = 1))(x)$' and then the second to what Frege views as the result of the predication.

not when they occur as components, and not, according to this option, when they occur as constituents either. It was precisely Frege's choice of Option 2, therefore, that is responsible for the conclusion drawn by Geach, Dummett, and others that these complex incomplete expressions are best thought of only as patterns among terms and sentences, rather than syntactic entities actually belonging to the language—that, as Dummett goes on to say later in the same paragraph cited above, a "complex predicate is thus not really an expression—a bit of language—in its own right" (p. 31).[5]

But what exactly is wrong with Frege's choice; what is wrong with Option 2? A quick answer is simply that it introduces syntactic ambiguity into our language. According to Option 2, as we saw, the result of applying the predicate '$\lambda x(3 > x)$' to the term '2'—that is, $P_{\langle e:t \rangle}$('$\lambda x(3 > x)$', '2')—turns out to be the sentence '3 > 2', but this sentence can also be analyzed as $P_{\langle e,e:t \rangle}$('>', '3', '2'). So this single sentence would have two different syntactic analyses, resulting either from an application of the predication rule $P_{\langle e:t \rangle}$ to a complex incomplete predicate and a term, or from an application of the separate predication rule $P_{\langle e,e:t \rangle}$ to a basic incomplete predicate and two terms.[6]

This objection, however, may be a bit too quick. Is syntactic ambiguity, in itself, such a bad thing? Usually, when people object to syntactic ambiguity, it is because the same expression, under its different syntactic analyses, is associated with different semantic values, of some kind or other. We have only two kinds of semantic values: referents and senses. Given our extension of the reference relation to complex incomplete expressions, it is easy to see that the sentence '3 > 2' would have the same referent under each of the two analyses set out above—both $\rho[P_{\langle e:t \rangle}$('$\lambda x(3 > x)$', '2')] and $\rho[P_{\langle e,e:t \rangle}$('>', '3', '2')] are Truth—and this particular case reflects the general fact: the reference function $\rho$ would assign the same referent to each expression under any of the different analyses of that expression provided by Option 2. Therefore, if expressions under these different analyses are to be associated with different semantic values of any kind, they must be associated with different senses.

Are they? What we need to ask is whether, for example, the sense of $P_{\langle e:t \rangle}$('$\lambda x(3 > x)$', '2') is identical with that of $P_{\langle e,e:t \rangle}$('>', '3', '2'), and obviously,

---

[5]An implicit reliance on Option 2 can also be found in some of the more recent literature on Frege, such as Bell's (1996, p. 593) assumption—which figures crucially in the argument of that paper—that an application of the complex predicate '$\xi$ is greater than 1 and, for all $n$, if $n$ divides $\xi$, then either $n = \xi$ or $n = 1$' to term '13' must result in the sentence '13 is greater than 1 and, for all $n$, if $n$ divides 13, then either $n = 13$ or $n = 1$'.

[6]And of course, many other analyses as well—as many different analyses, in fact, as it has components.

there are again two options: either these senses are different, or they are the
same. Let us refer to *these* options, respectively, as Option A and Option B.
In a way, Option B is the semantic analogue of the syntactic Option 2. Just
as Option 2 requires that, whenever $\pi$ is an incomplete expression analyzed as
$R_{\langle\alpha_1,\ldots,\alpha_n:\beta\rangle}(\text{`}[\kappa_1,\ldots,\kappa_n/\xi_1,\ldots,\xi_n]\psi\text{'})$, we should have the syntactic result

$$P_{\langle\alpha_1,\ldots,\alpha_n:\beta\rangle}(\pi,\tau_1,\ldots,\tau_n) = [\tau_1,\ldots,\tau_n/\xi_1,\ldots,\xi_n]\psi,$$

the most natural way to capture Option B is by requiring, likewise, that we
should have

$$\sigma[P_{\langle\alpha_1,\ldots,\alpha_n:\beta\rangle}(\pi,\tau_1,\ldots,\tau_n)] = \sigma[[\tau_1,\ldots,\tau_n/\xi_1,\ldots,\xi_n]\psi]$$

as a semantic result. Nevertheless, it is important to see that our choice between
the semantic Options A and B is, in fact, logically independent of our choice
between the syntactic Options 1 and 2. Each choice can go either way, no matter
which way the other goes; so all told, there are four mixed options, which it will
be helpful to have explicitly before us.

Option 1A combines the Option 1 treatment of predication, according to
which, for example, $P_{\langle e:t\rangle}(\text{`}\lambda x(3 > x)\text{'}, \text{`}2\text{'})$ and $P_{\langle e,e:t\rangle}(\text{`}>\text{'}, \text{`}3\text{'}, \text{`}2\text{'})$ result in
distinct expressions, with the semantic Option A, according to which these
distinct expressions are assigned distinct senses: $\sigma[P_{\langle e:t\rangle}(\text{`}\lambda x(3 > x)\text{'}, \text{`}2\text{'})]$
$\neq \sigma[P_{\langle e,e:t\rangle}(\text{`}>\text{'}, \text{`}3\text{'}, \text{`}2\text{'})]$.

Option 1B combines the Option 1 treatment of predication, according to
which $P_{\langle e:t\rangle}(\text{`}\lambda x(3 > x)\text{'}, \text{`}2\text{'})$ and $P_{\langle e,e:t\rangle}(\text{`}>\text{'}, \text{`}3\text{'}, \text{`}2\text{'})$ result in distinct expressions, this time, with the semantic Option B, according to which these
distinct expressions are assigned the same sense: $\sigma[P_{\langle e:t\rangle}(\text{`}\lambda x(3 > x)\text{'}, \text{`}2\text{'})]$
$= \sigma[P_{\langle e,e:t\rangle}(\text{`}>\text{'}, \text{`}3\text{'}, \text{`}2\text{'})]$.

Option 2A combines the Option 2 treatment of predication, according to
which $P_{\langle e:t\rangle}(\text{`}\lambda x(3 > x)\text{'}, \text{`}2\text{'})$ and $P_{\langle e,e:t\rangle}(\text{`}>\text{'}, \text{`}3\text{'}, \text{`}2\text{'})$ are simply two different analyses of the same expression, the sentence '3 > 2', with the semantic
Option A according to which the expression has the different senses under
these different analyses: $\sigma[P_{\langle e:t\rangle}(\text{`}\lambda x(3 > x)\text{'}, \text{`}3\text{'})] \neq \sigma[P_{\langle e,e:t\rangle}(\text{`}>\text{'}, \text{`}3\text{'}, \text{`}2\text{'})]$.

Option 2B combines the Option 2 treatment of predication, according
to which $P_{\langle e:t\rangle}(\text{`}\lambda x(3 > x)\text{'}, \text{`}2\text{'})$ and $P_{\langle e,e:t\rangle}(\text{`}>\text{'}, \text{`}3\text{'}, \text{`}2\text{'})$ are, again, simply
two different analyses of the same expression, the sentence '3 > 2', with
the semantic Option B, according to which the expression is assigned

the same sense under each of these analyses: $\sigma[P_{\langle e:t\rangle}(\text{‘}\lambda x(3 > x)\text{’}, \text{‘2’})] = \sigma[P_{\langle e,e:t\rangle}(\text{‘>’}, \text{‘3’}, \text{‘2’})]$.

Of these four logical possibilities, only Option 2A can be dismissed out of hand: this option leads to unacceptable syntactic ambiguity, since it results in the assignment of different semantic values of some kind—senses, in this case—to the same expressions under different syntactic analyses.

By these standards, at least, the syntactic ambiguity associated with Option 2B would be acceptable, since the ambiguous expressions would always be associated with the same semantic values, both referents and senses, under each of their different syntactic analyses. But Option 2B faces another kind of problem: if we were to select this option, what could we possibly say about the *point* of introducing complex incomplete expressions? As we have seen, Frege placed great emphasis on the operation of forming new concepts by removing constituents from thoughts, and on the grammatically analogous operation of forming complex incomplete expressions, such as predicates, by removing grammatical constituents from complete expressions. Presumably, then, we should be able to do something either with these new predicates or with the resulting concepts that we could not have done without them. Given the semantic Option B, however, we could not actually use these new predicates to express new thoughts, since any sense carried by a sentence containing complex incomplete expressions would already be carried by some sentence containing only basic expressions. And given the syntactic Option 2, we could not even use these new predicates to form new sentences, since any sentence constructible using complex incomplete expressions would be constructible already from basic expressions alone. Option 2B therefore entails that these complex incomplete expressions allow us neither to express new thoughts nor even to form new sentences, and so it is hard to see how their introduction could have any point at all.

We are now in a position to appreciate the real reason—as opposed to the quick answer, given earlier—why the choice of the syntactic Option 2 is mistaken. If we were to adopt Option 2, then the application of, say, the complex predicate ‘$\lambda x(3 > x)$’ to the term ‘2’, through the rule $P_{\langle e:t\rangle}$, would not result in a sentence distinct from ‘$3 > 2$’. But as we have now seen, the resulting sentence *has* to be distinct. In order for the construction of the complex predicate to have any point at all, it must allow us the possibility, at least, of forming sentences with new semantic properties, but then these had better be new sentences, or else the very possibility that gives the complex predicate its point turns into the possibility, also, of unacceptable syntactic ambiguity. Put more succinctly: if we were to choose Option 2, we would be committed either to Option 2A or to Option 2B, but 2A results in unacceptable syntactic ambiguity, while 2B renders the introduction of complex incomplete expressions pointless. Since the syntactic Option 2 is either unacceptable or pointless, it is mistaken.

### 7.2.2 Semantic options

The syntactic Option 1 must be correct, then, since it allows us the possibility, without introducing unacceptable syntactic ambiguity, of using complex incomplete expressions to form expressions with new semantic properties—sentences expressing new thoughts, for example. But maybe just the *possibility* that these sentences could express new thoughts is enough; maybe we do not actually need the new thoughts themselves. This intriguing idea is what lies behind the mixed Option 1B, according to which, although complex incomplete expressions can be used to form new sentences, these new sentences then express exactly the same thoughts as old sentences that were available all along.

Moreover, as we will now see, something like Option 1B suggests itself as a treatment, not just of ordinary incomplete expressions, but also of the defined expressions introduced through our variant form decompositional rules.

When it comes to defined expressions, it is worth noting, there is really no choice between the syntactic Options 1 and 2. Although it is still, in a sense, a logical possibility, Option 2 is not really a live option at all in the syntax of definitions. What Option 2 *would* say, in this case, is that, whenever the defined symbol $\pi$ is introduced through a variant form removal rule as $R^*_{\langle \alpha_1,\ldots,\alpha_n:\beta \rangle}(\text{`}[\kappa_1,\ldots,\kappa_n/\xi_1,\ldots,\xi_n]\psi\text{'})$, the syntactic result of predicating this new symbol of the expressions $\tau_1,\ldots,\tau_n$—that is, $P_{\langle \alpha_1,\ldots,\alpha_n:\beta \rangle}(\pi,\tau_1,\ldots,\tau_n)$—should then turn out to be $[\tau_1,\ldots,\tau_n/\xi_1,\ldots,\xi_n]\psi$, rather than $\pi(\tau_1,\ldots,\tau_n)$. To illustrate, suppose we were to introduce the new predicate '$F_9$' through the stipulation that

$$R^*_{\langle e:t \rangle}(\text{`}['1'/'x']('3 > x')\text{'}) = \text{`}F_9\text{'},$$

Then Option 2 would tell us that the result of applying this new predicate to the term '2'—that is, $P_{\langle e:t \rangle}(\text{`}F_9\text{'}, \text{`}2\text{'})$—should be '3 > 2', rather than something like '$F_9(2)$', and this is not even remotely plausible. Why would anyone bother to introduce the new defined predicate '$F_9$' if it is simply supposed to disappear, in favor of its defining phrase, whenever it is actually applied to a term?

On the other hand, it is not only plausible but a standard view, and a view explicitly endorsed by Frege, that an expression containing defined symbols and

its definitional reduction, although syntactically distinct, should carry exactly
the same sense. We have already seen this in the remarks from the *Grundgesetze*
cited just at the end of Chapter 2 and also in a passage from (1914) that was
cited in Chapter 3, part of which we repeat here for convenience:

> we have to distinguish between a sentence and the thought it ex-
> presses. If the *definiens* occurs in a sentence and we replace it by
> the *definiendum*, this does not affect the thought at all. It is true we
> get a different sentence if we do this, but we do not get a different
> thought. (Frege, 1914, p. 208)

What Frege is saying in this passage, applied to our particular example, is that,
even though '$F_9(2)$' and '$3 > 2$' are distinct sentences, the sense of the former
is what we would get if we were to eliminate the *definiens* '$F_9$' in favor of its
*definiendum*, and therefore agrees with that of the latter:

$$
\begin{aligned}
\sigma['F_9(2)'] &= \sigma[P_{\langle e:t\rangle}('F_9', '2')] \\
&= \sigma[['2'/'x']('3 > x')] \\
&= \sigma['3 > 2'].
\end{aligned}
$$

The key idea here—what justifies the transition from the first of these equations
to the second—is simply a variant form of our Option B proposal, according to
which, put generally, we should have

$$
\sigma[P_{\langle \alpha_1,\ldots,\alpha_n:\beta\rangle}(\pi, \tau_1, \ldots, \tau_n)] = \sigma[[\tau_1, \ldots, \tau_n/\xi_1, \ldots, \xi_n]\psi]
$$

whenever $\pi$ is a defined expression introduced through a variant form removal
rule, and analyzed as $R^*_{\langle \alpha_1,\ldots,\alpha_n:\beta\rangle}(' [\kappa_1, \ldots, \kappa_n/\xi_1, \ldots, \xi_n]\psi ')$.

It is important to note, however, that this variant form of the Option B proposal, as well as the original proposal itself, formulated for complex incomplete
expressions, both clash with the principle of compositionality for senses, set out
earlier, according to which

$$
\sigma[P_{\langle \alpha_1,\ldots,\alpha_n:\beta\rangle}(\pi, \tau_1, \ldots, \tau_n)] = \sigma[P_{\langle \alpha_1,\ldots,\alpha_n:\beta\rangle}](\sigma[\pi], \sigma[\tau_1], \ldots, \sigma[\tau_n])
$$

regardless of the derivational history of $\pi$. Compositionality tells us that
the sense of a complex complete expression depends, in a way determined by
$\sigma[P_{\langle \alpha_1,\ldots,\alpha_n:\beta\rangle}]$, on the senses of its parts, including whatever incomplete or defined expressions might occur as syntactic parts of that expression. What the
semantic Option B and its variant form tell us, on the other hand, is that the
senses of both complex incomplete and defined expressions are to be specified

*contextually*—that we should be able to assign a sense to each complete expression in which one of these new expressions occurs, without assigning senses to these new expressions themselves.

This kind of contextual treatment is, in fact, endorsed by Dummett, who argues that the sense of a complex predicate "is not to be explained in terms of the senses of its constituents, but, rather, in terms of the common feature of the senses of all sentences formed by inserting a name in its argument-place" (1981, p. 286; see pp. 282–288 for a full discussion). Dummett's approach to complex incomplete expressions is thus entirely contextual in both the syntactic and semantic departments: just as a complex incomplete expression is supposed to be nothing but a pattern among complete expressions, its sense, likewise, is no more than a pattern among the senses of these complete expressions.

Now, in general, the method of contextual definition raises a number of difficult problems. Its advantages are apparent in Russell's treatment of definite descriptions, for example, or Quine's use of virtual classes. Its disadvantages have been discussed by a number of writers, but the central intuition behind these various objections is that contextual definitions force us to abandon the ideal that logical form should correspond to syntactic form. This line of objection can be seen very clearly, for example, in Kaplan's (1966, pp. 234–236) complaint that a language allowing contextual definitions cannot be, as he says, "logically perfect." In Kaplan's terminology, each expression exhibits both a grammatical form and a logical form: its grammatical form is given by its syntactic analysis; its logical form is determined by the semantic evaluation rules, the rules that "tell us how to 'construct' the semantical value of an expression in terms of the values of its logically simple [constituents]."[7] And what makes a language logically perfect, he writes, is a certain kind of fit between the logical and grammatical form of its expressions:

> In a logically perfect language the logical form of an expression must always mirror the grammatical form. Therefore, for logical perfection we require that the logically simple expressions coincide with the grammatically simple expressions, and that to every formation rule there corresponds a unique evaluation rule such that any compound formed by applying the formation rule to given [constituents] is eval-

---

[7] Here and in the displayed quotation that follows, in order to avoid unnecessary confusion, I have replaced 'components', which is what actually occurs in this passage, with 'constituents'. Kaplan, of course, is not dealing with the technical distinction set out here between components and constituents, and the "components" he speaks of happen to correspond to our constituents, not our components.

uated by applying the corresponding evaluation rule to the values of the [constituents]. This has the desired result that the semantical evaluation of an expression exactly recapitulates its grammatical construction. (Kaplan, 1966, p. 236)

Since the basic expressions of our language are already assigned basic procedures as their senses, achieving this kind of logical perfection merely requires embracing the principle of compositionality, according to which each syntactic rule $P_{\langle \alpha_1,...,\alpha_n:\beta \rangle}$ is associated with the unique evaluation rule $\sigma[P_{\langle \alpha_1,...,\alpha_n:\beta \rangle}]$, which then forms the sense of a compound from the senses of its parts. Shifting instead to the contextual treatment provided by our Option B proposals—and so abandoning compositionality—means abandoning logical perfection as well.

Now, as I said, contextual definitions raise difficult problems. The cases in which these problems are most difficult, however, are those in which semantic evaluation rules map expressions into unstructured entities, such as objects or truth values, or else into entities that may be structured, but whose structure is not supposed to reflect that of the expressions themselves, such as sets, or sets of possible worlds.[8] What makes the matter so difficult in these cases is the fact that, although we do seem to feel that the semantic evaluation of an expression should conform to its grammatical construction, it is hard to find any firm justification for this feeling.

The point can be illustrated by considering our treatment of reference. As it happens, we did, in fact, provide explicit definitions of the referents of complex incomplete and defined expressions, so that the evaluation of the sentence '$\lambda x(3 > x)\,2$', for example, can proceed through the steps

$$
\begin{aligned}
\rho['\lambda x(3 > x)\,2'] &= \rho[P_{\langle e:t \rangle}('\lambda x(3 > x)',\,'2')] \\
&= \rho[P_{\langle e:t \rangle}](\rho['\lambda x(3 > x)'],\,\rho['2']) \\
&= \rho['\lambda x(3 > x)'](\rho['2']) \\
&= \text{Truth,}
\end{aligned}
$$

conforming to the ideal of logical perfection. But we could just as easily have extended our treatment of reference to these new linguistic items through contextual definitions, by stipulating that

$$
\rho[P_{\langle \alpha_1,...,\alpha_n:\beta \rangle}(\pi, \tau_1, \ldots, \tau_n)] = \rho[[\tau_1, \ldots, \tau_n/\xi_1, \ldots, \xi_n]\psi]
$$

---

[8]These are, in fact, the kind of cases Kaplan means to consider; he takes "semantical value to be what Carnap calls 'the extension,' that is: a truth value for sentences, an individual for names, a class of individuals for one-place predicates, and so on" (1966, p. 235).

whenever $\pi$ is a complex incomplete or a defined expression, analyzed either as $R_{\langle \alpha_1, \ldots, \alpha_n : \beta \rangle}(\text{'}[\kappa_1, \ldots, \kappa_n / \xi_1, \ldots, \xi_n] \psi\text{'})$ or through the variant form of this removal rule. And in this case, the evaluation of the same sentence would have proceeded through the steps

$$
\begin{aligned}
\rho[\text{'}\lambda x(3 > x)\,2\text{'}] &= \rho[P_{\langle e:t \rangle}(\text{'}\lambda x(3 > x)\text{'}, \text{'}2\text{'})] \\
&= \rho[[\text{'}2\text{'}/\text{'}x\text{'}](\text{'}3 > x\text{'})] \\
&= \rho[\text{'}3 > 2\text{'}] \\
&= \rho[P_{\langle e, e:t \rangle}(\text{'}>\text{'}, \text{'}3\text{'}, \text{'}2\text{'})] \\
&= \rho[P_{\langle e, e:t \rangle}](\rho[\text{'}>\text{'}], \rho[\text{'}3\text{'}], \rho[\text{'}2\text{'}]) \\
&= \rho[\text{'}>\text{'}](\rho[\text{'}3\text{'}], \rho[\text{'}2\text{'}]) \\
&= \text{Truth,}
\end{aligned}
$$

where the second line is justified by the contextual treatment of the incomplete expression '$\lambda x(3 > x)$' and the rest of evaluation follows our standard pattern. Here, although it does seem that the first of these methods of evaluation is more attractive than the second, in this kind of situation, where the semantic values have no structure, it is hard to find any real *reason* for this attraction, apart from a simple decision to prefer semantic evaluation rules that recapitulate syntactic form. After all, even though the first method of evaluation recapitulates syntax and the second does not, they both end up assigning exactly the same referent to the sentence. Why, it might be asked, should we worry about the precise method of assignment, as long as the assignments themselves agree?

This issue—the problem of finding some reason to value logical perfection— seems to have been implicit already in Kaplan's use of shudder quotes to describe semantic evaluation rules as rules telling us how to "construct" the semantic values of expressions. Unless semantic values themselves have a significant structure, the evaluation rules do not really construct them at all; they simply assign these values to expressions. If evaluation rules actually did construct semantic values, with the values assigned to expressions depending in some way on the sequence of rules used to calculate the assignment, there might then be a clear reason for insisting on logical perfection. But what is so important about logical perfection in those cases in which the construction of semantic values is just a metaphor? It may be that the demand for logical perfection here results only from taking the metaphor too seriously, or it may be that there are other reasons for it. To settle the problems raised by contextual definitions in this case, it would be necessary to locate these other reasons, if they exist, and then balance their importance against the real convenience of being able to work with contextually defined expressions.

Fortunately, we do not have to become involved in any of these difficult issues simply to decide whether the *senses* of complex incomplete and defined expressions can be specified through contextual definitions. Here, the rules assigning senses to expressions are exactly the kind of rules for which talk of constructing semantic values can be taken literally. Senses are structured semantic values, and the sense assigned to an expression really does reflect its method of construction, the exact sequence of rules through which the assignment is calculated. In this case, then, there are no delicate matters of balance to consider at all; the contextual approach suggested by our semantic Option B is simply wrong, assigning senses through a sequence of rules—and so, constructing these senses—in a way that violates Frege's requirement that the sense of an expression should mirror its structure.

Again, the point can be illustrated by tracing the assignment of a sense to the sentence '$\lambda x(3 > x)\,2$', which would proceed, according to the contextual Option B, as follows:

$$
\begin{aligned}
\sigma['\lambda x(3 > x)\,2'] &= \sigma[P_{\langle e:t\rangle}('\lambda x(3 > x)', \,'2')] \\
&= \sigma[['2'/'x']('3 > x')] \\
&= \sigma['3 > 2'] \\
&= \sigma[P_{\langle e,e:t\rangle}('>', \,'3', \,'2')] \\
&= \sigma[P_{\langle e,e:t\rangle}](\sigma['>'], \sigma['3'], \sigma['2']) \\
&= (\sigma['>']\ \sigma['3']\ \sigma['2']) \\
&= (\text{greater } 3\ 2).
\end{aligned}
$$

The contextual treatment would assign exactly the same sense to the sentence '$F_9(2)$', with '$F_9$' defined as above, and both assignments would be incorrect. Rather than reflecting the structure of '$\lambda x(3 > x)\,2$' or '$F_9(2)$', both one-place predications formed through an application of the rule $P_{\langle e:t\rangle}$, the assigned sense corresponds instead to the sentence '$3 > 2$', a two-place predication formed through the rule $P_{\langle e,e:t\rangle}$.

When it comes to the assignment of senses, then, there is good reason to maintain the compositionality principle, according to which the sense of an expression of the form $\sigma[P_{\langle \alpha_1,\ldots,\alpha_n:\beta\rangle}(\pi, \tau_1, \ldots, \tau_n)]$ is uniformly defined as $\sigma[P_{\langle \alpha_1,\ldots,\alpha_n:\beta\rangle}](\sigma[\pi], \sigma[\tau_1], \ldots, \sigma[\tau_n])$. What this entails, however—since the function $\sigma[P_{\langle \alpha_1,\ldots,\alpha_n:\beta\rangle}]$ takes $\sigma[\pi]$ as an argument—is that we must be able to assign a sense to $\pi$ as it occurs in isolation, even if $\pi$ is a complex incomplete or defined expression. In the case of the sentence '$\lambda x(3 > x)\,2$', for example, the compositional assignment of sense begins as follows:

$$
\begin{aligned}
\sigma['\lambda x(3 > x)\,2'] &= \sigma[P_{(e:t)}('\lambda x(3 > x)', '2')] \\
&= \sigma[P_{(e:t)}](\sigma['\lambda x(3 > x)'], \sigma['2']) \\
&= (\sigma['\lambda x(3 > x)']\ \sigma['2']) \\
&= (\sigma['\lambda x(3 > x)']\ 2).
\end{aligned}
$$

The first line, as usual, reflects syntactic analysis; the second, compositionality; and the third, an application of the appropriate mode of composition. The fourth line indicates our identification of $\sigma['2']$, the sense of '2', as the basic procedure 2. But in this case, we cannot complete our assignment of a sense to the sentence until we are able to identify $\sigma['\lambda x(3 > x)']$, the sense of the incomplete expression; and in just the same way, we would not be able to assign a sense to the sentence '$F_9(2)$' until we were able to identify $\sigma['F_9']$, the sense of the defined expression '$F_9$'. An adherence to logical perfection, and so compositionality, therefore forces us to identify the senses of defined and incomplete expressions in isolation, in such a way that these senses can then appear as real constituents of complex senses.

This is the general conclusion I have been aiming at, and since the argument leading up to it was somewhat complicated, a quick summary may be helpful. Basically, there are two reasons for thinking we might be able to get away without assigning senses to complex incomplete or defined expressions. First, we might suppose that complex incomplete expressions, at least, never occur as real syntactic constituents of complete expressions, but only as features or patterns, so that it would be possible to assign a sense to each complete expression without paying any explicit semantic attention to these incomplete expressions at all. This was the idea underlying the syntactic Option 2, which we rejected on the grounds that it either leads to unacceptable syntactic ambiguity or renders the introduction of these complex incomplete expressions pointless. Second, we might suppose that, even if complex incomplete expressions, and now defined expressions too, do occur as real constituents of complete expressions, we could avoid any direct account of their senses by treating them contextually, assigning senses to the complete expressions in which they occur without assigning senses to these incomplete or defined expressions themselves. This was the idea underlying the semantic Option B, which we rejected on the grounds that it violates Frege's conception of senses as semantic values reflecting the structure of expressions. Both complex incomplete and defined expressions must be able to appear as real constituents in complete expressions, and their senses must likewise appear as constituents in the senses of any complete expressions that contain them; so they must *have* senses.

# Chapter 8

# Senses of incomplete expressions

If complex incomplete and defined expressions, as we have now seen, must have senses—if they cannot be treated contextually, from either the syntactic or the semantic perspective—it becomes necessary to ask what their senses might be: how should the senses of these expressions be reified within the semantic framework set out here? This chapter considers two alternatives. The first is a kind of "de re" proposal, according to which these complex incomplete and defined expressions are assigned particular basic procedures as their senses, just as if they were basic expressions. Although this proposal satisfies our formal constraints, and has some surprising attractions, it is problematic as an interpretation of Frege. The second alternative, a refinement of the first, introduces complex incomplete senses, along the lines of "macros" in computer languages, to serve as the senses of complex incomplete and defined expressions. This alternative shares the attractions of the initial proposal but avoids its problems.

## 8.1 A de re proposal

The best way to appreciate the first alternative is to return to Kaplan's ideal of logical perfection, which combines two requirements: in order for a language to count as logically perfect, it must satisfy the principle of compositionality, but it must also satisfy the separate requirement that, as Kaplan writes, "logically simple expressions coincide with grammatically simple expressions" (1966, p. 236). Since it is now settled that our language should satisfy compositionality, we concentrate here on the second of these two requirements.

Within the present framework, the most straightforward interpretation would result from taking an expression to be "logically simple" if it has a basic procedure as its sense, and "grammatically simple" if it is basic, not constructed

through a syntactic rule.  On this interpretation, the force of the requirement that logically and grammatically simple expressions coincide would simply be that all and only the basic expressions should have basic procedures
as their senses.  In particular, the senses of complex incomplete and defined
expressions—such as the predicates '$\lambda x(3 > x)$' and '$F_9$', considered earlier—
could not be basic procedures, since these expressions are not themselves basic,
but are instead constructed, or introduced into the language, through syntactic
removal rules.

Given this interpretation, our initial proposal involves explicitly violating
the requirement of logical perfection: the proposal is simply that expressions
that are constructed syntactically through ordinary removal rules or their definitional variants should be regarded, semantically, just as if they were basic.  The
senses of basic expressions are the basic procedures that compute their referents,
and so the idea would be to treat the senses of complex incomplete or defined
expressions in exactly the same way.  Both '$\lambda x(3 > x)$' and '$F_9$', for example,
have as referents the function that maps a number into Truth just in case it is
less than 3; and so according to this proposal, these expressions would both take
as their senses the basic procedure that computes this function—which, for future reference, we can label less-than-3.  Since basic procedures are individuated
along with the functions they compute, the net effect of this initial proposal
is that the senses of complex incomplete and defined expressions, like those of
basic expressions, are little more than surrogates for their referents; and it is for
this reason that I refer to the idea as a *de re* proposal.

Now, although this de re proposal does violate Kaplan's requirement that
logically and grammatically simple expressions should coincide, at least under its
most straightforward interpretation, there is also another way of reading the requirement according to which the proposal involves no violation at all.  Suppose
that, as before, we understand the logically simple expressions as those taking
basic procedures as their senses, but that we now interpret the "grammatically
simple" expressions to include both basic expressions and those constructed
through syntactic removal rules, the incomplete and defined expressions.  Then,
of course, the logically and grammatically simple expressions could again be
said to coincide, even under the de re proposal, since all expressions that take
basic procedures as their senses would now be classified as grammatically simple.  Furthermore, I believe the idea behind this interpretation—grouping the
complex incomplete and defined expressions together with the basic expressions
as simple—is not just a verbal gimmick, but that it actually provides a useful
perspective on the matter.

In many ways, both complex incomplete and defined expressions really are very much like basic expressions, syntactically as well as semantically, so that it makes good sense to catch this similarity by classifying them all together as *simple*. For reasons that seem to be largely visual, it is easier to appreciate the similarity between basic and defined expressions, such as '$F_9$', than between basic and incomplete expressions, such as '$\lambda x(3 > x)$' or even '$\lambda xy(x > y)$'. Certainly, in the models of definitional practice touched on earlier, which treat the introduction of a defined symbol as a shift to an entirely new language, the defined symbol is then classified as a basic expression in the new language. What this means is that, in the new language, the syntactic analysis of any sentence containing the defined symbol halts once it reaches that symbol, just as it halts once it reaches any other basic expression. The analysis is then viewed as a complete analysis of that sentence into its syntactic atoms; it need not continue to trace the definitional history of the defined symbol itself.

There is no reason to lose track of this connection between defined symbols and basic expressions just because we have now decided to adopt a more realistic model of definitional practice, according to which defined symbols are injected directly into the language. Even in this case, it is still natural to imagine that the purely syntactic analysis of a sentence should halt with its defined symbols, rather than continuing to explore their definitional history; and indeed, that seems to be the way defined symbols are treated in natural languages. Suppose, for example, that I introduce the name 'Schmidt' into a dialect of English by stipulating that this term is to refer to the person who first proved the incompleteness of arithmetic. Of course, there are many different theories available about the *semantic* relations between the term 'Schmidt' and the description through which it is introduced. But it is hard to dispute that, from a purely *syntactic* perspective, this defined term will behave much like a basic expression: the purely syntactic analysis of any sentence containing the term—such as 'Schmidt was intelligent'—will halt once it reaches 'Schmidt', a syntactic atom.

So it is plausible, at least, that defined symbols should be classified as grammatically simple, along with basic expressions; and if defined symbols are nothing but variant forms of complex incomplete expressions, as I have suggested, it then follows that these expressions can plausibly be regarded as grammatically simple as well. The result is a novel but not unattractive view about the extent of syntactic analysis. According to this view, although both complex incomplete and defined expressions may themselves have nontrivial syntactic structure, reflecting the removal rules through which they are constructed, or introduced into the language, the structure assigned to these expressions need not figure into the analyses of more complex expressions containing them, where they are to be regarded, instead, as grammatically simple.[1]

The de re proposal, which assigns basic procedures to complex incomplete and defined expressions as their senses, can therefore be reconciled with the requirement of logical perfection, under an interpretation of this requirement that is at least not too unnatural. The proposal has, furthermore, the striking advantage of providing a robust interpretation of Frege's notion of fruitfulness for stipulative definitions, and at the same time, explaining the role of complex incomplete expressions in concept formation; for it is a consequence of this proposal that the introduction of these new expressions, defined and incomplete, will allow for the expression of genuinely new thoughts—thoughts that simply could not have been expressed without them.

This point can be illustrated through an example. As we have seen, both the complex incomplete predicate '$\lambda x(3 > x)$' and the defined predicate '$F_9$', according to the de re proposal, would take the basic procedure less-than-3 as senses; and so it follows that both the sentences '$\lambda x(3 > x)\,2$' and '$F_9(2)$', for instance, would express the thought (less-than-3 2), as we can verify by tracing the evaluation of the first sentence:

$$
\begin{aligned}
\sigma['\lambda x(3 > x)\,2'] &= \sigma[P_{\langle e:t\rangle}('\lambda x(3 > x)',\,'2')] \\
&= \sigma[P_{\langle e:t\rangle}](\sigma['\lambda x(3 > x)'],\sigma['2']) \\
&= (\sigma['\lambda x(3 > x)']\ \sigma['2']) \\
&= (\text{less-than-3 2}).
\end{aligned}
$$

But it is easy to see that this thought simply could not have been expressed by any sentence belonging to our original language, before the addition of removal rules allowed us to introduce complex incomplete and defined predicates. Any sentence expressing this particular thought would have to be formed through an application of the predication rule $P_{\langle e:t\rangle}$ to a one-place predicate—that is,

---

[1]This view concerning the extent of syntactic analysis of sentences containing defined expressions, at least, is hinted at by Dummett, when he writes at one point that the "dependence of the sense of ... defined expression[s] on those occurring in the definiens is not in doubt: but, when we are concerned with the essential structure of a sentence or of a thought, the analysis ought to terminate with simple expressions and their senses, not, in general with primitive ones" (1981, p. 340). If we read Dummett's "simple" expressions here as equivalent to our simple expressions—that is, as including both basic and defined expressions—and his "primitive" expressions as including only our basic expressions, then the idea expressed in this passage is, again, that the analysis of a sentence containing a defined symbol ought to halt once it reaches that symbol, rather than continuing to explore the way in which the defined symbol was introduced.

an expression from the category $\langle e : t \rangle$—and a single term, but our original language did not even contain any one-place predicates.

The de re proposal has certain attractions, then, but it also carries significant costs. Since, according to this proposal, the senses assigned to complex incomplete and defined expressions are nothing but surrogates for their referents, it follows that any such expressions with the same referents must have the same senses as well. And from this we can conclude at once that these de re senses cannot perform all the functions envisioned by Frege. It takes only a moment of thought to see, for example, that the complex predicate '$\lambda x(\neg(\neg(x = 2) \land \neg(2 > x)))$' has the same referent as '$\lambda x(3 > x)$', but for most of us, verifying this equivalence actually does take a moment of thought. As we have discussed earlier, in Chapter 2, Frege's conception of sense included a strongly cognitive, or psychological, component, according to which two expressions are supposed to be assigned distinct senses whenever it takes any thought, or reasoning, at all to discover that their referents coincide—whenever the identity of their referents is not self-evident, so that this discovery has some cognitive value. By this psychological criterion, the predicates '$\lambda x(3 > x)$' and '$\lambda x(\neg(\neg(x = 2) \land \neg(2 > x)))$' should carry different senses. But since these predicates have the same referents, the de re proposal would have to assign them the same senses as well: both predicates would express the sense less-than-3, so that the two sentences '$\lambda x(3 > x)\,2$' and '$\lambda x(\neg(\neg(x = 2) \land \neg(2 > x)))\,2$', for example, would both express the thought (less-than-3 2).[2]

Of course, this gap between sense and psychological significance does not

---

[2] Another treatment of complex incomplete expressions that is similar in some ways to the de re proposal is that advanced by Cresswell (1985, pp. 99–101), whose approach is guided by what he calls a "macrostructure constraint" (p. 80), according to which the structured meaning associated with an expression is supposed to reflect only its syntactic macrostructure, not any of its more delicate structural features. On this view, it could be argued that the assignment of the sense (less-than-3 2) to the two sentences '$\lambda x(3 > x)\,2$' and '$\lambda x(\neg(\neg(x = 2) \land \neg(2 > x)))\,2$' correctly represents their shared macrostructure, while brushing over microstructural differences. It is interesting to note, however, especially in light of Cresswell's defense of the macrostructure constraint for sentences containing complex predicates, that he explicitly abandons this idea when it comes to defined expressions: "In technical discourse I believe that a great deal more structure is often involved. And often we must attribute a structure to the meaning of single words and not just complex expressions ... [I]n technical subjects ... we have lexical items introduced by explicit definition. Each of these items actually abbreviates a complex structure" (p. 81). I am not entirely sure how the abbreviated complex structures carried by defined lexical items are to be represented, but it is natural to suppose that Cresswell is suggesting something along the lines of our semantic Option B, according to which the sentence '$F_9(2)$', for instance, would then be assigned a structured meaning like (greater 2 3). This suggestion would have the odd consequence that the sentences '$F_9(2)$' and '$\lambda x(3 > x)\,2$'

necessarily indicate a fatal defect in the de re proposal. As we saw in Chapter 4, considerations internal to Frege's own treatment of definitions suggest that the psychological significance of a defined expression should be separated from its sense. Indeed, if modern work in the philosophy of language has shown us anything, it is that no one notion can play all the roles attributed by Frege to that of sense; and writers exploring Fregean themes have partitioned the various aspects of our intuitive notion of meaning in a number of different ways, often assigning the role of tracking psychological significance to something other than sense.[3] Nevertheless, since the connection between sense and psychological significance was such an important component of Frege's own conception, any proposal that not only separates, but entirely severs these two ideas, as the de re proposal does, would have to be evaluated very carefully.

## 8.2   Complex incomplete senses

At this point, in order to motivate the next suggestion, it will be useful to contrast the de re proposal with the previous Option B, considered in Chapter 7, which provides a contextual treatment of the semantics of complex incomplete and defined expressions.

The de re proposal has the advantage of showing how the introduction of complex incomplete or defined expressions might allow for the formulation of new thoughts: the sentence '$\lambda x(3 > x)\, 2$' expresses the thought (less-than-3 2), which is distinct from any thought expressible in the base language, as we have seen, and in particular from the thought (greater 3 2), expressed by the sentence '$3 > 2$'. Moreover, in assigning the sense (less-than-3 2) to both the sentences '$\lambda x(3 > x)\, 2$' and '$\lambda x(\neg(\neg(x = 2) \wedge \neg(2 > x)))\, 2$', the proposal reflects at a semantic level the important structural similarities between these two sentences: both are constructed through the one-place predication rule, applied to co-referential predicates and identical terms. But it is hard to accept the idea that

---

would not only differ in meaning, but also that the meaning of '$F_9(2)$', which seems, at least visually, to displays less structure than '$\lambda x(3 > x)\, 2$', would actually be more complex.

[3]Familiar examples of this partitioning, mentioned earlier, include Kaplan's (1989) separations between "character" and "content" and Perry's (1977) distinction between the "thought" expressed by a sentence and its "sense." Burge discusses the relation between Frege's senses and the conventional linguistic meanings in a series of papers including (1979) and (1984). In the structured meaning literature, Salmon (1986) tries to explain how sentences carrying the same structured meaning (which he refers to as their "information content") might have a different psychological impact on a speaker by suggesting that they present this meaning in different ways; and Soames (1987) suggests that the relation between speakers and structured meanings is mediated by, or at least associated with, relations between speakers and sentences.

these two very different sentences should be assigned, not just similar senses, but exactly the same sense.

According to the previous Option B, as we recall, the sentence '$\lambda x(3 > x)\,2$' is supposed to share the sense of '$3 > 2$', while '$\lambda x(\neg(\neg(x = 2) \wedge \neg(2 > x)))\,2$' would share the sense of '$(\neg(\neg(2 = 2) \wedge \neg(2 > 2)))$'; the two sentences containing complex predicates are thus assigned (greater 3 2) and (not (and (not (equal 2 2)) (not (greater 2 2)))) as their respective senses. In contrast to the de re proposal, then, Option B does manage to distinguish the thoughts expressed by these two sentences, but only at the cost of entirely obscuring their structural similarities. And of course, this treatment makes it impossible to explain how sentences containing complex incomplete or defined expressions could carry new thoughts; neither of these two sentences expresses a thought that is not already carried by a sentence from our original language, prior to the introduction of removal rules.

Ideally, we would like a way of combining the advantages of these two approaches—the de re proposal and the previous Option B—while avoiding their disadvantages, a goal that can be separated into three criteria of adequacy. A correct treatment must, first of all, respect Frege's idea that the introduction of complex incomplete or defined expressions might allow for the formulation of new thoughts; the thought expressed by the sentence '$\lambda x(3 > x)\,2$', for example, should differ from that expressed by '$3 > 2$'. Second, a correct treatment should reflect the common structural features of expressions like '$\lambda x(3 > x)\,2$' and '$\lambda x(\neg(\neg(x = 2) \wedge \neg(2 > x)))\,2$', providing a perspective from which the thoughts expressed by sentences like these can be grouped together as equivalent. But, third, the treatment should not simply take sentences like these to express identical thoughts, ignoring the semantically important features of their substructures.

In attempting to develop a treatment that satisfies these three criteria of adequacy, it is helpful to begin by considering a similar problem found in the analysis of computer programming languages. Suppose that two high-level programs are line-by-line identical, except that at a certain point each calls a different subprocedure for executing the same function—perhaps it is necessary to sort a list, and one program does this using the bubblesort algorithm while the other uses mergesort.[4] Do the two programs then implement the same procedure, or not? The matter is vexed in the literature on programming language

---

[4]It is not, of course, necessary to understand the difference between bubblesort and mergesort to follow the present argument—the point is simply that there are different algorithms for sorting a list, with different properties—but for those readers who care, an introductory

semantics, and to a certain extent the answer seems to depend on the context of
the question. Because they call different subprocedures, the two programs will
be compiled into different sequences of machine language instructions, and since
the mergesort algorithm is more efficient than bubblesort, one of the programs
will run faster than the other. In any context in which things like speed or
precise patterns of register usage are a concern, then, it will make sense to distinguish the procedures implemented by these programs. But it is also possible
to adopt a perspective from which list sorting is taken as a basic operation, so
that the exact way in which this function is implemented lies below the chosen
level of analysis; and from this perspective, it would be natural to say that the
two programs do implement exactly the same procedure.

Because we are working with a model in which senses are interpreted as procedures, we can now draw on this analogy with programming language semantics
to enhance our basic model in such a way that it allows for these multiple perspectives. The general idea is simple. The sense of the expression '$\lambda x(3 > x)\, 2$'
will be interpreted explicitly as a procedure that applies a certain subprocedure,
corresponding to the sense of '$\lambda x(3 > x)$', to the number 2. In this way, it differs
from the sense of '$3 > 2$', which involves no call to a subprocedure and simply
applies the sense of '$>$' to 3 and 2. There is, likewise, a perspective from which
the senses of expressions like '$\lambda x(3 > x)\, 2$' and '$\lambda x(\neg(\neg(x = 2) \land \neg(2 > x)))\, 2$'
can be classified together as equivalent, since they both apply subprocedures
computing the same function—the function that maps 0, 1, and 2 into Truth,
and every other number into Falsity—to the same object. But in contrast to
the de re proposal, the two senses will also be distinguishable, on the grounds
that they implement the subprocedure in different ways.

The remainder of the section develops this general idea into a concrete proposal, and evaluates it against our three criteria of adequacy. What is important
here is not so much the particular details of this development, which could easily be carried out differently, but simply the demonstration that the procedural
model provides a framework within which the idea can, in fact, be developed in
detail.

### 8.2.1   Developing the proposal

We begin by introducing a class of *sense variables* ($\mathsf{x}, \mathsf{y}, \mathsf{x}_1, \mathsf{y}_1, \ldots$), whose precise role will become clear shortly, but which can be thought of to begin with

treatment can be found in Harel (1987), which also includes a discussion of levels of detail in
the analysis of algorithms.

as providing the senses of ordinary linguistic variables; the $\sigma$ function is then extended so that $\sigma['x'] = x$, $\sigma['y'] = y$, $\sigma['x_1'] = x_1$, and so on. This assignment of senses to variables now allows us, using our standard principles of compositionality for senses, to assign senses to open as well as closed expressions, as we can illustrate by calculating the sense assigned to the open expression '$3 > x$', for example:

$$
\begin{aligned}
\sigma['3 > x'] &= \sigma[P_{\langle e,e:t\rangle}('>', '3', 'x')] \\
&= \sigma[P_{\langle e,e:t\rangle}](\sigma['>'], \sigma['3'], \sigma['x']) \\
&= (\sigma['>'] \, \sigma['3'] \, \sigma['x']) \\
&= (\text{greater } 3 \text{ x}).
\end{aligned}
$$

This calculation follows our standard pattern, except that the sense variable x is assigned to the linguistic variable '$x$'. Just as open expressions are syntactic entities like expressions except that they may contain variables, we can now define *open senses* as tuples, such as (greater 3 x), that are like senses except that they may contain sense variables.

The next step is to extend our principle of sense compositionality, so far defined only for expressions generated by predication rules, so as to apply also to the complex incomplete and defined expressions generated by syntactic removal rules and their variants. In the case of ordinary removal rules, the appropriate principle of compositionality will be defined by stipulating that

$$
\sigma[R_{\langle\alpha_1,...,\alpha_n:\beta\rangle}('[\kappa_1, \ldots, \kappa_n/\xi_1,\ldots,\xi_n]\psi')] = \sigma[R_{\langle\alpha_1,...,\alpha_n:\beta\rangle}](\sigma[\xi_1],\ldots,\sigma[\xi_n], \sigma[\psi]),
$$

with the definitional variants of these rules handled in a similar way.[5] The point of this principle is to take seriously at the semantic level the syntactic idea that complex incomplete expressions—and so defined symbols as well—really do have some complexity. What the principle tells us is that the sense of a complex incomplete expression formed through an application of the rule $R_{\langle\alpha_1,...,\alpha_n:\beta\rangle}$ to the canonical description '$[\kappa_1, \ldots, \kappa_n/\xi_1, \ldots, \xi_n]\psi$' depends on the sense of the open expression $\psi$, as well as the senses of the variables $\xi_1, \ldots, \xi_n$, in a way determined by the function $\sigma[R_{\langle\alpha_1,...,\alpha_n:\beta\rangle}]$. It remains, therefore, only to define the function $\sigma[R_{\langle\alpha_1,...,\alpha_n:\beta\rangle}]$ itself, the particular mode of procedural

---

[5]For simplicity, we concentrate throughout the remainder of this chapter on complex incomplete rather than defined expressions—taking as our examples the complex predicate '$\lambda x(3 > x)$' and the sentence '$\lambda x(3 > x)\, 2$', rather than the defined predicate '$F_9$' and the sentence '$F_9(2)$'. But the account of complex incomplete senses developed here is supposed to apply equally to both kinds of expressions.

composition associated with syntactic removal rules; this is done through the stipulation that

$$\sigma[R_{\langle\alpha_1,\ldots,\alpha_n:\beta\rangle}](\mathcal{Z}_1,\ldots,\mathcal{Z}_n,\mathcal{Q}) \;=\; (\text{lambda } (\mathcal{Z}_1,\ldots,\mathcal{Z}_n)\,\mathcal{Q})$$

whenever $\mathcal{Z}_1,\ldots,\mathcal{Z}_n$ are sense variables and $\mathcal{Q}$ is an open sense.

The tuples assigned to complex incomplete and defined expressions by these principles can be referred to as *complex incomplete senses*. We illustrate by calculating the complex incomplete sense assigned to our sample predicate '$\lambda x(3 > x)$'—formed, we recall, through an application of the syntactic rule $R_{\langle e:t\rangle}$ to the canonical sentence description '['1'/'$x$']('3 > x')'—as follows:

$$\begin{aligned}
\sigma['\lambda x(3 > x)'] \;&=\; \sigma[R_{\langle e:t\rangle}(' \,['1'/'x']('3 > x')\,')] \\
&=\; \sigma[R_{\langle e:t\rangle}](\sigma['x'], \sigma['3 > x']) \\
&=\; (\text{lambda } (\sigma['x'])\,\sigma['3 > x']) \\
&=\; (\text{lambda } (x)\,(\text{greater } 3\ x)).
\end{aligned}$$

Again, the first of these equations simply reflects the syntactic analysis of the predicate; the second follows by our new principle of compositionality for predicates formed through removal rules; the third, from an application of the new mode of procedural composition associated with removal rules; and the fourth from our identification of the senses of '$x$' and '3 > x' as $x$ and (greater 3 x).

Once these new complex incomplete senses have been associated with complex incomplete and defined expressions, this assignment can then, of course, be appealed to in conjunction with our ordinary principles of compositionality and procedural composition, as we can see by calculating the sense of the sentence '$\lambda x(3 > x)\,2$', for example:

$$\begin{aligned}
\sigma['\lambda x(3 > x)\,2'] \;&=\; \sigma[P_{\langle e:t\rangle}('\lambda x(3 > x)', \text{'2'})] \\
&=\; \sigma[P_{\langle e:t\rangle}](\sigma['\lambda x(3 > x)'], \sigma['2']) \\
&=\; (\sigma['\lambda x(3 > x)']\,\sigma['2']) \\
&=\; ((\text{lambda } (x)\,(\text{greater } 3\ x))\ 2).
\end{aligned}$$

Here, the last line is justified by the identification of 2 as the sense of '2', but also by the identification, just established, of the complex incomplete sense ((lambda (x) (greater 3 x))) as the sense of '$\lambda x(3 > x)$'.

As suggested earlier, complex incomplete senses are to be interpreted, from an intuitive standpoint, as procedures that compute functions. Unlike basic procedures, however, complex procedures like these are to be individuated, not simply by the functions they compute, but by the particular ways in which they compute these functions, the particular arrays of basic procedures they employ to determine outputs from inputs. The complex incomplete sense (lambda (x) (greater 3 x)), for example, should be thought of as computing a function by returning Truth as an output just in case it can be determined that the number 3 is greater than the input. But a different complex incomplete sense, such as (lambda (x) (not (and (not (equal x 2)) (not (greater 2 x))))), will compute the same function in a different way: by returning Truth as an output just in case it can be determined that it is not the case that the number 2 is both not equal to the input and not greater than the input.

In order to give literal meaning to these intuitive ideas within the model developed here, allowing us to speak rigorously about the particular *way* in which a complex incomplete sense computes a function, it is necessary to show, as before, how these complex senses can be interpreted as sequences of basic procedure executions. This task, to which we now turn, is carried out in two stages. We begin by generalizing our background framework for describing procedure executions; working within this more general framework, we then present a richer set of expansion rules for implementing complex executions in terms of basic executions.

**Generalizations**

Our framework for describing procedure executions is generalized in three ways.

Previously, we had imagined an infinite set of registers, each of the form $\Gamma_i$ with $i$ a sequence, to act as pick-up and drop-off points for procedure inputs and outputs; these registers were thought of as arranged in a tree, with $\Gamma_1$ at the top, then $\Gamma_{i*1}, \Gamma_{i*2}, \Gamma_{i*3}, \ldots$ lying immediately below $\Gamma_i$, and with $\Gamma_{i*(n+1)}$ lying immediately to the right of $\Gamma_{i*n}$. As our first generalization, we move to a set of registers of the form $\Gamma_i^m$, with $i$ a sequence and $m$ a positive integer. It is helpful to picture these registers as arranged, now, in a sequence of trees, running from left to right; to guide visualization, portions of the first two trees in this sequence are depicted in Figure 8.1.

The leftmost tree in the entire sequence—which can be identified with our original register tree—consists of those registers of the form $\Gamma_i^1$. Again, $\Gamma_1^1$ lies at the very top of this tree, with $\Gamma_{i*1}^1, \Gamma_{i*2}^1, \Gamma_{i*3}^1, \ldots$ lying immediately below $\Gamma_i^1$, and with $\Gamma_{i*(n+1)}^1$ lying immediately to the right of $\Gamma_{i*n}^1$. But we should now imagine that each tree headed by a register of the form $\Gamma_1^m$ is followed in the sequence of trees by another headed by a register of the form $\Gamma_1^{m+1}$, so that the register tree headed by $\Gamma_1^1$ is followed by another headed by $\Gamma_1^2$, which is

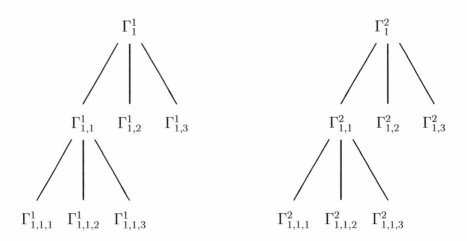

Figure 8.1: Parts of some register trees.

itself followed by another headed by $\Gamma_1^3$, and so on. Each of these new trees will be isomorphic to the original, with registers of the form $\Gamma_{i*1}^m, \Gamma_{i*2}^m, \Gamma_{i*3}^m, \dots$ immediately below any register of the form $\Gamma_i^m$, and with any register of the form $\Gamma_{i*(n+1)}^m$ immediately to the right of one having the form $\Gamma_{i*n}^m$. Because of this isomorphism, we can define a notion of correspondence between any register from any tree and one particular register from any other tree: each register of the form $\Gamma_i^m$ from the $m$-th tree can be said to correspond to the register of the form $\Gamma_i^n$ from the $n$-th tree.

The reason for this sequence of trees has to do, of course, with the interpretation of complex incomplete senses. Suppose that such a sense is assigned to the register $\Gamma_i^m$. Then, as we will see shortly, this sense is actually executed as a subprocedure in the corresponding register $\Gamma_i^{m+1}$ belonging to the next tree in the sequence, with the result reported back to $\Gamma_i^m$. Since complex procedures can be nested within one another to an arbitrary depth, with subprocedures calling subprocedures, the sequence of trees must be infinitely long.

As our second generalization of the background framework, we address the matter of binding the sense variables in open senses. Where $\mathcal{Z}$ is a sense variable and $\Gamma_i^m$ a register, we begin by defining an *assignment* as a pair of the form $\mathcal{Z}/\Gamma_i^m$; the intuitive idea is that $\mathcal{Z}/\Gamma_i^m$ assigns to $\mathcal{Z}$ whatever value is contained in the register $\Gamma_i^m$. A *binding* $B$ is then defined simply as a set of assignments, simultaneously assigning values from various registers to a number of sense variables. The binding $\{x/\Gamma^1_{1,1}, y/\Gamma^2_{1,1,3}\}$, for example, assigns to x whatever value is contained in the register $\Gamma^1_{1,1}$ and to y whatever value is contained in $\Gamma^2_{1,1,3}$.[6]

Where $\mathcal{P}$ is a sense and $B$ is a binding, we can refer to $(\mathcal{P})_B$ as a *bound sense*, in which certain sense variables in $\mathcal{P}$ may be assigned the values specified by $B$. Again, the precise way in which this works will be spelled out shortly, but as an example, the item (greater x y)$_{\{x/\Gamma^1_{1,1}, y/\Gamma^2_{1,1,3}\}}$ is a bound sense, which assigns the specified values to x and y, and is therefore to be interpreted as applying the basic procedure greater to those values. The empty set $\emptyset$, containing no assignments at all, is included among the bindings, and the bound sense $(\mathcal{P})_\emptyset$ is identified with $\mathcal{P}$.

As our third and final generalization of the framework, we introduce one further basic procedure, copy, which computes the identity function, mapping any object into itself. This new procedure is not used to interpret any particular expression of the language, but merely performs a bookkeeping function, allowing items to be copied from one register to another; the basic procedure execution

$$[\text{copy } \langle \Gamma^m_i \rangle \ \Gamma^n_j],$$

for example, has the effect of copying whatever value is contained in $\Gamma^m_i$ into the register $\Gamma^n_j$.

## Expansion rules

Before considering our new expansion rules in detail, it may be helpful to sketch the execution of a sample procedure. Let us begin, therefore, by considering the complex sense ((lambda (x) (greater 3 x)) 2), executed at the register $\Gamma^1_1$.

As before, arguments are always executed first, so that the initial step is the execution of the basic procedure 2, with its output deposited in $\Gamma^1_{1,1}$. The next step is the execution of the complex procedure (lambda (x) (greater 3 x)), with the content of $\Gamma^1_{1,1}$ taken as input and its own output deposited in $\Gamma^1_1$. Since this procedure is complex, however, its execution at $\Gamma^1_1$ will be implemented through the execution of a subprocedure—in particular, the bound procedure (greater 3 x)$_{\{x/\Gamma^1_{1,1}\}}$—at the corresponding register $\Gamma^2_1$. The execution of this subprocedure requires, again, first executing 3 with its output deposited in $\Gamma^2_{1,1}$,

---

[6]Our official definition thus allows for bindings in which multiple values are assigned to the same variable, but we need not concern ourselves either with interpreting these bindings or with complicating the definition to rule them out, since our rule for introducing bindings— the Expansion Rule 3, below—guarantees that bindings of this kind will never actually be introduced.

and then executing the sense variable x at $\Gamma^2_{1,2}$ under the binding $\{x/\Gamma^1_{1,1}\}$, which will have the effect, according to our rules, of simply copying the contents of $\Gamma^1_{1,1}$ into $\Gamma^2_{1,2}$. The basic procedure **greater** will then be executed at $\Gamma^2_1$, taking the contents of $\Gamma^2_{1,1}$ and $\Gamma^2_{1,2}$ as inputs. And finally, the content of $\Gamma^2_1$—that is, the result of the subprocedure execution—will be copied back to $\Gamma^1_1$, the register from which the subprocedure was called.

We turn now to the expansion rules through which this kind of behavior is achieved. In our earlier setting, where all complex senses were complete, we were able to expand complex procedure executions into sequences of basic executions through successive applications of a single rule, our Expansion Rule 0, defining the notion of an immediate expansion for procedure executions containing complex complete senses. Since the current setting is richer, allowing both complete and incomplete complex senses, as well as bindings, a number of different expansion rules will be required. Let us say, in this new setting, that a procedure execution of the form

$$[(\mathcal{P})_B \ \langle \Gamma_{i_1}, \ldots, \Gamma_{i_n} \rangle \ \Gamma_j]$$

is *complex* if $\mathcal{P}$ is a complex sense, either complete or incomplete, or else $B$ is a nonempty binding; the execution is *basic*, then, if $\mathcal{P}$ is a basic procedure and the binding $B$ is empty. What we need to show is how complex procedure executions, exhibiting any of these various forms of complexity, can be expanded into sequences of basic executions.

The particular expansion rules provided here correspond to a fourfold classification of the senses that might be contained in a complex procedure execution. If the sense $\mathcal{P}$ contained in the procedure execution is itself complex, then either (1) it is a complex complete sense of the form $(\mathcal{P}' \ \mathcal{Q}_1 \ \ldots \ \mathcal{Q}_n)$, or (2) it is a complex incomplete sense of the form (lambda $(\mathcal{Z}_1 \ \ldots \ \mathcal{Z}_n) \ \mathcal{Q}$); if the sense $\mathcal{P}$ is basic, then either (3) it is an ordinary basic procedure, or (4) it is a sense variable. The notion of an *immediate expansion* is now defined through four separate rules, covering each of these cases. These four rules are listed below, with the statement of each rule followed by a brief explanation.

- *Expansion Rule 1:* If $\mathcal{P}$ is a complex complete sense of the form $(\mathcal{P}' \ \mathcal{Q}_1 \ \ldots \ \mathcal{Q}_n)$ and $B$ is a binding, then the execution

$$[(\mathcal{P})_B \ \langle \rangle \ \Gamma^m_i]$$

has as its immediate expansion the sequence

$$\langle \quad [(\mathcal{Q}_1)_B \ \langle\rangle \ \Gamma^m_{i*1}],$$

.

.

.

$$[(\mathcal{Q}_n)_B \ \langle\rangle \ \Gamma^m_{i*n}],$$
$$[(\mathcal{P}')_B \ \langle\Gamma^m_{i*1}, \ldots, \Gamma^m_{i*n}\rangle \ \Gamma^m_i] \ \rangle.$$

Explanation: This first rule is the analogue of our original Expansion Rule 0, which it subsumes; the only difference is that, now, the binding $B$ is passed along from a complex complete sense to the constituent senses through which it is implemented.

- *Expansion Rule 2:* If $\mathcal{P}$ is a complex incomplete sense of the form (lambda $(\mathcal{Z}_1 \ldots \mathcal{Z}_n)$ $\mathcal{Q}$) and $B$ is a binding, then the execution

$$[(\mathcal{P})_B \ \langle\Gamma^m_{i*1}, \ldots, \Gamma^m_{i*n}\rangle \ \Gamma^m_i]$$

has as its immediate expansion the sequence

$$\langle \quad [(\mathcal{Q})_{B^*} \ \langle\rangle \ \Gamma^{m+1}_i],$$
$$[\text{copy} \ \langle\Gamma^{m+1}_i\rangle \ \Gamma^m_i] \ \rangle,$$

where $B^*$ is formed from $B$ as follows: first let $B'$ be the result of removing any assignments involving the variables $\mathcal{Z}_1, \ldots, \mathcal{Z}_n$ from $B$; then let $B^*$ be the result of adding the assignments $\mathcal{Z}_1/\Gamma^m_{i*1}, \ldots, \mathcal{Z}_n/\Gamma^m_{i*n}$ to $B'$.

Explanation: This rule captures the idea that the execution of a complex incomplete sense at any given register is implemented as the execution of a subprocedure at the corresponding register on the next tree in the sequence, with the result then reported back. The first line of the expansion sequence tells us that the execution of (lambda $(\mathcal{Z}_1 \ldots \mathcal{Z}_n)$ $\mathcal{Q}$) at the register $\Gamma^m_i$, with the values contained in $\Gamma^m_{i*1}, \ldots, \Gamma^m_{i*n}$ as inputs, is implemented as the execution of $\mathcal{Q}$ at the register $\Gamma^{m+1}_i$, with the binding shifted so that the values from $\Gamma^m_{i*1}, \ldots, \Gamma^m_{i*n}$ are now assigned to the variables $\mathcal{Z}_1, \ldots, \mathcal{Z}_n$.[7] The second line tells us, once this execution is complete, that the result is then copied back to $\Gamma^m_i$.

---

[7]Note that this shift takes place in two stages: first, in the move from $B$ to $B'$ any previous assignments to these variables are removed; the new assignments are then added in the shift from $B'$ to $B^*$. As a result of this two-stage process, we can be sure that no binding generated by these expansion rules assigns more than one value to the same variable.

- *Expansion Rule 3:* If $\mathcal{P}$ is a basic procedure that is not a sense variable and $B$ is a binding, then the execution

$$[(\mathcal{P})_B \ \langle\rangle \ \Gamma_i^m]$$

has as its immediate expansion the sequence

$$\langle \, [\mathcal{P} \ \langle\rangle \ \Gamma_i^m] \, \rangle.$$

Explanation: The point of this rule is simply that variable bindings have no effect on the execution of basic procedures that are not themselves sense variables.

- *Expansion Rule 4:* If $\mathcal{P}$ is the sense variable $\mathcal{Z}$ and $B$ is a binding containing the assignment $\mathcal{Z}/\Gamma_j^n$, then the execution

$$[(\mathcal{P})_B \ \langle\rangle \ \Gamma_i^m]$$

has as its immediate expansion the sequence

$$\langle \, [\text{copy} \ \langle\Gamma_j^n\rangle \ \Gamma_i^m] \, \rangle.$$

Explanation: This final rule tells us that the execution of a sense variable at the register $\Gamma_i^m$, within the scope of a binding that assigns the value from the register $\Gamma_j^n$ to this variable, is implemented by a basic execution that copies the value from $\Gamma_j^n$ to $\Gamma_i^m$.

Once the notion of an immediate expansion has been defined through these four new expansion rules, rather than the previous Expansion Rule 0, the definition of a *full expansion* of a sequence of executions can be carried over unchanged from our previous discussion, in Chapter 5. Where $\mathcal{P}$ is a complete sense, therefore, we can now define the *execution sequence associated with* $\mathcal{P}$ as the full expansion of the execution sequence $\langle[(\mathcal{P})_\emptyset \ \langle\rangle \ \Gamma_1^1]\rangle$; the notion remains well-defined, since it can again be verified that each such execution sequence leads to a unique full expansion. Since $(\mathcal{P})_\emptyset$ is identified with $\mathcal{P}$ and $\Gamma_1^1$ is identified with $\Gamma_1$, this definition again generalizes our earlier treatment. And as before, the association between senses and execution sequences justifies us in interpreting the sense of an expression as a procedure for determining its referent, a procedure through which the expression's referent is placed in the register $\Gamma_1^1$.

## 8.2.2 Examples and equivalencies

We begin with the tuple ((lambda (x) (greater 3 x)) 2), which serves as the sense of '$\lambda x (3 > x) \, 2$'. Using our expansion rules, we can now calculate the execution sequence associated with this sense, which is defined as the full expansion of the sequence

$$\langle \; [((((\text{lambda } (x) \, (\text{greater } 3 \, x)) \, 2))_\emptyset \; \langle\rangle \; \Gamma^1_1] \; \rangle.$$

By an application of Rule 1, this initial sequence expands to

$$\langle \; [(2)_\emptyset \; \langle\rangle \; \Gamma^1_{1,1}],$$
$$[(((\text{lambda } (x) \, (\text{greater } 3 \, x)))_\emptyset \; \langle \Gamma^1_{1,1} \rangle \; \Gamma^1_1] \; \rangle,$$

which itself expands to

$$(*) \qquad \begin{aligned} \langle \; & [(2)_\emptyset \; \langle\rangle \; \Gamma^1_{1,1}], \\ & [((\text{greater } 3 \, x))_{\{x/\Gamma^1_{1,1}\}} \; \langle\rangle \; \Gamma^2_1], \\ & [\text{copy } \langle \Gamma^2_1 \rangle \; \Gamma^1_1] \; \rangle \end{aligned}$$

by an application of Rule 2. The idea, once again, is that the execution of (lambda (x) (greater 3 x)) at $\Gamma^1_1$, with the content of $\Gamma^1_{1,1}$ as an input, is implemented by first executing the bound sense (greater 3 x)$_{\{x/\Gamma^1_{1,1}\}}$ as a subprocedure at $\Gamma^2_1$, and then copying the result from $\Gamma^2_1$ back into $\Gamma^1_1$.

The remaining expansions simply show how (greater 3 x)$_{\{x/\Gamma^1_{1,1}\}}$ is implemented as a subprocedure at $\Gamma^2_1$. A further application of Rule 1 to the second line of $(*)$ leads to

$$\begin{aligned} \langle \; & [(2)_\emptyset \; \langle\rangle \; \Gamma^1_{1,1}], \\ & [(3)_{\{x/\Gamma^1_{1,1}\}} \; \langle\rangle \; \Gamma^2_{1,1}], \\ & [(x)_{\{x/\Gamma^1_{1,1}\}} \; \langle\rangle \; \Gamma^2_{1,2}], \\ & [(\text{greater})_{\{x/\Gamma^1_{1,1}\}} \; \langle \Gamma^2_{1,1}, \Gamma^2_{1,2} \rangle \; \Gamma^2_1], \\ & [\text{copy } \langle \Gamma^2_1 \rangle \; \Gamma^1_1] \; \rangle. \end{aligned}$$

Several applications of Rule 3 then allow us to eliminate the bindings from the first, second, and fourth lines of this sequence, resulting in

$$\begin{aligned} \langle \; & [2 \; \langle\rangle \; \Gamma^1_{1,1}], \\ & [3 \; \langle\rangle \; \Gamma^2_{1,1}], \\ & [(x)_{\{x/\Gamma^1_{1,1}\}} \; \langle\rangle \; \Gamma^2_{1,2}], \\ & [\text{greater } \langle \Gamma^2_{1,1}, \Gamma^2_{1,2} \rangle \; \Gamma^2_1], \\ & [\text{copy } \langle \Gamma^2_1 \rangle \; \Gamma^1_1] \; \rangle. \end{aligned}$$

And finally, an application of Rule 4 to the variable in the third line yields

$$\langle \quad [2 \ \langle\rangle \ \Gamma_{1,1}^1],$$
$$[3 \ \langle\rangle \ \Gamma_{1,1}^2],$$
$$[\text{copy} \ \langle\Gamma_{1,1}^1\rangle \ \Gamma_{1,2}^2]$$
$$[\text{greater} \ \langle\Gamma_{1,1}^2, \Gamma_{1,2}^2\rangle \ \Gamma_1^2],$$
$$[\text{copy} \ \langle\Gamma_1^2\rangle \ \Gamma_1^1] \quad \rangle$$

as a full expansion of the initial sequence, and so as the execution sequence associated with the tuple ((lambda (x) (greater 3 x)) 2), which is assigned to the sentence '$\lambda x(3 > x)\,2$' as its sense. It should be clear that this sequence provides a more precise description of the procedure sketched earlier.

By comparison, let us now consider the tuple (greater 3 2), which is assigned to the sentence '$3 > 2$' as its sense, and which is associated with the execution sequence

$$\langle \quad [3 \ \langle\rangle \ \Gamma_{1,1}^1],$$
$$[2 \ \langle\rangle \ \Gamma_{1,2}^1],$$
$$[\text{greater} \ \langle\Gamma_{1,1}^1, \Gamma_{1,2}^1\rangle \ \Gamma_1^1] \quad \rangle.$$

This execution sequence is evidently distinct from the previous execution sequence associated with the tuple ((lambda (x) (greater 3 x)) 2). For one thing, the two sequences differ in length: the previous sequence contained five basic procedure executions, while this one contains only three. Both contain executions of 2 and 3, but in the previous sequence, 2 is executed first and 3 second, while in this one, the order is reversed. Again, the previous sequence executes greater in the course of a call to a subprocedure, at the register $\Gamma_1^2$, belonging to the second procedure tree, while in this one, there is no call to any subprocedure and greater is executed at $\Gamma_1^1$. Our interpretation of senses as execution sequences thus reinforces the idea that the introduction of complex incomplete expressions—and of course, defined expressions as well—allows for the formation of sentences that carry new thoughts: the two sentences '$\lambda x(3 > x)\,2$' and '$3 > 2$' are assigned different senses, which are themselves associated with different execution sequences.

Finally, we can consider the sentence '$\lambda x(\neg(\neg(\neg(x = 2) \wedge \neg(2 > x)))\,2$', whose sense is associated with the execution sequence resulting from the full expansion of

$$\langle \quad [(((\text{lambda (x) (not (and (not (equal x 2)) (not (greater 2 x))))) 2)})_\emptyset \ \langle\rangle \ \Gamma_1^1] \quad \rangle.$$

Two expansion steps, based on applications Rules 1 and 2, lead us from this initial sequence to the sequence

$$\langle \quad [(2)_{\emptyset} \ \langle\rangle \ \Gamma^1_{1,1}],$$

(**)         $[(((\text{not (and (not (equal x 2)) (not (greater 2 x))))))_{\{x/\Gamma^1_{1,1}\}} \ \langle\rangle \ \Gamma^2_1],$

$$[\text{copy} \ \langle\Gamma^2_1\rangle \ \Gamma^1_1] \ \rangle.$$

Already, then, even without completing the expansion, we can see the similarity between this sequence and the earlier (*), generated at the same stage by expanding the sense associated with '$\lambda x (3 > x) \, 2$'. Both sequences begin by executing 2 at the register $\Gamma^1_{1,1}$. Both then continue at $\Gamma^2_1$ by executing subprocedures that compute the same function—the function that maps only 0, 1, and 2 into Truth. And both conclude by copying the result from $\Gamma^2_1$ back to $\Gamma^1_1$. Since these two sequences compute the function at $\Gamma^2_1$ in different ways, through different subprocedures, they will lead to distinct full expansions. But if we adopt a perspective from which this function is regarded as basic, so that we are simply not concerned with the particular way in which it is implemented, then these distinct expansion sequences can reasonably be grouped together as equivalent.

This concept can be captured through the definition of an equivalence relation intended to represent the idea that two sequences are identical at the "top level" of execution—those procedure executions carried out in the first register tree—and that, although any subprocedures they call must compute the same functions, these subprocedures may be implemented in different ways. More precisely, let us stipulate that one execution sequence is $\Gamma^1$-*equivalent* to another sequence of the same length just in case, for any two procedure executions occupying the same position in each sequence, either (1) these executions both occur in the first register tree and they are identical, or (2) these executions both occur in the $m$-th register tree, for some $m$ greater than 1, and they are executions of procedures that (a) compute the same function and (b) have the same binding. Thus, for example, the execution sequence (*) is $\Gamma^1$-equivalent to (**), because the first and third executions belonging to each of these sequences satisfy clause (1), while the second executions from each sequence satisfy clause (2).

It is easy to verify that the concept of $\Gamma^1$-equivalence really is an equivalence relation: reflexive, symmetric, and transitive. The concept, furthermore, can be lifted in a natural way from execution sequence to sense tuples, and also generalized to capture deeper notions of equivalence, though still short of identity, among execution sequences, and so among sense tuples. We can say, first of all, that the sense $\mathcal{P}$ is $\Gamma^1$-*equivalent* to the sense $\mathcal{P}'$ whenever $\langle[(\mathcal{P})_{\emptyset} \ \langle\rangle \ \Gamma^1_1]\rangle$ and $\langle[(\mathcal{P}')_{\emptyset} \ \langle\rangle \ \Gamma^1_1]\rangle$ can themselves be expanded into $\Gamma^1$-equivalent execution sequences—from which it now follows, for example, that the two sense tuples

((lambda (x) (greater 3 x)) 2)

((lambda (x) (not (and (not (equal x 2)) (not (greater 2 x)))))) 2)

are $\Gamma^1$-equivalent. And second, for $m$ greater than 1, we can define one execution
sequence as $\Gamma^m$-*equivalent* to another of the same length just in case, for any
two procedure executions occupying the same position in each sequence, either
(1) these executions both occur in the $i$-th register tree, for some $i$ less than or
equal to $m$, and they are executions of the same basic procedure, or (2) these
executions both occur in the $j$-th register tree, for some $j$ greater than $m$, and
they are executions of procedures that (a) compute the same function and (b)
have the same binding. It is easy to see that $\Gamma^m$-equivalence is likewise an
equivalence relation, and that, for $n$ less than $m$, two execution sequences that
are $\Gamma^m$-equivalent must be $\Gamma^n$-equivalent as well.

### 8.2.3   Evaluating the proposal

The strategy of interpreting complex incomplete and defined expressions through
complex incomplete senses carries a number of advantages, as we can see by
evaluating it against the three criteria of adequacy formulated earlier.

We wanted, first of all, to respect Frege's idea that the introduction of complex incomplete or defined expressions should allow for the formation of sentences expressing thoughts that could not otherwise have been expressed. Like
the de re proposal, the current strategy satisfies this requirement: the thought
expressed by the sentence '$\lambda x(3 > x)\,2$', for example, is indeed new, differing
from that expressed by the previously available sentence '$3 > 2$'. Second, we
wanted to recognize at the semantic level the structural similarities between
sentences such as '$\lambda x(3 > x)\,2$' and '$\lambda x(\neg(\neg(x = 2) \land \neg(2 > x)))\,2$', formed by
the application of identical syntactic rules to co-referential expressions. Like
the de re proposal, again, the current strategy allows us to satisfy this requirement as well: the thoughts expressed by these two sentences can be classified
together as $\Gamma^1$-equivalent. But, third, we did not want to take sentences like
these as expressing exactly the same thought, entirely ignoring the semantically
significant features of their substructures. And unlike the de re proposal, the
current strategy also allows us to meet this requirement: although the thoughts
expressed by these two sentences are classified together as $\Gamma^1$-equivalent, they
are not even $\Gamma^2$-equivalent, let alone identical.

And what about logical perfection? As we have seen, the de re proposal runs
afoul of this ideal—at least under the most straightforward interpretation—by

assigning basic procedures as senses to expressions that are, in fact, grammatically complex. But the appeal to complex incomplete senses now allows us to specify the semantics for a language containing complex incomplete or defined expressions in a way that meets the standards of logical perfection: all and only basic expressions are assigned basic procedures as their senses, and compositionality is uniformly adhered to. And it helps us also, I think, in understanding Frege's own project of constructing an ideal language, designed to provide an accurate representation of the structure of thoughts.

The de re proposal does indeed violate the ideal of logical perfection, but it does so in a particular way, by assigning basic procedures as senses to complex expressions, with the result that thoughts might actually end up exhibiting less structure than the sentences that express them. This possibility is not one that ever troubled Frege. Instead, he was worried about the opposite possibility, that natural languages might conceal structure that is actually present in thoughts, by containing simple lexical items—for example, 'number'—that carry complex senses. Now that we have introduced complex incomplete senses, we can understand Frege's concern by imagining a language in which logical perfection is violated in this way, by the assignment of these complex incomplete senses to apparently primitive predicates and function symbols, with the result that the thoughts carried by sentences might be considerably more complex than the sentences themselves. This is the situation Frege believed he confronted, and that he hoped to escape from by the design of an ideal language, one whose sentences represent the real structure of thoughts.

# Chapter 9

# Afterword

The goal of this book has been to explore the difficulties presented for Frege's semantic theory by the mundane capacity—found in natural languages as well as many formal languages, and certainly those that Frege considered—of allowing for the introduction of new expressions through stipulative definition.

In the first four chapters of the book, I concentrated on the psychological constraints governing Frege's notion of sense and argued that, given these constraints, the introduction of defined expressions alone, apart from any considerations of context or contingency, already forces a break between the sense and the psychological significance of an expression. In the next four chapters, after introducing a simple model of senses as procedures, I focused on Frege's requirement that the sense of an expression should mirror its grammatical structure. The requirement can be satisfied, I argued, only if defined expressions—and complex incomplete expressions as well—are assigned senses of their own, rather than treated contextually, and I explored one way in which these senses might be reified within the procedural model.

In this final chapter, I simply want to mention a few of the remaining open issues and suggest some directions in which the work presented here might be developed. I concentrate on two such issues. First, the procedural model of senses presented in the second part of the book may have some independent interest; but it is developed here only for a very restricted language, and as I said earlier, it would have to be applied much more broadly in order to justify any claim to plausibility. And second, it is important to understand the tension between the treatments of defined expressions offered in the two parts of this book.

## 9.1 Developing the procedural model

To begin with, then, there are three areas in which the procedural model is most notably lacking: its application to empirical predicates, to quantification, and to higher-order predication and function application.

Nothing is ever as straightforward as it should be, of course, but I see no special problems in extending the kind of procedural model set out here to a language expressing empirical properties. Suppose, for example, that Timer is a cat and Maddie is a dog, and imagine that our language contains 'cat' as a basic predicate. The sense of this basic predicate could then be represented as a basic procedure—cat, say—computing a function that maps Timer into Truth and Maddie into Falsity. And likewise, just as the sense of the numeral '1' is represented through the basic procedure 1, the sense of 'Timer' could be represented through the basic procedure timer, computing the function that maps the empty sequence into Timer. The sense of the simple sentence 'Timer is a cat' could then be identified with the tuple (cat timer), which would be associated with the execution sequence

$$\langle \quad [\text{timer } \langle\rangle \ \Gamma_{1,1}],$$
$$[\text{cat } \langle\Gamma_{1,1}\rangle \ \Gamma_1] \ \rangle.$$

And it is easy enough to see how, by introducing appropriate procedures to act as the senses of function and relation symbols, we could then represent the thoughts expressed by more complicated empirical sentences as well, such as 'The father of Timer plays with Maddie'.

In a way, quantifiers pose no real problems either, at least if we adopt the "infinite conjunction" and "infinite disjunction" view of expressions like 'all' and 'some', since there is no particular reason—given the level of idealization we have already accepted—for insisting that the execution sequences associated with our senses must be finite. Suppose, for example, that all and some are basic procedures computing functions from the infinite Cartesian product $(D_t \times D_t \times \cdots)$ into $D_t$, where all computes the function mapping an infinite sequence of truth values into Truth just in case each of its members is Truth, and some computes the function mapping such a sequence into Truth just in case one of its members is Truth. And consider to begin with the statement '$\forall x(x > 2)$', telling us, incorrectly, that every number is greater than 2. Then, without getting into details of the various mappings, it would be natural to think of the sense of this statement as a tuple along the lines of (all (x) (greater x 2)), which could be associated with the execution sequence

$$\langle\quad [(\text{greater } 0\ 2)\ \langle\rangle\ \Gamma_{1,1}],$$
$$[(\text{greater } 1\ 2)\ \langle\rangle\ \Gamma_{1,2}],$$

.

.

.

$$[\text{all}\ \langle\Gamma_{1,1},\Gamma_{1,2},\ldots\rangle\ \Gamma_1]\ \rangle.$$

This sequence, whose length is $\omega + 1$, involves, first, executing each procedure of the form (greater n 2) where n ranges over the senses of the numerals, with the outcomes arranged in the registers $\Gamma_{1,2}, \Gamma_{1,2}, \ldots$, and then executing the procedure all with the resulting sequence of outcomes as input, and with its own outcome deposited in the register $\Gamma_1$.

Nested quantifiers could be handled in a similar fashion. Consider, for example, the statement '$\forall x \exists y (y > x)$', telling us that, for every number, there is a greater number. This statement might be assigned a sense along the lines of (all (x) (some (y) (greater y x))), leading to the execution sequence

$$\langle\quad [(\text{some (y) (greater y 0))}\ \langle\rangle\ \Gamma_{1,1}],$$
$$[(\text{some (y) (greater y 1))}\ \langle\rangle\ \Gamma_{1,2}],$$

.

.

.

$$[\text{all}\ \langle\Gamma_{1,1},\Gamma_{1,2},\ldots\rangle\ \Gamma_1]\ \rangle.$$

as an intermediate stage, and to a final sequence in which each particular execution of the form

$$[(\text{some (y) (greater y n))}\ \langle\rangle\ \Gamma_{1,j}]$$

is itself expanded into the sequence

$$\langle\quad [(\text{greater } 0\ \text{n})\ \langle\rangle\ \Gamma_{1,j,1}],$$
$$[(\text{greater } 1\ \text{n})\ \langle\rangle\ \Gamma_{1,j,2}],$$

.

.

.

$$[\text{some}\ \langle\Gamma_{1,j,1},\Gamma_{1,j,2},\ldots\rangle\ \Gamma_{1,j}]\ \rangle.$$

The length of the resulting sequence would then be $((\omega + 1) \cdot \omega) + 1$.

There are two general problems with the approach to quantification sketched here, neither particularly serious, but both suggesting the need for certain changes in our overall architecture for describing procedures.

The first is the obvious problem concerning quantification over sets of objects large enough that they cannot be arranged in a denumerable sequence. I mention this problem here only to acknowledge it. I do not feel that it poses any insurmountable difficulties for the procedural approach, but an adequate treatment would force us to generalize our underlying notion of a procedure considerably, possibly introducing operations that return sets of values when applied to sets of arguments and appealing to other ideas from parallel computation. The issues involved in developing a suitably general notion of a procedure are largely technical, and the work remains to be done.

The second difficulty with the current approach to quantification is more broadly conceptual; we can appreciate the problem by looking again at the execution sequence associated with the generalization '$\forall x(x > 2)$' and noting that this sequence actually contains senses for each of the individual sentences '$0 > 2$', '$1 > 2$', and so on—that is, the sense tuples (greater 0 2), (greater 1 2), and so on—even though these individual sentences do not occur as grammatical parts of the generalization itself. This kind of discord between the grammatical parts of a generalization and the senses contained in its execution sequence may seem, once again, to threaten Frege's idea that the thought expressed by a sentence should mirror its grammatical structure. Moreover, we have Frege's clear denial that the thought expressed by a generalization should contain constituents of this kind: he writes at one point, for example, that the sense of the sentence 'Cato is mortal' is not contained in that of 'All men are mortal', and somewhat more dramatically, that, by uttering this generalization, he should not be understood as asserting anything about a "chieftain from darkest Africa who is wholly unknown to me" (1914, p. 213; see also 1895b, p. 454). The problem that Frege sees here appears to be this: if the sense of 'All men are mortal' were to contain the sense of some term referring to the African chieftain, but Frege is not even aware of this individual—and if grasping the sense of a complex involves grasping the senses of its parts—then it is hard to see how he could grasp the thought expressed by this generalization at all.

In the case at hand—the generalization '$\forall x(x > 2)$'—the problem is not that the execution sequence contains the basic procedure greater, since the predicate '$>$' occurs in the statement, but that it contains senses of all the individual numerals—0, 1, and so on—while only the numeral '2' occurs in the statement itself. Now it is true that, as we discussed earlier, basic procedures can be thought of as surrogates for referents. Still, it may seem odd for any senses at all of terms that do not occur in a sentence to appear in the execution sequence associated with that sentence, even if those senses are nothing more than surrogates for referents; and it is often thought, in any case, that quantification involves a sort of immediate connection with objects themselves, without the mediation of senses.

One way to capture this idea might be to introduce an entirely new style of procedure execution: just as

$$[\mathcal{P} \; \langle \Gamma_{i_1}, \ldots, \Gamma_{i_n} \rangle \; \Gamma_j]$$

represents the action of executing the procedure $\mathcal{P}$, with the contents of the registers $\Gamma_{i_1}, \ldots, \Gamma_{i_n}$ taken as inputs, and with its own output deposited in $\Gamma_j$, we might take the new execution

$$[\mathcal{P} \; \langle \langle o_1, \ldots, o_n \rangle \rangle \; \Gamma_j]$$

to represent the action of executing $\mathcal{P}$ with the objects $o_1, \ldots, o_n$ themselves taken as inputs, and its output again deposited in $\Gamma_j$. Of course, our overall framework would then have to be enriched in various ways to accommodate this new style of procedure execution: we would have to generalize the notion of an assignment so that objects themselves, not just the contents of registers, could be assigned to sense variables; and we would have to formulate new expansion rules governing the new executions. Once this work had been carried out, however, it would then be possible to associate a sentence such as our '$\forall x(x > 2)$' with an execution sequence along the lines of

$$\langle \quad [(\text{lambda } (\text{x}) \; (\text{greater x } 2)) \; \langle \langle 0 \rangle \rangle \; \Gamma_{1,1}],$$
$$[(\text{lambda } (\text{x}) \; (\text{greater x } 2)) \; \langle \langle 1 \rangle \rangle \; \Gamma_{1,2}],$$
$$\cdot$$
$$\cdot$$
$$\cdot$$
$$[\text{all } \langle \Gamma_{1,1}, \Gamma_{1,2}, \ldots \rangle \; \Gamma_1] \quad \rangle,$$

in which no senses occur apart from those of expressions contained in the sentence itself.

There is, then, work to be done in extending the kind of procedural model set out here to cover empirical language and ordinary quantification, but at least certain clear avenues of exploration remain open. A more serious difficulty is posed by higher-order predication and function application, and this would have to encompass quantification as well, if we were to adopt the familiar view of quantifiers as higher-order predicates. Suppose, for example, that 'Π' is a universal quantifier conceived of along these lines—a second-order predicate that applies to a first-order predicate just in case that first-order predicate applies to every object in the domain. Using this new predicate, we can then form statements such as 'Π($\lambda x(x > 3)$)', for example, telling us that '$\lambda x(x > 3)$' applies to every object in the domain. And we can understand the difficulty presented by higher-order operations by contrasting the procedure that would be involved in determining the truth value of this sentence with the procedures associated with ordinary first-order statements, such our earlier '$3 + 2 = 5$'.

In the case of the statement '$3 + 2 = 5$', the procedure for determining truth value—which was described in detail in Chapter 5—can naturally be broken down into two parts. The procedure first determines the referents of the two terms to which the predicate is applied, '$3 + 2$' and '5'. Then, once the referents of these terms have been identified—once we know what they refer to—the procedure determines whether or not these items satisfy the predicate '='. In the case of the sentence 'Π($\lambda x(x > 3)$)', the analogous procedure would involve, first, determining the referent of the first-predicate '$\lambda x(x > 3)$', and then, once we know what it refers to, determining whether the referent of this first-order predicate satisfies the second-order predicate 'Π'.

The problem in this case is not that the latter procedure involves an appeal to ideal capacities; we have already accepted this kind of idealization. The problem is that it is difficult to understand what could be involved in determining the referent of a predicate like '$\lambda x(x > 3)$'—difficult, not just to find a systematic procedure for determining the referents of predicates like these, but even to figure out what determining, or identifying, the referent of such a predicate might amount to. This difficulty may be what underlies the considerable tension in Frege's own discussion of reference for predicates and function symbols, and it has led Dummett to conclude that Frege's "attribution of reference to incomplete expressions appears in the end unjustified" (1973, p. 243). At the very least, the difficulty shows that a procedural model of sense for higher-order languages would have to take a very different form from the account of sense for first-order languages set out here.

## 9.2 Two approaches to defined expressions

Let us now turn to a comparison between the semantic accounts of defined expressions set out in the two parts of this book.

Our overall discussion was cast against the background of a conflict among three broad ideas, all of which figure prominently in Frege's thought. The first is the idea that the notion of sense should be closely correlated with the psychological states of language users. The second is the thesis of eliminability, according to which a sentence containing defined expressions must share its sense with the sentence that results when each of these defined expressions is eliminated in favor if its defining phrase. The third is the thesis of fruitfulness, according to which the introduction of defined expressions should allow us to prove things that we could not have proved without them.

In the first part of the book, based on a weak understanding of fruitfulness, I developed a reading according to which Frege adheres to eliminability but abandons the correlation between senses and psychological states. On the view explored there, sentences containing defined expressions provide cognitive leverage by allowing speakers to present the same senses, the same thoughts, to themselves in different ways. Since these different sentences, all expressing the same thought, might have distinct syntactic structures, it follows as a corollary of this view that sentences need not correspond in structure to the thoughts they express.

In the second part of the book, by contrast, I take seriously Frege's idea that there should be such a correspondence and show how this idea can be implemented in a simple semantic model. The resulting view respects fruitfulness, of a much stronger sort, abandons eliminability, and again abandons any correlation between senses and psychological states.

At this point, the difference between these two approaches to defined expressions should be apparent, but it is nevertheless useful to highlight these differences with a concrete example. Let us begin, then, with the two sentences

$$(1) \quad 3 + 2 = 5,$$
$$(2) \quad 3 + 3 = 6.$$

Now suppose the three new predicates $F_1$, $F_2$, and $F_3$ are introduced through the following definitions, where we again use Frege's double-stroke notation to indicate the introduction of a defined expression:

$$\Vdash (3 + x = 5) \;=\; F_1(x),$$
$$\Vdash (x + 2 = 5) \;=\; F_2(x),$$
$$\Vdash (x + 3 = 6) \;=\; F_3(x).$$

And consider the sentence pairs

$$(3a) \quad F_1(2),$$
$$(3b) \quad \lambda x(3 + x = 5)2,$$
$$(4a) \quad F_2(3),$$
$$(4b) \quad \lambda x(x + 2 = 5)3,$$
$$(5a) \quad F_3(3),$$
$$(5b) \quad \lambda x(x + 3 = 6)3.$$

Evidently, both the sentences (3a,b) and (4a,b) reduce to (1) when defined expressions and $\lambda$-expressions are eliminated. According to the theory developed in the first part of the book, therefore, all of these sentences—(1), (3a,b), (4a,b)—would express the same sense, the same thought. What the sentences (3a,b) and (4a,b) provide are simply different ways of presenting this thought to ourselves, allowing for the possibility that we might be in different psychological states while grasping the same sense. And by the same token, the sentences (5a,b) would share the sense of (2), differing only in psychological significance.

According to the theory developed in the second part of the book, by contrast, the sentences (3a,b) as well as (4a,b) would differ in sense from (1), since they differ in structure; and likewise, (5a,b) would differ in sense from (2). In fact, apart from the three (a,b)-pairs, which do agree in sense, each of the sentences displayed here would be taken to express a distinct thought. There is, however, one significant equivalence. On this latter view, the sentences (4a,b) and (5a,b)—which bear no relation at all according to the earlier account—are now classified as $\Gamma^1$-equivalent, since they involve the application of co-referential predicates to identical terms, differing only in the way the procedures corresponding to these predicates are implemented.

The two parts of this book, then, set out two distinct approaches to the semantics of defined expressions. And as this example shows, these two approaches are not only distinct, but conflicting: sentences that are classified as expressing the same thought according to the first approach express different thoughts according to the second, while the second approach allows equivalence relations that are not recognized by the first. Both of these approaches are, I feel, coherent, and both develop ideas that can be found in Frege. It would be good to arrive at a deeper understand of the conflict between them.

# Bibliography

(Ayer, 1936) A. J. Ayer. *Language, Truth, and Logic.* Victor Gollantz, Ltd., 1936. Second edition (1936) reprinted by Dover Publications, Inc., in 1952.

(Ayer, 1959) A. J. Ayer, editor. *Logical Positivism.* MacMillan Publishing Co., Inc., 1959.

(Baker and Hacker, 1984) G. P. Baker and P. M. S. Hacker. *Frege: Logical Excavations.* Oxford University Press, 1984.

(Bell, 1987) David Bell. Thoughts. *Notre Dame Journal of Formal Logic,* 28:36–50, 1987.

(Bell, 1996) David Bell. The formation of concepts and the structure of thoughts. *Philosophy and Phenomenological Research,* 66:583–596, 1996.

(Belnap, 1993) Nuel Belnap. On rigorous definitions. *Philosophical Studies,* 72:115–146, 1993.

(Benacerraf, 1981) Paul Benacerraf. Frege: the last logicist. In Peter French, Teodore Uehling, and Howard Wettstein, editors, *The Foundations of Analytic Philosophy,* volume VI of *Midwest Studies in Philosophy,* pages 17–35. University of Minnesota Press, 1981.

(Burge, 1979) Tyler Burge. Sinning against Frege. *The Philosophical Review,* 88:398–432, 1979.

(Burge, 1984) Tyler Burge. Frege on extensions of concepts, from 1884 to 1903. *The Philosophical Review,* 93:3–34, 1984.

(Bynum, 1972) Terrell Bynum, editor. *Conceptual Notation and Related Articles.* Oxford University Press, 1972.

(Carnap, 1947) Rudolph Carnap. *Meaning and Necessity: A Study in Semantics and Modal Logic.* The University of Chicago Press, 1947.

(Church, 1941) Alonzo Church. *The Calculi of Lambda Conversion.* Princeton University Press, 1941.

(Cresswell, 1982) M. J. Cresswell. The autonomy of semantics. In S. Peters and E. Saarinen, editors, *Processes, Beliefs, and Questions,* pages 69–86. D. Reidel Publishing Company, 1982.

(Cresswell, 1985) M. J. Cresswell. *Structured Meanings: The Semantics of Propositional Attitudes.* The MIT Press, 1985.

(Davies and Isard, 1972) D. Davies and S. Isard. Utterances as programs. In D. Michie, editor, *Machine Intelligence.* Edinburgh University Press, 1972.

(Dummett, 1973) Michael Dummett. *Frege: Philosophy of Language.* Harvard University Press, 1973. Second edition, 1981.

(Dummett, 1975) Michael Dummett. Frege. *Teorema*, 5:149–188, 1975. Translated, revised, and reprinted as "Frege's distinction between sense and reference" in Dummett (1978); pagination refers to this version.

(Dummett, 1978) Michael Dummett. *Truth and Other Enigmas.* Harvard University Press, 1978.

(Dummett, 1981) Michael Dummett. *The Interpretation of Frege's Philosophy.* Harvard University Press, 1981.

(Dummett, 1984) Michael Dummett. An unsuccessful dig. In Crispin Wright, editor, *Frege: Tradition and Influence*, pages 194–226. Basil Blackwell Publisher, Inc., 1984.

(Dummett, 1989) Michael Dummett. More about thoughts. *Notre Dame Journal of Formal Logic*, 30:1–19, 1989.

(Dummett, 1990) Michael Dummett. Thought and perception: the views of two philosophical innovators. In David Bell and Neil Cooper, editors, *The Analytic Tradition: Meaning, Thought, and Knowledge.* Basil Blackwell Publisher, Inc., 1990. Reprinted in Dummett (1991a); pagination refers to this version.

(Dummett, 1991a) Michael Dummett. *Frege and Other Philosophers.* Harvard University Press, 1991.

(Dummett, 1991b) Michael Dummett. Frege and the paradox of analysis, 1991. In Dummett (1991a), pp. 17–52.

(Fodor, 1975) Jerry Fodor. *The Language of Thought.* Harvard University Press, 1975.

(Fodor, 1978a) Jerry Fodor. Propositional attitudes. *The Monist*, 61, 1978. Reprinted in Fodor (1981b); pagination refers to this version.

(Fodor, 1978b) Jerry Fodor. Tom Swift and his procedural grandmother. *Cognition*, 6, 1978.

(Fodor, 1979) Jerry Fodor. Three cheers for propositional attitudes. In William Cooper and Edward Walker, editors, *Sentence Processing: Psycholinguistic Studies Presented to Merrill Garrett.* Lawrence Erlbaum Associates, 1979. Reprinted with extensive revisions in Fodor (1981b), pp. 100–123; pagination refers to this version.

(Fodor, 1981a) Jerry Fodor. The present status of the innateness controversery, 1981. In Fodor (1981b), pp. 257–316.

(Fodor, 1981b) Jerry Fodor. *Representations: Philosophical Essays on the Foundations of Cognitive Science*. The MIT Press, 1981.

(Fodor, 1987) Jerry Fodor. *Psychosemantics: The Problem of Meaning in the Philosophy of Mind*. The MIT Press, 1987.

(Frege, 1879) Gottlob Frege. *Begriffsschrift, eine der arithmetischen nachgebildete Formelsprache des reined Denkens*. Halle, 1879. Translated as *Begriffsschrift, a formula language, modeled upon that of arithmetic, for pure thought* in van Heijenoort (1967); pagination refers to this version.

(Frege, 1879 to 91) Gottlob Frege. Logik, 1879 to 91. Translated as "Logic" in Hermes *et al.* (1979); pagination refers to this version.

(Frege, 1881) Gottlob Frege. Booles rechnende Logik und die Begriffsschrift, 1881. Translated as "Boole's logical calculus and the concept-script" in Hermes *et al.* (1979); pagination refers to this version.

(Frege, 1882) Gottlob Frege. Über die wissenschaftliche Berechtigung einer Begriffsschrift. *Zeitschrift für Philosophie und philosophische Kritik*, 81:48–56, 1882. Translated as "On the scientific justification of a concept script" in Bynum (1972); pagination refers to this version.

(Frege, 1884) Gottlob Frege. *Die Grundlagen der Arithmetik*. Breslau, 1884. Translated by J. Austin as *The Foundations of Arithmetic*, Basil Blackwell, 1950; pagination refers to this version.

(Frege, 1891a) Gottlob Frege. *Function und Begriff*. Hermann Pohle, Jena, 1891. An address given to the *Jenaische Gesellschaft für Medicin und Naturwissenschaft*. Translated as *Function and Concept* in McGuinness (1984).

(Frege, 1891b) Gottlob Frege. [On the concept of number], 1891. Translated in Hermes *et al.* (1979); pagination refers to this version.

(Frege, 1892a) Gottlob Frege. Über Begriff und Gegenstand. *Vierteljahrsschrift für wissenschaftliche Philosophie*, 16:192–205, 1892. Translated as "On concept and object" in McGuinness (1984).

(Frege, 1892b) Gottlob Frege. Über Sinn und Bedeutung. *Zeitschrift für Philosophie und philosophische Kritik*, 100:25–50, 1892. Translated as "On sense and meaning" in McGuinness (1984).

(Frege, 1893) Gottlob Frege. *Grundgesetze der Arithmetik*, volume 1. Verlag Hermann Pohle, 1893. Partially translated in Furth (1964).

(Frege, 1895a) Gottlob Frege. [Comments on "Über Sinn und Bedeutung"], 1895. Translated in Hermes *et al.* (1979); pagination refers to this version.

(Frege, 1895b) Gottlob Frege. Kritische Beleuchtung einiger Punkte in E. Schröeder, Vorlesungen über die Algebra der Logik. *Archiv für systematische Philosophie*, 1:433–456, 1895. Translated as "A critical elucidation of some points in E. Schröeder, *Vorlesungen über die Algebra der Logik*" in McGuinness (1984).

(Frege, 1897) Gottlob Frege. Logik, 1897. Translated as "Logic" in Hermes *et al.* (1979); pagination refers to this version.

(Frege, 1906a) Gottlob Frege. Einleitung in die logik, 1906. Translated as "Introduction to logic" in Hermes *et al.* (1979); pagination refers to this version.

(Frege, 1906b) Gottlob Frege. Was kann ich als ergebnis meiner arbeit ansehen?, 1906. Translated as "What may I regard as the result of my work?" in Hermes *et al.* (1979); pagination refers to this version.

(Frege, 1914) Gottlob Frege. Logik in der Mathematik, 1914. Translated as "Logic in mathematics" in Hermes *et al.* (1979); pagination refers to this version.

(Frege, 1918) Gottlob Frege. Der gedanke: eine logische untersuchung. *Beiträge zur Philosophie des deutschen Idealismus*, 1:58–77, 1918. Translated as "Logical investigations I: Thoughts" in McGuinness (1984).

(Frege, 1919) Gottlob Frege. [Notes for Ludwig Darmstaedter], 1919. Translated in Hermes *et al.* (1979); pagination refers to this version.

(Frege, 1923) Gottlob Frege. Logische Untersuchungen, ditter Teil: Gedankengefüge. *Beiträge zur Philosophie des deutschen Idealismus*, 3:36–51, 1923. Translated as "Logical investigations III: Compound thoughts" in McGuinness (1984).

(Frege, 1925) Gottlob Frege. Erkenntnisquellen der Mathematik und der mathematischen Naturwissenschaften, 1925. Translated as "Sources of knowledge of mathematics and the mathematical natural sciences" in Hermes *et al.* (1979); pagination refers to this version.

(Frege, VII3) Gottlob Frege. Letter to E. Husserl, 30 October to 1 November 1906, VII3. Translated in Gabriel *et al.* (1980); pagination refers to this version.

(Frege, VII4) Gottlob Frege. Letter to E. Husserl, 9 December 1906, VII4. Translated in Gabriel *et al.* (1980); pagination refers to this version.

(Frege, VIII12) Gottlob Frege. Draft of a letter to P. Jourdain, undated, VIII12. Translated in Gabriel *et al.* (1980); pagination refers to this version.

(Frege, XIV11) Gottlob Frege. Draft of a letter to G. Peano, undated, XIV11. Translated in Gabriel *et al.* (1980); pagination refers to this version.

(Frege, XIV7) Gottlob Frege. Letter to G. Peano, 29 September 1896, XIV7. Translated in Gabriel *et al.* (1980); pagination refers to this version.

(Frege, XV14) Gottlob Frege. Letter to B. Russell, 28 December 1902, XV14. Translated in Gabriel *et al.* (1980); pagination refers to this version.

(Frege, XV18) Gottlob Frege. Letter to B. Russell, 13 November 1904, XV18. Translated in Gabriel *et al.* (1980); pagination refers to this version.

(Furth, 1964) Montgomery Furth, editor. *Frege: The Basic Laws of Arithmetic.* University of California Press, 1964.

(Gabriel *et al.*, 1980) Gottfried Gabriel, Hans Hermes, Friedrich Kambartel, Christian Thiel, and Albert Veraart, editors. *Gottlob Frege: Philosophical and Mathematical Correspondence.* The University of Chicago Press, 1980.

(Geach, 1961) Peter Geach. Frege. In Peter Geach and G. E. M. Anscombe, editors, *Three Philosophers*, pages 127–162. Cornell University Press, 1961.

(Hahn, 1933) Hans Hahn. *Logik, Mathematik und Naturerkennen.* Gerold and Company, 1933. Translated and partially reprinted as "Logic, mathematics, and knowledge of nature" in Ayer (1959); pagination refers to this version.

(Harel, 1987) David Harel. *Algorithmics: The Spirit of Computing.* Addison-Wesley Publishing Company, 1987. Second edition published in 1993.

(Heim and Kratzer, 1998) Irene Heim and Angelika Kratzer. *Semantics in Generative Grammar.* Blackwell Publishers Inc., 1998.

(Hermes *et al.*, 1979) Hans Hermes, Friedrich Kambartel, and Friedrich Kaulbach, editors. *Gottlob Frege: Posthumous Writings.* The University of Chicago Press, 1979.

(Hindley *et al.*, 1972) J. R. Hindley, B. Lercher, and J. P. Seldin. *Introduction to Combinatory Logic*, volume 7 of *London Mathematical Society Lecture Note Series.* Cambridge University Press, 1972.

(Horty, 1987) John Horty. *Some Aspects of Meaning in Mathematical Language.* PhD thesis, Philosophy Department, University of Pittsburgh, 1987.

(Horty, 1993) John Horty. Frege on the psychological significance of definitions. *Philosophical Studies*, 72:223–263, 1993.

(Jeshion, 2001) Robin Jeshion. Frege's notions of self-evidence. *Mind*, 110:937–976, 2001.

(Johnson-Laird, 1977) Philip Johnson-Laird. Procedural semantics. *Cognition*, 5:189–214, 1977.

(Kant, 1781) Immanuel Kant. *Kritik der reinen Vernunft*, 1781. Second edition, 1787. Translated by Norman Kemp Smith as *Critique of Pure Reason*, St. Martin's Press, 1929.

(Kant, 1783) Immanuel Kant. *Prolegomena zu einer jeden künftigen Metaphysik die als Wissenschaft auftreten können*, 1783. Translated by Lewis White Beck as *Prolegomena to any Future Metaphysics*, Bobbs-Merrill, 1950; pagination refers to this translation.

(Kaplan, 1966) David Kaplan. What is Russell's theory of descriptions? In *Physics, Logic, and History.* Plenum Publishing Corporation, 1966. Reprinted in Pears (1972).

(Kaplan, 1989) David Kaplan. Demonstratives: an essay on the semantics, logic, metaphysics, and epistemology of demonstratives and other indexicals. In Joseph

Almog, John Perry, and Howard Wettstein, editors, *Themes from Kaplan*, pages 481–563. Oxford University Press, 1989.

(King, 1995) Jeffrey King. Structured propositions and complex predicates. *Nous*, 29:516–535, 1995.

(King, 1996) Jeffrey King. Structured propositions and sentence structure. *Journal of Philosophical Logic*, 25:495–521, 1996.

(King, 2001) Jeffrey King. Structured propositions. In Edward Zalta, editor, *The Stanford Encyclopedia of Philosophy (Fall 2001 Edition)*. Stanford University, 2001. Available at http://plato.stanford.edu/archives/fall2001/entries/-propositions-structured/.

(Kripke, 1979) Saul Kripke. A puzzle about belief. In A. Margalit, editor, *Meaning and Use*, pages 239–283. D. Reidel Publishing Company, 1979.

(Lewis, 1972) David Lewis. General semantics. In Donald Davidson and Gilbert Harman, editors, *Semantics of Natural Language*, pages 169–218. D. Reidel Publishing Company, 1972.

(Linsky, 1967) Leonard Linsky. *Referring*. Routledge and Kegan Paul, 1967.

(McGuinness, 1984) Brian McGuinness, editor. *Gottlob Frege: Collected Papers on Mathematics, Logic, and Philosophy*. Basic Blackwell Publisher, 1984.

(Montague, 1970) Richard Montague. Universal grammar. *Theoria*, 36:373–398, 1970. Reprinted in Richmond Thomason, editor, *Formal Philosophy: Selected Papers of Richard Montague*, pages 222–246, Yale University Press, 1974.

(Moschovakis, 1994) Yiannis Moschovakis. Sense and denotation as algorithm and value. In *Proceedings of Logic Colloquium '90*, Springer-Verlag Lecture Notes in Logic #2, pages 210–249. Springer-Verlag, 1994.

(Partee, 1982) Barbara Partee. Intensional logic and natural language. In T. Simon and R. Scholes, editors, *Language, Mind, and Brain*, pages 65–74. Lawrence Erlbaum Associates, 1982.

(Pears, 1972) D. F. Pears. *Bertrand Russell: A Collection of Critical Essays*. Doubleday and Company, 1972.

(Perry, 1977) John Perry. Frege on demonstratives. *The Philosophical Review*, 86:474–497, 1977.

(Resnik, 1980) Michael Resnik. *Frege and the Philosophy of Mathematics*. Cornell University Press, 1980.

(Salmon, 1986) Nathan Salmon. *Frege's Puzzle*. The MIT Press, 1986.

(Sluga, 1980) Hans Sluga. *Gottlob Frege*. Routledge and Kegan Paul, 1980.

(Soames, 1987) Scott Soames. Direct reference, propositional attitudes, and semantic content. *Philosophical Topics*, 15:47–87, 1987.

(Steiner, 1975) Mark Steiner. *Mathematical Knowledge.* Cornell University Press, 1975.

(Stenlund, 1974) Sören Stenlund. Analytic and synthetic arithmetical statements. In Sören Stenlund, editor, *Logical Theory and Semantic Analysis: Essays Dedicated to Stig Kanger on his Fiftieth Birthday,* pages 199–211. D. Reidel Publishing Company, 1974.

(Suppes, 1957) Patrick Suppes. *Introduction to Logic.* D. van Nostrand Publishing Company, 1957.

(Suppes, 1980) Patrick Suppes. Procedural semantics. In R. Haller and W. Grassel, editors, *Language, Logic, and Philosophy,* pages 27–35. Hölder-Pichler-Temsky Publishers, 1980.

(Suppes, 1982) Patrick Suppes. Variable-free semantics with remarks on procedural extensions. In T. Simon and R. Scholes, editors, *Language, Mind, and Brain,* pages 21–34. Lawrence Erlbaum Associates, 1982.

(Tappenden, 1995) Jamie Tappenden. Extending knowledge and 'fruitful concepts': Fregean themes in the foundations of mathematics. *Nous,* 29:427–467, 1995.

(Thomason, 1974) Richmond Thomason. Introduction. In Richmond Thomason, editor, *Formal Philosophy: Selected Papers of Richard Montague,* pages 1–69. Yale University Press, 1974.

(van Heijenoort, 1967) Jean van Heijenoort, editor. *From Frege to Gödel: A Source Book in Mathematical Logic, 1879–1931.* Harvard University Press, 1967.

(van Heijenoort, 1977) Jean van Heijenoort. Sense in Frege. *The Journal of Philosophical Logic,* 6:93–102, 1977.

(Waismann, 1956) Friedrich Waismann. How I see philosophy. In H. Lewis, editor, *Contemporary British Philosophy.* George Allen and Unwin, Ltd., 1956. Reprinted in Ayer (1959); pagination refers to this version.

(Weiner, 1984) Joan Weiner. The philosopher behind the last logicist. In Crispin Wright, editor, *Frege: Tradition and Influence,* pages 57–79. Basil Blackwell Publisher, Inc., 1984.

(Weiner, 1990) Joan Weiner. *Frege in Perspective.* Cornell University Press, 1990.

(Whitehead and Russell, 1910) Alfred North Whitehead and Bertrand Russell. *Principia Mathematica,* volume 1. Cambridge University Press, 1910.

(Wittgenstein, 1956) Ludwig Wittgenstein. *Bemerkungen über die Grundlagen der Mathematik.* Basil Blackwell, 1956. Translated as *Remarks on the Foundations of Mathematics,* The MIT Press (1967); pagination refers to this version.

(Woods, 1975) William Woods. What's in a link: foundations for semantic networks. In D. Bobrow and A. Collins, editors, *Representation and Understanding: Studies in Cognitive Science,* pages 35–82. Academic Press, 1975.

(Woods, 1981)  William Woods. Procedural semantics as a theory of meaning. In A. K. Joshi, B. L. Webber, and I. A. Sag, editors, *Elements of Discourse Understanding*, pages 300–334. Cambridge University Press, 1981.

# Index

a priori and a posteriori truths, 12–14, *see also* informative and uninformative truths

analysis and decomposition, *see* constituents and components

analytic and synthetic truths, 27–33, *see also* informative and uninformative truths

Anderson, Alan, 35

assignment, *see* senses, sense variables

associations, *see* senses, association with expressions; procedures, procedure executions, execution sequences associated with expressions; referents, association with expressions

Ayer, Alfred Jules, 11, 12, 15, *see also* Ayer-Hahn monsters

Ayer-Hahn monsters, *see* informative and uninformative truths, models of the speaker and, Ayer-Hahn monsters

Baker, Gordon, 92

Bell, David, 92, 108

Belnap, Nuel, ix, 34, 35

Benacerraf, Paul, 29, 40–41

binding, *see* senses, sense variables

Boole, George, 19, 30–32, 89

Brandom, Robert, ix

Burge, Tyler, 44, 58, 124

Carnap, Rudolph, 6, 83, 114

Church, Alonzo, 95

cognitive value, *see* informative and uninformative truths

compositionality, *see also* decomposition
  for referents, 72–73
  for senses, 76–77, 93–94, 112–117, 119, 126–128
  of semantic content, 2

concept formation, 87–98, 107, *see also* definition, concept formation and

constituents and components, 92–93, *see also* compositionality; decomposition
  components, 94–98
  constituents, 93–94

Cresswell, Max, 4, 83, 123

Davies, Julian, 65

decomposition, 85–93, *see also* compositionality

definitions, *see also* expressions, defined
  concept formation and, 30–33
  eliminability and fruitfulness, viii, 33–34, 50, 145
  explicative definitions, 34–36
    eliminability of, 36–39
    fruitfulness of, 39–40
  stipulative definitions, vii, 34–36, 140
    eliminability of, 40, 50–54
    fruitfulness of, strong interpretation, 65, 122–123, 129, 135–138, 145

fruitfulness of, weak interpretation, 40–53, 145
Dummett, Michael, 6, 9, 24, 40, 66–68, 85, 91–94, 97–98, 106–108, 113, 122, 145

expressions, *see also* syntax
    basic
        complete, 69, 70
        incomplete, 70
    complex
        complete, 70–71
        incomplete, 85–98, 102, 104–140
    defined, 98–102, 111–139
    linguistic variables, 71, 102–104, 127
    open, 71

Fodor, Jerry, 11, 58–65
full expansions, *see* procedures, procedure executions, expansion rules

Geach, Peter, 107, 108

Hacker, Peter, 92
Hahn, Hans, 11, 12, 15, *see also* Ayer-Hahn monsters
Harel, David, 126
Haugeland, John, ix
Heim, Irene, 95
Hindley, J. Roger, 95
Horty, John, 24, 51
Husserl, Edmund, 14, 22

immediate expansions, *see* procedures, procedure executions, expansion rules
indexicals, 56–58
information value, *see also* informative and uninformative truths
    semantic content and, 2

informative and uninformative truths
    compared to a priori and a posteriori truths, 12–14
    compared to analytic and synthetic truths, 27–33
    definition of, 9
    general discussion of, 7–9
    models of the speaker and, 10–17
        Ayer-Hahn monsters, 11–14, 17, 52–53, 62
        limited intellects, 14–17
Isard, Stephen, 65

Jeshion, Robin, 9
Johnson-Laird, Philip, 65
Jourdain, Philip, 86

Kant, Immanuel, 27–33, 87, 89–90
Kaplan, David, 56–58, 113–115, 119–120
King, Jeffrey, 83
Kratzer, Angelika, 95
Kripke, Saul, 52

Leśniewski, Stanisław, 34
Leibniz, Gottfried, 18, 20
Lercher, Bruce, 95
Lewis, David, 83
Linsky, Leonard, 6, 17

Maddie, 141
Montague, Richard, 70
Moschovakis, Yiannis, 65

*P*-rules, *see* syntax, predication rules (*P*-rules)
paradox of analysis, 36–39
Partee, Barbara, 65
Peano, Giuseppe, 14
Perry, John, 56–58, 124
Pietroski, Paul, ix
predication rules, *see* syntax, predication rules (*P*-rules)

procedures, *see also* senses
    basic, 73–76, 120–124, 131
    complex
        complete, 76–84
        incomplete, 126–139
    effective, 67–68, 73
    ideal, 68–69, 73–75, 141–144
    procedure executions
        basic, 79
        complex, 81
        execution sequences, 79
        execution sequences associated
          with senses, 82, 134
        expansion rules, immediate expansion, 81–82, 131–134
        full expansion, 82, 134
        registers, 77–79, 83, 129–130
propositional attitudes, *see* senses, psychological states and

$\rho$ function, *see* senses, association with expressions ($\rho$ function)
$R$-rules, *see* syntax, removal rules ($R$-rules)
$R^*$-rules, *see* syntax, removal rules, variant form ($R^*$-rules)
referents, 145
    association with expressions ($\rho$ function), 72–73, 102–104
    distinguished from senses, 3
    for basic expressions, 72
    for complex expressions
        complete, 72–73
        defined and incomplete, 102–104, 145
registers, *see* procedures, registers
removal rules, *see* syntax, removal rules ($R$-rules)
removal rules, variant form, *see* syntax, removal rules, variant form ($R^*$-rules)
Russell, Bertrand, 14, 23, 25, 66

$\sigma$ function, *see* senses, association with expressions ($\sigma$ function)
Salmon, Nathan, 8, 13, 83, 124
Scott, Dana, ix
Seldin, Jonathan, 95
self-evidence, *see* informative and uninformative truths
senses, *see also* procedures
    argument for introduction of, 1–9
    as procedures, 66–69, 141–145
    association with expressions ($\sigma$ function), 76–77, 108, 112, 116, 126–128
    basic, 75–76
    complex
        complete, 80–81
        incomplete, 124–139
    grasp of, 37–38, 42–49, 85–91, 93, 98, 143
    psychological states and, viii, 4–7, 50–56, 123–124, 140, 145
    sense variables, 126, 130–131
    standards for sense identity
        definitions and, 24–26
        models of the speaker and, 12–17
        the strict interpretation, 17–26
Sluga, Hans, 20, 87, 88
Soames, Scott, 83, 124
Steiner, Mark, 99
Stenlund, Sören, 25
substitution, 95
Suppes, Patrick, 65, 95
syntax, 69–71, *see also* expressions
    predication rules ($P$-rules), 70–71, 104–118
    removal rules ($R$-rules), 96–97
    removal rules, variant form ($R^*$-rules), 99–100
    syntactic categories, 69–70
    syntactic rules, 70

Tarski, Alfred, 103
Thomason, Richmond, ix, 70
Timer, 141
Trendelenburg, Adolf, 20

understanding, *see* senses, grasp of

Van Heijenoort, Jean, 65
variables, *see* expressions, linguistic vari-
        ables; senses, sense variables

Waismann, Friedrich, 49
Weierstrass, Karl, 39
Weiner, Joan, 40
Whitehead, Alfred North, 25
Wittgenstein, Ludwig, 48–49
Woods, William, 65